Bird School

Bird
School

A BEGINNER IN THE WOOD

ADAM NICOLSON

**WILLIAM
COLLINS**

William Collins
An imprint of HarperCollins*Publishers*
1 London Bridge Street
London SE1 9GF

WilliamCollinsBooks.com

HarperCollins*Publishers*
Macken House, 39/40 Mayor Street Upper
Dublin 1, D01 C9W8, Ireland

First published in Great Britain in 2025 by William Collins

3

A catalogue record for this book is
available from the British Library

ISBN 978-0-00-849083-6

Set in Adobe Garamond Pro
Printed and bound in the UK using 100%
renewable electricity at CPI Group (UK) Ltd

MIX
Paper | Supporting
responsible forestry
FSC™ C007454

This book contains FSC™ certified paper and other controlled
sources to ensure responsible forest management.

For more information visit: www.harpercollins.co.uk/green

For all my much-loved Ravens

Contents

1.

Bird School

LEARNING

The first time I met a bird close-up, it was dead. A raven. Even seeing it on the side of the mountain road in Crete was a shock: a large, dark splayed body the size of a small dog. I stopped the car and got out, not quite certain if I would find a wounded animal, enraged at its fate and frenzied in pain. But it was properly dead. Whatever it had once been had left. Holding its rigid form – all looseness and flexibility gone; it was as stiff as a dried cod – feeling my way around it, rustling open its wing feathers, pushing through the soft plumage on its nape and back, was like exploring a derelict house. Rafters, furnishings, upholstery, timbers, abandonment. It had been shot and its bill was bloodied in gouts towards the point, yet the midnight blue of its back and wing shimmered in my hands, each sheathing layer overlapping the next in soft-edged scales.

The bird felt like a miracle of construction: the splitting-axe of its bill, more palaeo than any piece of bird-body I had ever seen, capable of crushing the skull of a rabbit in one slow, final closure; the nape that it ruffles and raises in both anger and desire; the spread of the primary feathers in the wing, no matter wasted, each rib as structural as a medieval vault, as fine as necessary, graded in width and strength from outer to inner and from tip to root.

And then the claw, dirty from life, knobbled like a Malacca cane, the darkness giving way, as an undertaker's shoe might when muddied beside the grave, to a leathered practicality, armoured against the world and padded against rock.

The dead bird was not the bird. The body seemed only to have been the means by which the bird could have become itself. But that moment of closeness to such an animal was the beginning of something for me.

I had never paid much attention to birds. For whatever reason – perhaps because everyday birds were too small, too evasive, too difficult to know, requiring too much patience and too much submission to

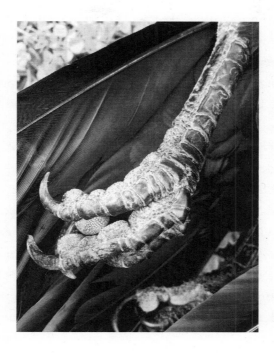

their ticky little habits – I had not cared about them. Or not bothered to care.

My family had never been troubled by them. My father – no naturalist – was always more interested in looking across a bit of country than in what it might be made of. The *view* was the thing, not the plants or animals in it. As a boy I never chose to understand the birds or tried to learn the songs or calls. I did love seabirds – big, obvious, loud, heraldic, unmistakable – and came to know them on our annual holidays in Scotland, but the birds in the wood or the garden at home remained a blank, a flicker of nothing much, like motes in sunlight.

Why this indifference? Perhaps because attending to the birds seemed marginal to the bigger stories. Perhaps because my father looked down on anything like that. He built himself a gazebo – an eighteenth-century joke: 'I will gaze', as a fusion of Latin and English – on the corner of the garden from which he could survey a stretch of country 'unchanged since Jane Austen saw it', as he would often say. A view, or a landscape as it was always more grandly described, precludes a love of anything else and as the naturalist Mark Cocker described in *Our Place*, his excoriating 2018 account of the failure of modern nature organisations to attend to the well-being of nature, this view-addiction has presided over a destruction of everything else. Perhaps because of an inherited taste for parkland, carpet has seemed better than vitality, smoothness than mess. The Britain Cocker portrayed has fetishised a 'landscape beauty almost devoid of biodiversity … Nature is slipping away from these islands … Not since the last ice age has Britain been so stripped bare of its natural inhabitants.' In common with that presiding culture, I had walked thousands of miles across a diminished Britain without ever truly recognising what was or wasn't there.

Later, when I encountered bird people who had spent their years of apprenticeship learning and attending to the birds, I slid past them. I remember in Turkey, making a radio programme on Homer with my friend and lifelong birder Tim Dee. As we stood together on the Trojan plain, perched on the slopes of a Bronze Age tumulus known as the Tomb of Achilles, he said he could hear a woodlark singing above us. I began to talk into his woolly microphone about the beauties of that place, its oak woods, its leaning, creaky olive groves, the lionskin of late summer grasses, the endless, homeless north wind blowing across from the steppes, and said something about 'the song of a lark high above us'. Tim stopped me: 'Not a lark, a woodlark.' He can never watch a film without agonising over the presence of the wrong birds at the wrong time of year on the soundtrack.

We started again and I said 'lark' again and I remember his frustrated, raised eyebrows and the pursed lips of the radio producer who remains silent, his eyes on the horizon, as his contributors mouth idiocies.

It is a reproachful memory, symptomatic of a certain frame of mind. And so a couple of years ago I decided to embark on an attempt to encounter birds, to engage with a whole and marvellous layer of life that I had lived with in a kind of blindness and deafness for decades.

I wanted to look and listen, to return to Bird School and see what it might teach me. I knew it would be long, slow and bitty. Birds don't easily offer themselves up and in that way differ from our modern experiences in which the wanted or desired is almost constantly available. Birds move too fast or are too far away. We summon their alarm. Their concealment is occasionally interrupted only by a flickering, transient, uncertain presence. 'Nature likes to be hid,' Heraclitus wrote in Ephesus 2,600 years ago and as such birds are the opposite of a landscape view that lays itself out in a kind of horizontal, placid seductiveness. Birds refuse that subjugation. They are often on the run, intent on a life in which the human observer is merely a threat or annoyance. They know how to fly away, neatly like owls or buzzards, with a kind of disdainful calm, or like pigeons with a grand fluster of feathers and noise, or blackbirds with a car-alarm-disturbed-terror-shriek; or to hide and creep, to stay still and silent, like the snipe or woodcock in the most anxious stillnesses in nature, to warn each other of some alien mammal in the neighbourhood and to observe us far more than we ever observe them.

Experiments have shown how much they dislike the threat that a human eye represents. They don't like being looked at, and birds, if you look at them too hard, will fly away. The eye-spots on butterfly wings are designed to alarm bird predators and the reaction of most birds, especially in the young, is to take flight. The response is more powerful when it is a watching face; a pair of eyes is more frightening to them than a single eye-shaped form and one can experiment with this: watch with your hand over one eye and the birds might be untroubled. Remove it and they will flee. Deep in their adaptive minds is the knowledge that predators have their eyes in the front of their heads, giving them the necessary, wide, binocular gaze, and it is that double, watching, hungry vision that birds fear and avoid.

We bring terror in our wake. Charles Foster, the English writer on the wildness of animals, has said that whenever he wanders into the section of a bookshop called 'Birdwatching', he looks for those books that might describe or try to describe the experience of birds watching us.

What do they make of us? What is that large mammal that likes to stop on its walk through the wood and somehow transform its little eyes into a pair of bug-eyed predatory lenses with which it tracks us as we pass? Could we ever trust it? What is its world, its intention? What does it want?

I have come to think that the inaccessibility of birds is the heart of their marvellousness. Both concealment and their capacity for distance and height is their form of pride. We do not own them. They possess themselves, even as their indifference makes us long for them. 'You don't hear birds, you hear worlds,' Olivier Messiaen, the great French composer, once wrote. That unknowable otherness, the way in which they represent the complex, involved presence of entire life systems that are not-us but are somehow interleaved with our own, is the source of the birds' beauty. They are unknowability itself alive in front of us, coloured, feathered, voluble, quick, inaccessible, with something fractal about them, so that the more you look, the less you know. Or perhaps the more you look, the more you know how little you know. You can only be led towards them, as if into a mystery.

2.

Birdhouse

ABSORBING

I slowly developed a double thought: not only to learn something of birds but to make a place, despite the general crisis, that might be accommodating and receptive to them. I live in the Sussex Weald, damp and tree-thick country. We first came here thirty years ago, on the run from London and looking for a refuge, somewhere my wife Sarah and I felt we could be happy. We found a small, slightly abused dairy farm in the rough country on the borders of two ancient parishes, Brightling and Burwash. It was called Perch Hill, meaning stick hill, because the high clay soils of the fields were good for growing little else. Over the previous decades, as the economics of modern dairying pinched on small farms, it had been driven increasingly hard, its trees felled, hedges and even small woods taken out and pastures re-sown with dominant modern rye-grasses. By the early 1990s, when we arrived, the farmer had finally given up, having sold the cattle and let out the whole place as grazing for sheep.

It should be – and probably always was – somewhere that is congenial to birds, but, along with the rest of the country, the bird life here had diminished. Could it be made better? Was that even possible?

I began to feel that to learn about birds and to make a bird-friendly place might be two halves of one idea. Learn the birds and their needs, understand the deep story and disciplines of this farm, and the two goals could coalesce. A good place could make its birds, just as birds could make a place, not only as key ingredients in its ecology, playing their part in its complex trophic structures, but by making it 'hum with the frequencies of the unconscious', as the poet and novelist Kapka Kassabova has said of her much-loved homeland in Bulgaria. Birds are the voice of a wood early in the year and the form in which that wood takes wing as the fledglings leave the nest in summer. They are the upper register in the music of anywhere that is vital and flourishing. And so, I hoped, as I became alive to the birds, the place might become alive to them.

History is thick here. Much of the land on this farm and its neighbours is not unlike a rough, overgrown garden. The ways down into the woods are narrow and arched. Oak trees hang their limbs over the gateways and ancient many-stemmed hazels push up towards them. The midwinter sunshine comes between the trees and spreads its broken beams over the gates, throwing shadows on the grass in parallelograms of light and shade.

Choose any one of these entrances into the hidden and sunken lanes that cross this woody country and the place closes over, moss-lined, in spring wallpapered with primroses and wood anemones, coming to the little tree-roofed streams that are creased into the clays and sandstones.

Most of that wooded lowland of the Sussex Weald has been almost forgotten now, the coppiced trees neglected for decades so that each stem from their ancient stools has become a full-grown forest plant, which here and there has crashed out in winter gales to lie horizontal among its neighbours.

I do not know of a landscape that is so full of the suggestions of the past, perhaps because modernity has abandoned so much of it. Many of the woods have returned to a wildness they have not had since the

Mossy medieval woodbank and lane on the edge of High Wood with overgrown chestnut coppice

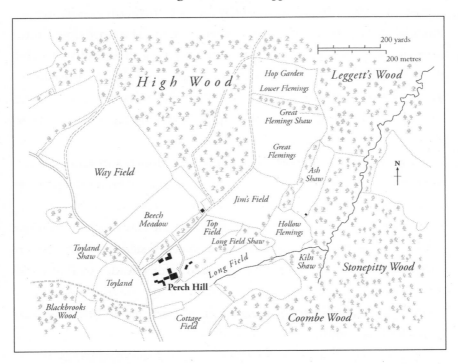

The fields of Perch Hill Farm surrounded by the ancient woodland from which they were cut in the late Middle Ages

Dark Ages. The old handmade structures moulder – not only the lanes, but the woodbanks that once protected the young trees from the deer, the coppice stools themselves, the jigsawed outlines of field and wood, the remote abandoned ponds long ago dammed for ironworks, the pits where the farmers dug for the limy marl to sweeten their acid soils.

It still bears in its bones memories of deep poverty and hard labour. Try digging a posthole in the clay or even burying a pet or a dead lamb in the corner of a field and you soon know how intractable the land is: the lanes were mostly impassable all winter, or would have needed a team of oxen to drag a wagon through their clag; and hardly a day of sunshine passes before that stolid stickiness transmutes into an equally unaddressable concrete. No one who could have chosen to farm else-where would have opted for these difficulties.

The need for intense, body-racking work created a landscape of interlinked privacies, a place infused with human life, with the woods planted some with hornbeam, for its strength and its ability to make the best of hot-burning charcoal; with ash, for the all-important light-ness in the handles of rakes or scythes; and oak for everlasting robustness, to make the thatched houses, barns and byres of which each separate farmstead consisted. Historically, fields were tiny, often no more than one or two acres. And farms were small, twenty or thirty acres, with a few cows, some pigs and chickens. Oxen were the draught animals of choice but this was farming on the level of gardening.

Here human enterprise and the natural world are braided together. Nothing is entirely wild or unwild and the generations of farmers who lived and worked this land have moulded the farm in a way that was always accommodating of natural life. Their system was cyclical and only intermittently disruptive. Each part of the wood in turn would be coppiced every twelve or fifteen years and otherwise allowed to grow on in peace. In some years, the grass in the meadows would be left to grow until July so that hay could be made there. In the intervening years the fields would be grazed by the pasturing animals. In winter those animals would be housed and the hay fed to them. All winter the farm would be left wet and empty and only in the following spring the dung spread across it.

The impact of those farmers was not relentless or even continuous. In both space and time, the human influence was irregular and patchy, scarcely imposing for a while, but then – in the hay harvest, in the laying or pleaching of a hedge that had outgrown itself as a barrier to stock or in the coppicing of a few acres of wood – radically invasive, entirely changing the environment in which plants and creatures lived, at least for a while.

There is no evidence that the making in the Middle Ages of small Wealden farms like this one involved a diminution of their wildlife. It is impossible to be sure but in many ways the traditional shape of Perch Hill is not unlike that of the natural, post-glacial world – the one to which the modern rewilding movement often looks – with the difference that human beings were an integral part of it.

The ecologist Ben Macdonald has described the benefits brought to birdlife by the interventions of medieval man.

Perch Hill: a farm buried in a wood

In place of aurochs-grazed pastures, we put to work tiny groups of cattle and pigs. In place of wild wood-pastures, we planted orchards. An organic orchard holds twice as many earthworms per square metre as dense woodland. If you were a blackbird or any other pasture-feeding species, you were winning. Birds that evolved in scrub-grasslands, whether red-backed shrikes or turtle doves, thrive under extensive grazing … Coppicing woodlands, as the late Oliver Rackham observed, recreates the tree-breaking actions of bison – or the zealous activity of beavers. If you were a nightingale or a willow tit, you were winning.

Charcoal burners in the hornbeam woodlands kept the right conditions going for nightjars and woodlarks. Hay meadows were perfect for corncrakes and other insect eaters. When in July I walk across one of our bigger fields called Great Flemings, named after the man who farmed it in the sixteenth century, it can be thick with grasshoppers, meadow brown butterflies and other insects fizzing out of the stems in front of me. I reckon there can be fifty or even a hundred in every square yard. The meadow is big, two hundred yards by three hundred, so it must hold hundreds of thousands of grasshoppers, an enormous resource for insect-eating birds across a summer.

This pattern of maintenance and dependence that came and went is unlike the repetitive and constant impositions of modern agriculture but it is intriguingly like the world described in an idea of natural richness that emerged in the 1970s. The theory has a clumsy name – the intermediate disturbance hypothesis – but it enshrines the understanding that natural life thrives not in a world of brutal and constant change, nor in unbroken calm, but somewhere in the middle of those extremes. Too much destruction reduces biodiversity. If a field is ploughed every year, or if a hurricane regularly destroys a forest, a natural world of any richness will not develop. Only the plants and animals that can rapidly recolonise a place would be given a chance before the next round of demolition and dismantling. Counterintuitively, the same is true of too little destruction. Dominant competitors outreach everything else. In Sussex, nothing but a solid, shady oak wood would grow. First, the birds of the open grassland – the skylarks – would fade away. For a while birds of a rich scrubby undergrowth – the warblers and nightingales – would come and sing but as the oak cover thickened they too would disappear and you would be left only with the remnants of tits and finches.

The bit-by-bit practices of Wealden farming enabled a kind of heterogeneity that was patchy in both time and space, precisely the environment in which a wide variety of natural life can thrive. If there was any place in which to come to understand birds, this careful, knitted and half-broken farm was it.

I had always loved one of our smallest fields at the bottom of the farm called Hollow Flemings, named after the man who also farmed its neighbour Great Flemings long ago. For many years we used it as rough grazing, the cows picking at the grasses and shoving their noses into the edges of the wood. It is tucked away in one of the small side valleys with which the land is pleated here. Dyer's greenweed grew in the summer and meadow brown butterflies used to flitter across it in June and July, pairs of them dancing around themselves as they fled across the hillside in dark, double, guttering flames.

Then, one wet winter, two things happened. The stream at the foot of the field, gorged with rain, started to cut down into its bed. At the same time the springs in the field itself were running hard, lubricating the upper layer of clay. One morning I found about three acres of Hollow Flemings had slipped, leaving a little cliff at the top of it, two or three feet high, and a tumble of fallen and half-fallen trees at the bottom where the clay was now clogging the stream. Over the next weeks, still more of the land slumped downwards. It was clear that the use of that field was over. We couldn't mow it or even fence it and so we let it go. It was no longer any part of the farmed world.

Brambles bubbled up into thickets that no deer could enter. Willows and alders sprouted beneath them, followed by the blackthorn and birches. Within a year or two young ash trees were raising their heads above the thorns. Now young oaks, some fifteen feet high, stand around the old landslip, the tips of their branches just beginning to touch, perhaps the product of jays forgetting a cache of acorns they had buried there.

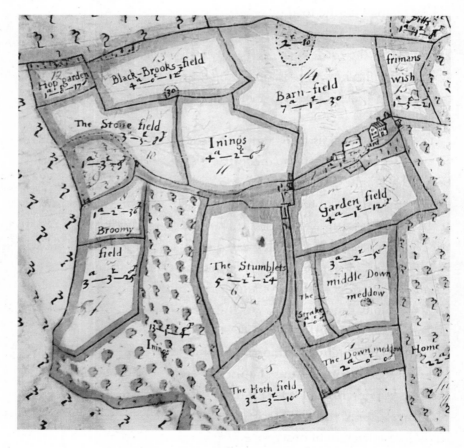

Garden-scale farming: part of a 1600 map of the Sussex Weald now in East Sussex Record Office

Deer graze in the narrow tongues of grass that persist between the clumps of new woodland. And then, one spring, two nightingales made the brambly thickets their territories, one at each end of the landslip, sigh-shouting at the night sky for any wives that might be passing.

In one way, that field is a ruin; in another it is reaching for a kind of wholeness, a reassertion of itself that shows abandonment is not abandonment but a form of emergence and release. The forgotten field, years before anyone much spoke of rewilding, had rewilded itself.

I met a man on the road one day – we were both out walking – and started to chat. He had worked at Perch Hill as a boy in the 1940s, looking after the cattle, making the hay. He looked at me quizzically when I told him how much I loved being there and after a pause asked the question that had been on the tip of his tongue. 'Perch Hill, still slipping, is it?'

Yes, still slipping, as fields of other farms in this valley are. When I went to the local county record office I searched through the documents that might describe this farm. It was a detailed story, going back through a sequence of tenants and landowners, fifty-one names over six centuries, their mortgages and debts, their legacies and inheritances. In the 1820s it had belonged to a local estate and a surveyor had mapped it, listing one of our fields as Slide Field. Neighbouring farms were equally rough, their sixteenth-century parcels labelled as Slidden Mede, Little Bramble, Broomy Field, the Stumblets, the Wagmires. None was easy.

Despite the roughness, an organised life was being lived here. Over and over again, copying out the listings from the earlier documents, the lawyers described Perch Hill's 'Stables Outhouses Edifices and Buildings Closes yards gardens pastures arable orchards and woodlands' like a diagram of order, an embroidered sampler of rural life. But twice in among them, in seventeenth- and eighteenth-century documents, a phrase jumped out at me: *rough grounds*.

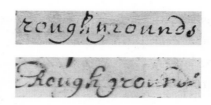

Rough grounds, the half-accommodated land, neither woodland nor pasture, nor orchard nor arable, but something that still had one foot in the unchanged, pre-anthropic world. Not rewilded but wild nonetheless, pre-cultured, living in the borderlands of nature and culture. Rough grounds was the early modern term for a place where the intermediate disturbance hypothesis held sway.

The oldest document of all came from that marginal territory, an act of transfer between father and son but describing a place that had scarcely been taken in from the wild. The deed is a beautiful thing, a small document, folding up to the size of a postcard and written on stiff parchment, with a seal still hanging from it. It was drawn up on Monday 7 June 1419, four years after the English archers had destroyed the French nobility at Agincourt. By it, a Burwash man John Ringmer

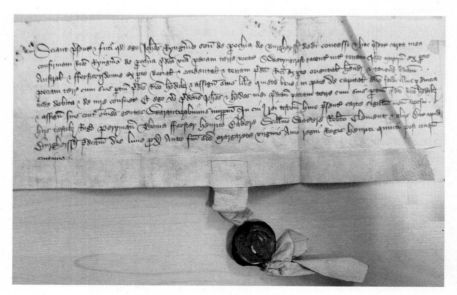

gave the land to his son Richard, a transaction witnessed by four of their neighbours, and calling the place not Perch Hill (a name it acquired only in the late sixteenth century) but something older and more visceral: Sweating Croft, or as it is spelled by the medieval clerk, Swetyngcroft.

What did it mean? A piece of land so hard to work that it could be identified by the sweat it drew from the farmer? Or land, as Perch Hill still is, so wet with springs, dripping like a man swinging his scythe at the hay all one long summer morning? Or both? A place so wet that only unrelenting work could bring it within the human fold? There is no telling but in the subtle, oblique way of ancient documents, which hint at and rarely describe, these were the pointers for me. Nature and culture interfold here. The whole place is an act of companionship across generations and species. It is a place to make good but not a place to make neat. Both it and you will sweat in it.

If I was to come to know the birds as I had resolved to do, this boundary condition was what to aim for and cultivate. The ideal was immersion.

Hollow Flemings, the self-rewilding field – perhaps the original Swetyngcroft – was the place. There is no view to speak of there. Resurgent nature is crowding back in. Young trees are proliferating in the brambles and up out of the bracken. This is where the nightingales had chosen to sing. If I was to learn about the birds, this was where I should base myself, away from any house, far from any road or disturbance, embedded in the edge country.

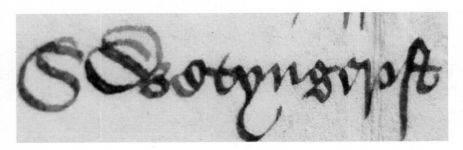

The tool was to be a shed in that forgotten field, a cabin with fold-down windows. It should be a small shelter, big enough to sleep in but little more, a birdhouse, a place for a day and a night, and a hide from which to see and hear the yearly show unfold. I did not want to observe the birds but to be with them. Not a gazebo or an observatory, to stare out from or to gaze at any view, but something closer and subtler than that, an *absorbatory*, a place to take it in, to dissolve, if such a thing is possible, the boundary between self and world.

There is nothing new about the idea of a shed as a revelatory place. Anything I made would, consciously or not, be a descendant of a long history of the shed as a way of encountering the world, not quite domestic and yet verging on domesticity, neither settled nor unsettled, out in nature but not of nature, poised between conditions. Every hut is a hide, an outer covering – it is no chance that we use the same word for the skin of a cow and a place of concealment: they have the same etymology – a shield and shelter, but one that is semi-permeable, a room into which the outside world could be allowed to enter as a welcome guest.

And so one autumn, I embarked on making a shed for Hollow Flemings. It was to be close up against the young trees, their branches no more than a foot and a half from the windows. It should be wooden and raised up on stilts, because being up in the trees feels more engaged with them. A tree, once you are among its leaves, is no longer an object but an environment. Where possible, the shed's materials – oak, chest-nut, birch – should come from nearby. The windows should be wide and shallow so that nothing outside could see in – to see but not be seen; to hide – but they must be on all sides so that where the trees stepped away, there could be a longer look down into the valley. It needed a woodburner for winter days and early mornings. I thought at first bird feeders could hang off struts from the corners and drew a sketch from which my daughter draughted the rough idea of a woven-feeling building – she made it hexagonal, with a corrugated hemp roof. An engineer designed the foundations required to stop the whole structure sliding downhill. Tim Dee suggested that what we were all now calling the Bird House should become a birdhouse and that nest boxes could be incorporated into the walls, accessible to birds from outside through the usual openings, and visible from inside through glass behind small wooden doors. But if we were to have nest boxes, we shouldn't have feeders nearby, as the two need to be separate for the birds' safety.

Nick Walsh, a joiner just down the road in Frant, agreed to make the little building with an oak frame and to fit it out with windows, nest boxes, benches and shutters. Colin Pilbeam, who manages the farm at Perch Hill, hired a digger and with Richard Lambden dug the trenches, screwed in the steel groundscrews and poured the foundations.

Nick arranged for a woodman down the road to make the chestnut hurdles for the walls. And then slowly over the autumn and early winter, Nick and his friend Gary Parker hammered and hauled together the wonderful structure. By January, the woodburner had been installed. The benches were finished. Sarah had given me a set of bird pictures for the sloping roofs inside the shed and I arranged a network of wires and pulleys in the trees from which to hang the feeders. The birdhouse was ready for the world to come.

I first sat in there on 19 January, soaking up the pleasure of occupying a newly made place for the first time. It was a room in the wood, a little capsule dedicated to the intermediate disturbance hypothesis, a hide for silence, a permeable place, designed to allow the world to enter it, a shed for the rough grounds, Swetyngcroft Hall.

I had been reading *Humankind* by Timothy Morton, the English philosopher and ecocritic. In a sequence of essays Morton argues for the virtues of 'solidarity with nonhuman people'. The heart of the problem is what Morton, who uses the pronouns 'they' and 'them', calls 'the Severing', a deep disconnectedness in our idea of the world that separates reality into two 'shrink-wrapped' categories: ourselves and Nature. This severing might have begun with the invention of agriculture in ancient Mesopotamia, but it remains a constant, ever-active principle, 'a wave that ripples out in many dimensions, in whose wake we are caught'. To bridge that gap, the best move is to stop imagining or assuming that human thought is 'the top access mode' to reality and instead believe that 'brushing against, floating through, licking or irradiating are also access modes as valid (or invalid) as thinking'. We need to be in the world with as little conceptualisation of it as the animals or maybe even the stones.

Modern thought assumes that we experience only what our own minds allow us to experience. We are said to live within the filter of our own perceptions, encountering not the actual things of the world, the 'noumena', but things as they appear to us, the 'phenomena' of a perceived world. Morton is insistent on the reality of things beyond our perception of them. Of course there is going to be a boundary between us and that reality – it is difficult to meet the noumenal world of actual things – as there is between every organism and the reality in which it is embedded, but the task of understanding is to make that boundary 'spongy', to recognise that 'there is a loose, thick, wavy line between things and their phenomena'. Only because the world and its categories are 'perforated and permeable' can we understand them at all. If everything existed in sealed categories, we would know nothing.

Fuzziness is a necessary openness to the reality of other lives.

It is the core ecological idea. Solidarity – 'the fact of being perfectly united or at one with something' – is the means of crossing or even living in that spongy boundary, so that *permeation*, the flooding in and through of all things by all things, is the foundational act of engaging with a reality that is 'necessarily ragged and pock-marked'. It also chimes with the intermediate disturbance hypothesis and with the traditional practices of Wealden farming. In all three, there is no permanent presence or exclusion. Everything comes and goes, everything is permeated, in the ragged and pock-marked way that Hollow Flemings embodies.

A conceptualised plea for de-conceptualisation may be paradoxical but there are deep rewards in it. We may all be alarmed by passivity, by the prospect of setting aside for a moment our agency, even our self-hood, and allowing all kinds of other realities to permeate through us. But with a glow of recognition I realised that the building of the bird-house was a folding out into the material world, a concretising, of just these ideas. It was a small laboratory for passive connectedness, allow-ing the birds to project a sense of the uncontrolled reality of their lives a few inches from my nose.

It is not as if Timothy Morton was the first to recognise the allure of the half-defined or the transient. There should be a portmanteau word in English to mean the-beauty-of-the-thing-almost-grasped-as-it-passes. I found myself looking again and again online at a drawing by Leonardo of a small stand of self-regenerating trees and shrubs, clearly growing on unmanaged or abandoned land, and perhaps twenty or thirty years old. They were curiously like the little copse of young birches, oaks and hazels next to the birdhouse. It is one of the subtle treasures of our world, made one morning in about 1500, bequeathed by Leonardo to his pupil and probable lover Francesco Melzi, finding its way in the early seventeenth century into the collection of Thomas Howard, Earl of Arundel and from him to Charles II. It is now ensconced in the Royal Collection at Windsor.

I felt, looking at it, as if Leonardo had drawn my own tiny patch of wood, with a miraculous ability to do what Morton had suggested. Leonardo's copse, filled with the shimmer of early summer light, seems alive. Here with the breeze moving among the branches is the-thing-almost-grasped-as-it-passes, some elements of those trees quite still, drawn with the sharp point of the chalk, others blurred and softened, muddled into motion where the chalk was lightly wetted on Leonardo's tongue.

Leonardo da Vinci (1452–1519), A stand of trees c. 1500

Earlier artists had drawn nature as if it consisted of solid and distinct objects disposed around the world, removed from any perception of them. Here the small wood was something that had been drawn as seen. It was as much Leonardo's apprehension of the copse that morning as the existence of the copse itself, as much alive as when first committed to its few square inches of paper, a model of the perforated boundary between self and world.

In the cold of the day and with the heat of the fire, I opened all the windows of the birdhouse, latching them up so that it felt as if I were sitting both inside and outside, warm with the fire to one side, cold with the air on the other, a small wooden building half-embraced by a Sussex wood, with the high-pitched rattling of the blue tits and great tits in the branches beside me.

I had Morton's and other books on the desk, a cup of coffee from a gas ring in my hand, no internet connection, passivity the chosen condition, the Leonardo-trees stirring in the light wind outside and thought that this was as near as I could hope to come to a permeated, category-defusing condition.

And then into the house, through the window on to one of the fold-down desks beside me, came my first co-occupant, unsummoned, claiming the place as its own, soon jumping down behind my buckets and sacks of bird food, tucking in behind the woven chestnut panels: *Troglodytes troglodytes*, the Cave-dweller Cave-dweller, a wren.

3.

Wrens

SURVIVING

That first winter, the little cave-dweller – it is his name in French: *le troglodyte mignon*; in Breton 'the cheerful one' – came to live in the birdhouse. Nick Walsh had made a shallow louvre at the top of the roof, to aerate the interior, and on cold nights the wren managed to slip in through that gap, the narrowest of entrances for this speleologist, looking for shelter from the weather and the residual night-warmth from the fire I had kept up all day. I took to stoking it late each afternoon before I left.

A balloon of cold had dropped on England. In the frost, the old oak leaves still fixed to the trees looked sugar-glazed. The ink froze in my pen and only started to flow when I held the barrel near the fire. The bowl of water for the dogs was crusted with ice and the frost made maps and diagrams on the window glass. Whole etched landscapes appeared, an alluvial plain marked with woods and single trees, and alleys of clear ground between them. Fronds and branch-lines of frost lasted all day on the glass of the north side.

The snow came in its different modes. Cold drizzle, then wide flakes, drifting in through the windows when I had them open, slowly dropping on to the desks and benches like people settling in for a play.

Then a hard and whistling wind that drove the snow in through the roof vent, filling the volume of the shed inside, a globe of specks that melted as they turned in the air above me.

The trees were heavy with it. Oak boughs came down in the wood, cracked off in the cold, lying, many of them still fully leaved, on the snow-dusted floor. On one of these mornings, as I arrived at the bird-house, I found a female bullfinch sitting quite still in a little pit of snow scarcely bigger than its own body. Black cap, pale-pink brown on its chest. A big atmosphere about it. I thought maybe its own heat had melted the space around its body, so that it was resting in its own thaw. Its eye was bright but its energy had gone and as I picked it up it lay calmly in my hand, opening and closing its stubby black bill, weakened with cold. No cry. I took it inside the birdhouse to warm up and set it on a bed of old moss I had peeled from the trunk of an ash. It sat watching me with the brilliant globes of its black eyes. I lit the fire and wondered if I had found it too late and was witnessing the death of this beautiful thing, the colours of its plumage on chest and back shifting from pink to brown and an almost chestnut grey so that no boundary was visible between them – unlike the glamorous and severe definition

of the black on its strong bull head, its wings and tail. A miraculous, watchful creature, sleek in its perfection but too diminished by the cold to show any fear.

It sat on the moss nest for ten minutes or so before it began to flutter and then strike out with its wings, still feeling at my fingers gently and weakly with its bill. I held it gradually warming in my hand and when it was ready took it outside and as I opened my hand it flew off into the trees.

The wren was not like that. It was alacrity made flesh and claimed this house from the beginning. I would arrive to find it scuttling from one bench and chest to another. Edward Armstrong, the best of all wren-describers, liked how 'it perks, bobs, teeters and frequently presses forward as if it had an appointment in mind'. The acorns and old oak sprigs I had gathered on the desks were all turned upside down. Sarah had given me a tiny collection of little model birds made in the 1960s by a gamekeeper a few villages away, each half an inch tall, and they were stirred about, shoved on to the floor, no respect shown.

The wren's droppings were all over the desks, especially where it had sat on the tie-beams in the roof, leaving a dripped line of white dabs below them. It had played with bits of an old blue tit nest that I had found so that tufts of moss and wool were scattered about the room. Every time I tidied everything up and set the model birds back on their shelf and wiped away the droppings, I would find the same thing the next day. I was servicing a wren hotel.

The bird was a little frightened of me and always gave its sharp alarm cry as I came up through the trapdoor in the floor. Sometimes it would walk along one of the windowsills, then hop from book to book. Or fly across the room, with incredible acuity, at ankle height – no rhythm in the flight – in an unbroken beeline three inches above the floor. Sometimes it flitted from one corner to another like a pinball in an arcade game and then stood on its tiny sprung legs, bouncing up and down, tail cocked, looking this way and that as if testing its own suspension. There seemed to be nothing longitudinal about it, more like a ball in flight, which like a helicopter might as well fly in reverse as forwards.

It was not the easiest of relationships but in these cold days we learned to live together, contented enough as long as we didn't try to meet. The bird didn't like being photographed and the only picture I have of it was snatched in an out-of-focus moment as it scuttled across the top of my edition of Gilbert White's journal.

If unlooked-at, the wren seemed all right. Better inside, even if accompanied by a human being, than out in the cold. He fluttered and clicked around the birdhouse and into the gaps in the chestnut panels on the walls, liking to sit on the floor between my splitting axe and the broom. We spent many hours together like that. The whole place was filled with his tiny presence. I once put the pen down and picked it up to find it sticky with his droppings. The true rewilding.

I wanted to call my new companion Emily Wren after Emily Dickinson. 'I am small, like the Wren,' she wrote in an early letter to T.W. Higginson, her mentor and encourager, 'and my Hair is bold, like the Chestnut Bur – and my eyes, like the Sherry in the Glass, that the Guest leaves.' And like the wren, she would have been at home in the birdhouse. Higginson had asked her what companions she had in life. She replied:

Hills – Sir – and the Sundown – and a Dog – large as myself,
that my Father bought me – They are better than Beings –
because they know – but do not tell – and the noise in the Pool,
at Noon – excels my Piano.

But Emily Dickinson had a rival. John Clare, her equal as the poet of birds, loved wrens for their bright, everyday ordinariness, the quality in his poetry that Seamus Heaney called 'an unspectacular joy and love for the inexorable one-thing-after-anotherness of the world'. Perhaps,

if he had been asked, Clare would have said he was a wren. Sitting with
my wren in the frost, I read for the first time, in another moment of
recognition, Clare's poem in which he remembered how, when he was
a boy-labourer in Northamptonshire, a wren

> many a time hath sought
> Shelter from showers in huts where I did dwell
> In early Spring, the tenant of the plain,
> Tenting my sheep.

And so this bright refugee-companion acquired a double name: John-
Emily Wren, half-Clare, half-Dickinson.

It hid most of the time. Often I didn't dare turn round for fear of
disturbing its calm and merely sat there listening to its scratchings as it
ate the remains of lacewings and other insects that had fallen into the
cracks between the floorboards. It often chattered to me. Usually very
quietly, it sang in the frost, as if it were thawing, a tiny whistling and
fluting so light I could hardly hear it, a little clickety wren, a wren
peeping off when it felt like it. The song was not machine-like, but
with an occasional trill interrupting its staccato notes, and with long
silences between phrases, sometimes squeezing out the notes as if closing the opening in his throat. The ending of the song was always a bit
inconclusive. It reminded Edward Grey, the distinguished British poli-
tician-cum-naturalist in the early twentieth century, of the efforts of
the lady who concluded her address of a public meeting with the words
'But still …' and sat down.

The wren summoned a kind of fondness in me in the way Clare
described – he loved it more than the nightingale – but I know now
that quietness is not the wren's default mode. A wren at full belt sings
with a desperate and loud urgency, a vehement blast of repeating notes.
Its percussive stream seems larger than its own tiny sharp-billed, carefully delineated body and something about that combination of

stridency and smallness, the sheer sweetness of the wren and its loud ferocity, made it the perfect beginning for my lessons: what was this little feathered life beyond the anxious flickering I could hear behind me as I sat listening, pretending to read?

Wrens are among the very lightest of our birds, weighing one third of an ounce or ten grams, about the weight of two sheets of paper, too small to survive cold for long. The frost is murderous for them. In hard winters, they can be found roosting together, usually not more than ten in one place, but sixty-one were once found crammed into a sheltered nook. No wren spends the winter anywhere that January temperatures drop below –7 degrees Celsius and many in Europe migrate to escape the cold, either southwards – Swedish wrens have been known to fly 1,500 miles to northern Italy for a Mediterranean winter – or in the Alps down off mountains where they have summered.

British wrens are not so mobile and there can be little doubt that the birdhouse and its louvre-entrance had been a life-saver for this bird. At regular intervals, frost devastates them. Between January and March 1963 England suffered its coldest winter since 1740. There were widespread reports of high numbers of dead and dying birds. Moorhens, lapwings, mistle thrushes and song thrushes all died in numbers. Thousands of robins and blackbirds were found dead in the fields and under hedges. But no bird suffered more than the wren, whose population fell by 79 per cent in that one winter. It took until 1967 for their numbers to recover.

There is no need to be sentimental about this. Perhaps the birdhouse had saved John-Emily, but whatever the winter, three-quarters of all wren chicks will die in their first year of life and almost 70 per cent of the survivors will die the following year, and 70 per cent of those survivors the year after that. Most wrens can expect to live no more than two years. The oldest recorded was seven years and four months old.

The pattern repeats. After that harsh winter, there was a steep increase up to the mid-1970s, when a series of cold winters slashed the numbers again, with parts of the country seeing a mortality rate of more than two-thirds, only for the wrens to recover once more. The population went through a sleigh ride, crashing again in the winter of 1996, peaking in 2006, crashing in 2011, reaching an even higher peak in 2017, dipping again, before rising in Britain and Ireland in 2023 to a record eleven million wren territories (each with a male bird and potentially several mates). The wren is now the commonest bird in the British Isles. They may summon our nurturing instincts but we need have no fear for them. They combine spectacular vulnerability with spectacular resilience, and it is a successful genetic strategy. They remain small because it is less costly to maintain a small body, even if smallness makes them vulnerable to the cold. Wren genes can risk mass destruction at regular intervals on the assumption that after the crash growth will return. Averaged out over decades, wren populations are almost stable.

The motor for this multi-generational life pattern is an urgent erotic energy. The answer to death is sex. If the wrens suffer in cold winters, their full-on approach to breeding will start to refill the niches the following spring, a fierce compulsion to propagate that has driven it to world success. Like many other wrens, ours began as an American species, and the sheer vehemence of its tiny life has driven it, drop by drop, territory by territory, across the whole of Eurasia.

Look at a wren and you are not seeing a sweet little fragmentary being but the demands of life itself, the product of tens of millions of generations bundled into a tiny round cocktailed package. Its evolutionary history is scarcely believable. It flies at a little more than twelve miles per hour, and is known in Shetland as 'the wee brown button … too much like a mouse to lay eggs', but wrens have spread from the Atlantic coast of Canada to the Pacific Northwest of the United States, across the Aleutians, island by island, each one with a different subspecies, to Japan, and on to Tibet and the Himalayas, thriving in Sikkim

and Kashmir, to the shores of the Caspian and Turkestan, on into
Europe, up to 7,700 feet in the snows of Psiloriti in Crete, where I have
seen them at six o'clock on a frosty August morning, to the High Atlas
in Morocco, to France, Britain and Iceland and only stopping short of
the shores of Greenland. Wrens have landed and developed into separate subspecies on St Kilda and Fair Isle. It is the first lesson I learned
from the little creature in the winter birdhouse with me: its essence is
not vulnerability but vibrancy.

The spectacular life-drive of the wren has long been recognised deep
within European culture, having played a part in a pair of rituals that
survived until the twentieth century. The first took place either on 26
December, St Stephen's Day, or Twelfth Night, 6 January. Men and
boys would beat the hedgerows until they caught or killed a wren. The
bird would be nailed to a pole or put in a cage dressed with ribbons
that were tied into holly and ivy and other winter greens. The shrine
would then be taken from house to house, where the 'wren boys' would
sing at the door and ask for food and drink. In return the householders
would be given 'lucky feathers from the bird'. At the end of the day the
wren, by now almost naked, would, if not already dead, be solemnly
killed and buried.

In the depths of winter, a tiny radiant creature was captured, sacri-
ficed, reverenced and buried. This was the remains of a fertility rite, a
ritual to banish the deathliness of winter and, like all sacrifices, to offer
up the beautiful in the hope of appeasing the brutal and destructive
forces of the world.

Winter sacrifice of the wren was accompanied by a spring version,
when the bird was again captured and displayed in little boxes deco-
rated with leaves and spring flowers, though this time not killed but
honoured before being released back into the wild. These May festivi-
ties were sexualised, a celebration of the power of the procreative drive
in people as much as in birds. And the wren was well chosen because it
does indeed turn out to be the most lustful of creatures.

Shakespeare knew it so that when King Lear looked for a symbol of the sexuality that ruled the world, it was the insects and the wren he chose:

The wren goes to't, and the small gilded fly
Does lecher in my sight.
Let copulation thrive ...
To't, luxury, pell-mell ...

Sheer procreative energy and sexual demand on the wing is what the little cocked tail and the bright habits of the wren's darting, dancing body, popping in and out of the shadows, now say to me. It is a ten-gram bundle of desire.

With the last of the frosts, John-Emily left the birdhouse. But all year, I was never without a wren. John-Emily and the millions of cousin wrens were with me wherever I went – in the oaks outside the birdhouse, in the pile of fallen timber by our kitchen door, fizzing through shadows in the brambles of Hollow Flemings, silently foraging, hopping around behind the barn doors, occupying every part of the rough grounds.

They were soon on their spring drive. The winter damage had to be made good. As the bullfinches returned to feast on the blackthorn blossom, and as other birds found their way into the birdhouse through the open windows, including one angry, anxious chaffinch, radiating the black, blue, green and amber brilliance of his spring breeding plumage, the wrens set to it.

The growing light levels were making deep physiological changes in them, as in all birds. In the females, as the days lengthen and brighten, the egg-laying mechanism grows and thickens. In the males, the testicles start to grow by a factor of a hundred or more. A winter testicle that might occupy less than a cubic millimetre – a mustard seed – could be almost one hundred cubic millimetres – the size of a pea – by

A male chaffinch

mid-April, having increased in size by four or five cubic millimetres a day until it occupies 3 per cent of the wren's body, pumping it full of aggressive male hormones.

Wrens now begin their preparations for breeding. They re-establish the boundaries of their territories by singing their hard, metallic territorial songs at any of up to seven neighbouring rivals. When not singing, the males start to build what are called cock nests, often made only of sticks roughly laid together, or in this wood of moss torn from the boles of fallen trees.

These nests are signals of their own excellence made to the females, who have much larger and overlapping territories and who in early spring roam the woods and rough grounds looking for suitable mates. Nests are expensive to make. Each one can take between half a day and five days to build. By the time it is finished, the cock nest weighs on average four times as much as the bird that created it.

This expense is part of the point. A high-quality cock is one that builds strings of nests (the most that have ever been found is twelve on one wren's territory) and female wrens judge a male by how many candidate nests he has made. The more a wren has built, the more likely it is that a female will mate with him. He controls an acre or even two – a lot of land for a small bird. Other, bigger songbirds tend to hold less ground: a reed warbler only five hundred square yards, a willow warbler about a third of an acre, a blackcap or a garden warbler a little more. It seems that a wren in particular depends for his well-being on making something of a show in the world, part of the widespread phenomenon in nature of the displayed handicap: if a male peacock can cope with such a tail, or a wren waste so much energy on unused nests, he is a mate worth having.

He sings and displays high in his territory, with his tail erect. Scientists have found a correlation between the length of that tail and high breeding success. Huge testicles, a long upright tail standing high above him and an extensive, nest-filled territory with plenty of cover in which to hide: these are the foundations of wren triumph.

Tail cocked up, mid-summer assertion

Once he has filled his spreading acres with potential homes, he finds a female prospecting and takes her on a tour, showing her nest after nest with a sweet cooing, quite unlike the machine-gun rattle he fires off at his male rivals. He sings outside or on top of each one and then inside to demonstrate its qualities. He is advertising to her the genetic likelihood that her offspring will also be top birds, capable of controlling and furnishing a territory as splendidly as he has. She is choosy. Female wrens have been seen flying from one territory to another, taking the tour and moving on to see if they could improve their chances. Her investment, after all, is in the even more energy-expensive process of creating, laying and incubating eggs.

On the farm, I found one wren cock nest rather roughly shoved into the housing of a hose reel next to the cow shed, another in the chassis of a van, and a third, more carefully made, of moss fronds that had been pushed into a hole in a barn wall where half a brick had fallen out, usually concealed by the barn door being kept open. All the nests had tiny openings and a long shallow passageway leading to the nest cavity.

Neither the van nor the hose-reel housing had met with the approval of any female but the nook in the dark behind the barn door had seemed suitable enough and that nest a wren-hen had lined with feathers and tufts of wool into which her five, six or seven eggs could be laid.

Wren coupling is less like a marriage than a merger. Both birds are more interested in profitable outcomes than the lovability of their partner. The fact that he has persuaded her to fit out and lay in one of his nests does not stop him courting other females or showing them the other nests he has made, nor mating with them and fathering several further broods that summer, each with a different hen. Individual cock wrens can have up to nine wives in one year. She too, having raised her chicks in May or June, will not hesitate to find another cock in another territory (almost never the same wren again) to lay and raise a second, third or fourth brood before the summer comes to an end. Polygyny rules, the male wrens holding their accommodating territories, the females cruising between them, the genetic material proliferating through the woods.

In this way, even though a variety of predators take a fifth of all nests, if not more, removing both eggs and nestlings, the population pump restores the damage the winters have wrought.

It is as if the wrens are the matadors of the songbird world. Each time they add a stick or a piece of moss to their cock nests, the wren will sing snatches of song at steady intervals beside it. Here I am! This is me! Look at Nest 7! It is one way in which birders can locate the otherwise well hidden and disguised structures the birds have made.

It is a paradox. Make every effort you can to conceal the precious nest and then shout about its location to all enemies and predators. The ornithologists Matthew Evans and Joe Burn have speculated that this is a flamboyant gesture by the male wrens. If they are doing something that carries with it a high possibility of harm, they are demonstrating to any passing hen a quality that might be called courage, or at least bravado. Who but a top wren would dare in the omnipresent face of the enemy to sing about his nests so clearly?

In the shrubland of Hollow Flemings, the kind of territory a wren likes to inhabit, with plenty of bramble and bracken, I was surrounded by unseen nests. Its acre or two would have been the size of a city block for a wren, full of hidden alleyways and rewarding corners, its geography and resources intimately known by the bird who would have spent nearly all its life there, familiar with the routes through, the resting places, the convenient bypasses. Only the occasional sight of a wren hop-skipping in the shadows between the leaves and the insistent territorial song gave their pervasive presence away.

Hollow Flemings was a cockpit of competition. The boundaries of wren territories seemed to meet around it, so that different wrens sang in the high ash wood above the birdhouse, in the young oak wood to the east, in the big old hazel shaw around the stream below and in the strip of rough hedgerow that stepped up the field to the west.

The male wrens were singing to keep their rivals away. Undoubtedly, the competition is real. As you might expect, sexual fidelity is not high on a wren's list of virtues. Hens paired with a low-quality male will often choose to mate with a more alluring neighbour or stranger. And top males seem to be attractive to a large number of females. When DNA analysis is done on the eggs and chicks in wren nests, it turns out that two out of every five nests contain eggs that have been fertilised by a wren other than the father of the rest of the brood.

Nevertheless, wren fathers seem to be better at keeping their rivals at bay than other species. Among reed buntings, nearly three-quarters of all nests had eggs in them that had been fertilised by different fathers, with more than half of all chicks being the offspring of stranger or neighbour birds. In several sad-sounding nests, every single one of the eggs had been fertilised by a reed bunting that was not the notional father of the brood. In wrens, although 40 per cent of nests showed evidence of some adultery, only 16 per cent of the chicks were not the offspring of the cock wren whose nest it was.

What explains the male wrens' relative success in keeping rivals out of the domestic nest? It looks as if they have a ferocious form of neighbour hatred. In many species, territory owners respond aggressively to strangers, recognising that they are probably on the look-out for a territory of their own. Neighbour birds they have known for some time, perhaps since the previous autumn, who are already settled in their own territory and won't be in need of invading another, are treated more gently. This higher tolerance of neighbours than strangers was recognised in the 1950s when it was called the 'dear enemy effect'. Skylarks, for example, deny the intrusions of skylark neighbours at the beginning of the breeding season, when boundaries are not known for sure, but by high summer the birds settle down and recognise, in effect, that good fences make good neighbours and that it is not worth spending the energy fighting over boundaries.

Wrens are different. Bird songs contain many variations that are scarcely audible to our ears but which allow them to discriminate between different rival singers. Usually, neighbour birds sing songs that are quite like each other's – local dialects that extend across a farm or around the edges of a single wood – and serve as a marker for those birds that are based locally. Strangers don't know the local dialect and so it is possible for birds to tell when a marauding interloper has turned up.

But wrens don't discriminate between strangers and neighbours. Unlike the larks, neighbour wrens continue to engage in intense vocal contests throughout the breeding season, making no distinction between the song of a long-established neighbour and that of a stranger flying in. Each stands either in the centre of their territories or on the border, quivering their wings, perched on bushes or singing posts at the peak of the undergrowth, directing their song at their rivals next door. Wren song, under ideal conditions, can be heard six hundred yards or even half a mile away. They listen to each other. And it is possible to stand between two of them in high summer, hearing the antiphonal response from one side and then the other, each wren waiting for the other to finish before he begins his response.

Trust plays no part in wren world. Everyone remains an enemy. Sexual partners cannot be trusted, nor neighbours. Everybody is out for the main chance, your children may well not be your children, your future is not assured. It is world in which trustlessness alone makes sense. And because wrens don't trust their neighbours, the level of extra-pair paternity is lower than among other species. It is a form of highly expensive exclusion made necessary by the almost unequalled sex drive of the bird.

Much later in the summer, with the bramble, the briar rose, the dog rose and the elderflower all out, I happened to be passing the door of the barn just at the moment of the fledgling wrens' emergence from their nest. The little birds as round as bumble bees were dropping like drips from a tap out of the mossy cushion their parents had pushed into the gap in the brickwork. One after another they came, each one a gobbet of life. One was too small to fly – it was the last to emerge – and it fell softly to the ground, scarcely heavier than a feather, landing in the gap between the open barn door and the wall. The others had left but from there it scuttled, like a young turtle making for the safety of the ocean, out across the yard to the cattle trough, which for drainage is set on a layer of tiles above the ground. In that narrow slice of dark under the trough, the young wren, for a moment anyway, found its refuge.

A week or two after that, early one evening, I was sitting in the birdhouse with the windows open, looking out at the young oak trees beside me. One robin was in pursuit of another, slaloming through the lacework of the branches. Coal tits, marsh tits, blue and great tits were flickering around the feeders, when without warning out of the darkening leaves, a wren flew into my face. It was a sudden flustering muddle of wing and feather, no claw or bill, but the breast of the little bundle of bird hurtling into my cheek. It wasn't painful, but I jumped and recoiled at the shock, confused that what had seemed like half-real bird images beyond the open window had surged into the third dimension. The wren was flung back at first on to the desk where it sat stunned at the accident, its eyes closed. I saw then how young it was, its age given away by the little yellow flange at the corner of its beak and the way its breast feathers were flecked as adults' are not.

Then it flew, in the wren's bright, immediate, cheerful, pulseless way, to a leafed branch of the oak outside, where it sat recovering, its tail cocking up and down, body flicking left and right, its head and peaky beak looking this way and that.

I sat there wishing an apology might be possible, the kind one makes to a person or a dog, saying repeatedly that it had been a mistake and that this young wren, perhaps John-Emily's offspring, was never more welcome than now. But you can't apologise to a wren. We do not know each other and their lives are invisible to us. They remain wrapped in their distances.

4.

Songbirds

PROCLAIMING

I wake in the dark of a night late in the spring, as Robert Louis Stevenson once did in the Cévennes, with the sky at the blue end of black, and like him feel beyond the windows 'the open world as it passes lightly, with its stars and dews and perfumes …'

It is four o'clock and nothing is lit. I am familiar with this moment; Stevenson called it 'the stirring hour'. Just now the cattle and sheep on the farm move in their beds, shifting the ache in their limbs, standing for an awkward moment, resettling, re-finding their rest.

I slide into yesterday's clothes, go downstairs, shrug on the coat and boots by the back door and walk out into the morning. It is raining. I feel it spit by spit on my cheeks and nose. It is not quite so dark that no deeper dark is apparent within it. This farm is far from street lights, buried in its fat belt of woodland. Everything is thick. The hedges are bent and burdened nowadays, twenty, thirty feet tall, dense with ivy and honeysuckle and bowed over around me as hunchbacked shadows. Only the leafless limbs of the stag oak beside the stream in the field below the house stand up against the sky beyond it. On the ground nothing is clear. The woods are no more than presences, known but unseen, the fields grey, unlit openings between them.

I stand, listen and hear the silence of the night as a high ringing. Thousands of feet above me, the engines of an early jet sigh as it slows towards the airport thirty miles to the west, rolling and groaning across the woods, down into the valley of the River Dudwell, leaving in their wake a shapeless rumbling, before that too fades.

The silence drops again and I stand unmoving under the curve of an old ivied blackthorn that leans out across the opening of a gate. I put my hands on its top bar but the metal is cold and wet and so instead rest there with my elbows. The sheep in the pasture beyond, a reedy bit of ground called Long Field, are pale, half-seen, soft-edged, as formless as gnocchi. As the minutes and half-hours pass I stand there suspended from the everyday.

The blackbird starts to sing. He is just above me, sitting high in the top of the hedge. The rain is still ticking against my waterproof but in the dark, I stand under him as he sings so that there in the gateway, I am four or five feet away, awash with his song. I cannot see him but the juice of his life is running around me, a blackcurrant liquid of song in the cold and wet, a gift from nothing, forever repeating the syrup of his phrases.

The farmers on the far side of the valley are starting to turn on their bedroom lights. The wind is coming hard through the tops of the big oaks but the morning is as still and dark as a pond.

There is a hint of a cackle in the bird's song. And while the wind is blowing and gusting now and then through the hedge, the blackbird's song is like the sound of someone enjoying a lovely dinner, rolling around in his mouth the deliciousness of everything life has given him, sometimes trilling out towards the end of a phrase, compressing the notes as if they were cream pushed through the nozzle of a tube, but otherwise full, unfiltered.

I must have heard this performance ten thousand times before but have never listened. It is better for being in the dark, so close and so loud, for the bird not knowing I am there to love what he has to offer.

That May, it became something I would look forward to every day, getting up in the night, creeping from the bedroom not to disturb Sarah, wanting to get out to where I would find the blackbird flinging his song into the silence around him.

Morning after morning I was up before dawn to hear him. Every time I heard something different. If a cherry could sing, I thought one day, it would sound like a blackbird, rounded and full and fleshy, that dark sugar-juice. Or a pot of apricots bubbling over, the sharpness in the sweetness, a sudden asperity. Or something matronly about it, a full embonpoint of song, as if a contralto were running through her scales in a drawing room somewhere at the far end of the house, and thinking to herself what pleasure there was to be had from life. Or maybe it was meaty, the music that boeuf bourguignon would make after it has been long bubbled on the heat. Or at other times, the laziness of a master toying with his instrument, the phrases played on the keys of a piano neglected in the corner of a bar, a cigarette in the mouth or smoking on the side. Or a slide guitar: no frets, all slip.

One description after another floated up into my mind with each familiar phrase. It was all too much, this way of talking or thinking about a bird, but what else do we have?

Ted Hughes once wrote a dazzling account of a crow in flight. With each inventive phrase, Hughes relished and disparaged his own brilliance:

It is not enough to say the crow flies purposefully, or heavily, or rowingly, or whatever. There are no words to capture the infinite depth of crowiness in the crow's flight. All we can do is use a word as an indicator, or a whole bunch of words as a general directive. But the ominous thing in the crow's flight, the bare-faced, bandit thing, the tattered beggarly gipsy thing, the caressing and shaping yet slightly clumsy gesture of the down-stroke, as if the wings were both too heavy and too powerful, and the headlong sort of merriment, the macabre pantomime ghoulishness and the undertaker sleekness – you could go on for a very long time with phrases of that sort and still have completely missed your instant, glimpse knowledge of the world of the crow's wingbeat. And a bookload of such descriptions is immediately rubbish when you look up and see the crow flying.

That paragraph was never out of my mind as I listened again and again to the effortless music of the blackbird, that looping liquidity, the slowness, its turning through its notes. However inadequate the language, those were the elements of what Hughes called the 'instant, glimpse knowledge' that both flight and song can give. We come to recognise the bird but we do not know exactly what it is we recognise.

I knew the blackbird's song as the music of summer. Any filmmaker would only have to put a blackbird in full song on the soundtrack of his film and warmth would fill the screen with images of sunlight falling through leaves, the round bosom of summer. I realised that the summer moments I remembered, like the warm wind making its way between shirt and skin, were often, at root, memories of blackbird song. I had always known it without knowing it.

The blackbird in the wide hedge running down from our polytunnels to the stream at the bottom of Long Field would sing for twenty minutes at a time. As the spring moved on, I would come out into the dawn dark with no shoes or boots and walk with cold feet through the wet of the grass and listen to him toying with song, a rolling shapeliness from the hedgerows as if a plum and its stone were being passed back and forth between teeth and tongue.

When daylight came, I hid beside the gate and watched him sing. Of course it was no casual laid-back performance. The song summoned a physical quivering in the bird; the whole of its body poured itself into song. What might have reached me as the strumming on a loose-stringed guitar began as a shuddering muscular spasm, with the phrases made not in the mouth but in the depth of the body, in the way that organ notes come not from the mouths on the visible tubes but from the whole metal and timber structure that supports them.

Listen to a blackbird and all you get is waves of ineffable enriched sweetness. But watch a blackbird singing and you will see something approaching a life-or-death performance.

On these first spring mornings, I started to acquire the birds around me. One wet cloudy dawn after another, I was up to hear them before the daylight leaked in. Out in the pastures, the grass was crusted with frost, bleaching it a pale sky-blue, but somehow the frost did not penetrate the wood. Instead its floor began to fill with a salad coat of garlic leaves, glossed with rain after a wet night, as gleamy as a showroom of new cars. Mist filled the alder carr at the bottom of Long Field. The hollows in the field where the cattle had sunk into the wet autumn surface had filled with water and each now was closed off with a half-opaque, half-transparent lid of ice, contoured in pale and dark. I had read somewhere that in summer these poach marks would make perfect skylark nests. That seemed a long way off. On moonlit dawns, each of the raindrops hanging from the tips of the birches and hazels held a bright white moon inside it like a fly in amber.

I had with me something that would transform my relationship to the birds, a modern miracle: a free program on a mobile phone that can identify birdsong in real time. Turn it on and even if many birds are singing at one time it can tell you what they are. The sound app was developed in 2021 by a young American AI specialist called Grant Van Horn. He had done a doctorate at the Visipedia lab at Caltech in California, which for years has specialised in the ability of computers to recognise visual patterns, and in 2019 joined forces with the venerable Lab of Ornithology at Cornell University in upstate New York. Cornell has been gathering data on the world's birds since 1915 and has assembled an archive from tens of thousands of citizen scientists.

As a result it knows where nearly all eleven thousand-odd of the world's bird species are to be found, when they are there and what they both sound and look like. The data on which this knowledge relies is derived from more than eight hundred million sightings submitted to the university's eBird website.

Van Horn's expertise is what, rather densely, he calls 'human-in-the-loop, machine-learning-powered community science apps … crafting real-world systems that integrate human expertise and large-scale datasets'. As those phrases might imply, there is some complexity at source, manipulating vast amounts of information, using AI to integrate new observations and refine what it knows.

A photo-based version of the app, drawing on Van Horn's research at Caltech, had been launched in 2017, using the kind of image recognition software that chooses large or small potatoes in a packing plant or the licence plates of speeding cars. Users could take a photograph with their phone and the app would tell them what bird they had seen. But to do this is difficult. Birds tend to disappear.

Sound, though, is different. Birds themselves use it to be present when they can't be seen, and to extend their presence beyond the limited physical space their bodies occupy. Birdsong is an extension of the bird's self into the air. The very qualities that lie at the root of birdsong – advertised life within a concealing environment – can be used by us to know the birds we cannot see. It had long been a dream of birders that a computer might recognise birdsong in real time. No one had managed it because computers find it more difficult to analyse the aural than the visual. The breakthrough came when Van Horn and the Cornell team turned to the electronic traces of songs known as spectrograms, spectrographs or sonograms. These graphs of song, which can show their loudness, duration and pitch, are an old technology. Before the Second World War, the Bell Laboratory in the United States had used spectrographs to produce pictures of human speech intended to be used by the deaf. They didn't work. Only one person ever managed to read them, but the American Navy realised that the Bell device could be used for another purpose: the engines of friendly and enemy submarines made different sounds underwater. The Bell spectrographs could distinguish between them.

Alongside the magnetic tape recorder developed by the Germans in the war, spectrographic analysis of birdsong was first used in the 1950s. When combined with the modern digital technology that could bring the spectrograms to a phone, this ability to analyse the look of songs was a breakthrough.

Many songs are similar but in detail every one is unique. The same tools that can analyse a picture of a bird can be used on the picture of its voice. To reduce the choices available, the app has to know where and when you are listening, but with those filters applied, each heard spectrogram can be checked against those in Cornell's memory bank and in that way the bird can be known.

Van Horn spent the first six months of 2021 creating the Sound ID, working in his parents' spare bedroom in California. He wrote the code in the early mornings, from six to ten, going for cycle rides to tease out recalcitrant problems with bugs in the system, not dependent on the team at Cornell but working remotely, to his own deadlines and with no more than a basic software program to write and edit the code. It was quick and intense work but by June that year he had finished and the app was released to the world a month later, with a name that could be applied to both wizard and bird: Merlin.

Merlin in the pocket expanded my own embryonic knowledge. I downloaded the appropriate part of the Cornell archive (Western Europe), told the app the date and where I was standing and asked it to listen. No need to be online or have a signal. The phone itself could do all the work and so, newly equipped, still feeling a little sceptical, I walked out across the farm for the first time with the wizard in hand. It was as if my ears had acquired binoculars. Birds I did not know sang to me. I could hear where birds I did know had taken up their singing posts. I was embedded in a world of familiars. I could walk around the farm and meet my bird companions.

Morning after morning, I was living in a bowl of song. Identifiable beings surrounded me. No longer did I have to pick through the pitiable attempts at transcribing the voice of birds that have plagued enthusiasts for centuries. I had read a brutal review of a book written by the naturalist Charles Witchell who in 1899 attempted to transcribe the calls of the birds he loved.

A thrush says 'chick', a dipper 'ching', a tree pipit 'chip', a house-martin 'jigg', a cirl-bunting 'sip', a hawfinch 'sit', a chaffinch 'twit', a dabchick 'whit', the Great Spotted Woodpecker 'gick', the Lesser Spotted Woodpecker 'kink', a redwing 'quilp', a reed-bunting 'tink', a chaffinch 'pink'.

'Bearing in mind that in all these cases the consonants are imaginary,' the reviewer concluded,

the same calls must too often, to different ears, seem like totally different words. How many of us, for instance, would say with Mr Witchell that 'shushushushu' is the common cry of the Magpie?

Merlin and Van Horn made all that unnecessary. A combination of citizen science, artificial intelligence, machine-learning and the miniaturisation of the modern mobile phone and its microphone released us all into a new relationship with nature. Just as binoculars changed our connection to birds – Tim Dee says that the poetry of Ted Hughes, for example, would be unthinkable without binoculars, and that even Edward Thomas's sense of birds was changed by them in the early years of the twentieth century – Merlin has made the birds paradoxically nearer and more knowable than they have ever been, except perhaps by the expert few.

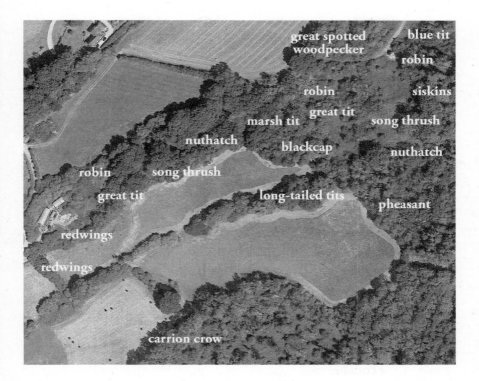

I knew even at the beginning that Merlin did not always get it right. It thought at one point we had an oystercatcher living in our oak woods, followed by a common sandpiper. But mistakes were rare and as I walked around the woods and fields I could map the birds that were singing or calling around me. The redwings, an unsuspected presence here, thrushes that had come as winter refugees from Scandinavia, were in the early days of spring still in the hedges by the blackbird gate; one robin was sopranoing in the first part of the shaw above the Long Field, another above Hollow Flemings and a third down by the birdhouse. A great tit was sawing away at the most boring of all bird songs – *and me and me and me and me and me and me* – below the robin in Long Field Shaw. Beside them was the peeping of a nuthatch and the whipped *fwheeet, wheep-wheep, wheep-wheep* of a song thrush, jazz-riffing like a joker with a violin. A crow cawed over on the edge of Coombe Wood to the south and from further off in the ash shaw above Hollow

Flemings came the beautiful resonant love-siren song of the mistle thrush, four notes, then five, practising the same phrase again and again with a kind of long, loud solemnity. In the mist of early mornings, I thought it the most beautiful thing I had ever heard, a compressed aria, briefly and repeatedly said, as it were a lament reduced to a single phrase: '*Don't leave me now, don't leave me now, don't let me die*', a voice lost in melancholy.

It was almost too much: fifteen identifiable birds, of which I knew almost nothing, coming at me in a clamorous crowd, needing and demanding attention. In the further wood, a buzzard mewed. The bright silver song of an overwintering blackcap, the first time I ever knew that wonderful bird for what it was, filled the lower slopes of Hollow Flemings. A blue tit scratched out a grating warning call beside it. A marsh tit sounded for a moment like a small and lighter version of a great tit, finer and more delicate. A coal tit sang *chick-a-dee, chick-a-dee, chick-a-dee* over and over again as if calling for its American cousin, the black-capped chickadee, to which the first English settlers gave that name. And in the stand of Western Hemlocks beyond the Perch Hill boundary, the siskins, little yellow, pine-loving finches, sang a high unbroken rivulet of song, almost without force or substance, like a stream running over pebbles, until I stood on a piece of fallen wood which cracked under me and they stopped.

A big woodpecker drilled into the trunk of a dying ash and, unheard by me but known to Merlin, some long-tailed tits peeped among the willows at the foot of the Long Field. For all that I tried, my hearing could not catch the sound they made.

Nevertheless, it was as if an entire term's-worth of birds had been laid out for me in the first week at school. 'We listen to be elsewhere,' Walter Benjamin once wrote of the experience of music, but this was sudden immersion in the hereness of here. I was living in a more populated and variegated world than I had ever understood, a richer place, more layered and more inhabited than I could have guessed.

Until now I had never known what magic there was in life before daylight and so to catch it I decided to sleep in the birdhouse. Nick Walsh had built three benches and a low desk that, if pushed together, could make a good bed. A mattress in a bag could be stored away in the daytime and rolled out at night.

And so one day in early summer I walked down through the wood in the last of the light after supper. Darkness was coming in like smoke. The greens were still distinguishable, the new oak leaves from the old, the birch from the hornbeam, and I felt as if I were swimming in quiet, the softness of the night thickening over me. At the birdhouse, it was cool and I lit the fire, rearranged the benches and the mattress, rolled out my sleeping bag, opened all the windows and lay down in the light of the flames as they burned down.

The dogs were curled up and calm on the bed, and we lay together in a wooden tent, sunk in a green sea, the only sound our breathing. A fox barked and the dogs sat up for a moment, alert, but soon curled back into their nose-to-tail doughnuts. I had my phone and Merlin beside me and fell asleep in a well of extraordinary peace.

At 3.51 I woke. A song thrush was singing. A few plain repeated notes, nothing more. Three minutes later a nuthatch, a near-electronic, telephonic beeping. Still no light in the sky.

3.56 a blackbird in the ash shaw to the north, a brief beginning, a beaded drop. The song thrush started again, in the oaks to the south and the wood pigeon now further away. The nuthatch again in among the hornbeams.

Parts of the morning air were just lightening to a pigeon grey.

At 3.58 a robin and a great tit sang as the light seeped into the birdhouse. Beyond the windows, looking from my sleeping bag, I could begin to see the greyed-out greens of the wood world.

Long pauses between these first snatches of song. At 4.01 a marsh tit and a minute later a chiffchaff. Again some silence and then at 4.06 a wren and a blackcap. The chorus was beginning and I dozed off as it grew around me, only waking half an hour later to hear it in concert, not quite a wall of sound but a garden of it, a woodful of it, pools and streams of it, a world crocheted in song, needleful after needleful as daylight started to colour the world around me.

The song thrush was singing sometimes two phrases, sometimes three, each of two parts, the first low on the sonograph and then full spectrum across it. But that was only part of it. The wood was a compendium of song: harshness, fullness, richness, gentleness, slightness, assertion, full-bloodedness and alarm.

Against the background of the chorus, a robin stood on the branch outside the window above my head. Without moving in my bed I could watch him, dark on his back, flecked on the chest, paling to grey, a certain redness only apparent in the plumage when he flew out of the shadow into the light.

It was a young one, making potent alarm calls like a thin steel comb on a railing, but no song. The testosterone fuel of birdsong had yet to

A coal tit

get hold of him. And so in his anxious state, he remained there, bending at the knee, looking at me carefully, hoverflies in the air between us, taking a little shit, flicking up the tail, like a finger in contempt, or a signal to a waiter, a turn, a flicker of the wings, as if preparing to leave, a turn on to another branch, then a turn on the spot, a tiny half-flight between two branches three inches apart. One of his bright interrogative eyes was always on me, first one side and then the other. Occasionally a straight binocular stare.

Further away, a blackbird shrieked in the wood, but another sang its fullness and a wren beside it. The lambs were bleating in Jim's Field beyond the ash shaw. St Francis thought lambs were always crying out for *Beee-th-le-heeem, Beee-th-le-heeem*. I was in a kind of paradise.

It has long been known that different birds start to sing each morning at different times. In 1913, Francis Allen, the editor of Thoreau's *Journals*, published an account of this staggered start to the bird day, having been recording them for almost fifty years in the woods around Boston. Others have done the same. The British artist-naturalist George Marples on the edge of the New Forest at Sway in Hampshire in the 1930s and Diego Llusia in the Île-de-France in the last few years both produced tables that ranked the birds in terms of the minutes before sunrise at which they first sang. How did my Perch Hill sequence compare with theirs?

The minutes before sunrise at which different birds start to sing

Perch Hill, 2022		Île-de-France, 2019		Hampshire, 1939	
43	song thrush	56	robin	44	blackbird
40	nuthatch	45	song thrush	43	song thrush
38	blackbird	40	blackbird	42	wood pigeon
36	robin	39	wren	34	robin
35	great tit	36	coal tit	23	pheasant
33	marsh tit	32	great tit	22	wren
32	chiffchaff	31	blue tit	17	great tit
28	wren	30	chaffinch	10	blue tit
27	blackcap	26	chiffchaff	9	chaffinch

The lists do not cover the same birds and are not in the same order, with a longer sequence in both Hampshire and France (thirty minutes or more from start to finish) than in Sussex (sixteen minutes), but nevertheless they are roughly equivalent. And a single striking fact emerges: one set of birds – robins, blackbirds, song thrushes (and a nuthatch for me) – all start singing earlier than tits, finches and, to a lesser extent, wrens. The French wrens seem to be early risers, but the Sussex and Hampshire wrens appear to stay quiet for longer.

This order in which the birds join the daily chorus seems to be a universal fact. Edward Armstrong, the wren expert, could always know that if he 'dressed quickly on hearing the first robin [he] could be out of doors in time to hear the first wren'.

Not until 2002 was the reason understood. Robert Thomas, then at the University of Bristol, and his colleagues measured the diameter of the exposed eye surfaces of a set of songbirds, and matched them to the times at which the birds first sang. Their paper published by the Royal Society made the connection clear: the bigger a bird's eyes, the earlier it could detect the light and so the earlier it started singing. In effect, birds with big eyes see the day earlier. From what is called nautical twilight, when the sun is still at twelve degrees under the horizon but its rays are spreading up over the rim of the earth, when sailors in the reflective conditions out at sea can begin to make out their surround-ings, the big-eyed birds know that day is starting. One by one, in what Thomas called 'a rather orderly fashion', the birds with ever-smaller eyes join the chorus of song until sunrise quietens them.

By the time birds such as chaffinches *Fringilla coelebs* and blue tits *Parus caeruleus* begin to sing, the earliest species are already beginning to fall silent.

Go for a walk in spring before sunrise and what you are hearing is not an anarchy of song but a set of aural flags being run up the flagpoles.

The genetic patterns of a sequence of birds allow them one by one to announce their recognition of the day. The songs are bird-sensibility and bird-identity translated into dawn music

Vision is of overriding importance in the life of birds. Compared with those of most animals, their eyes are large in relation to their bodies, to cope with the speed of flight, because eyes with a longer focal length and a wider aperture can both resolve objects at greater distances and recognise things more easily in low light. As a result, birds' eyes – of which we see only the exposed pupils – so completely fill the skull that they almost touch at the midline and together weigh nearly as much as the brain.

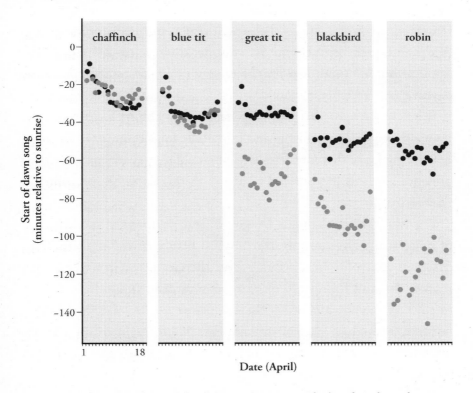

From Bart Kempenaers' wood outside Vienna: darker dots show the natural start times for birds singing in the unlit wood, paler dots the start times dragged forward by human light pollution

Light pollution is catastrophic for this dawn sequence. The behavioural ecologist Bart Kempenaers at the Max Planck Institute in Seewiesen near Munich measured the different start times for five different songbirds in an oak wood near Vienna. The edges of the wood were lit by street lights but the middle was dark. Kempenaers found that the unlit birds began to sing when expected, in the normal big-eye/small-eye sequence, starting about an hour before sunrise and ending around forty-five minutes later, but the street lights confused birds. Where lights shone into the wood, robins began an hour and twenty minutes earlier than normal; and the blackbirds and great tits advanced their start times by almost an hour. Only the chaffinches and blue tits kept to their usual pattern. The order in which they started to sing remained the same, and as the experiment continued, robins, blackbirds and great tits began to resume their natural habits. The implications are unknown for the energy expenditure of birds whose daytime is so roughly extended.

It isn't only light that can play havoc with the basic pattern. The urgency to sing is undeniable and it is vitally important for birds to get heard. Any noise that interferes with their ability to communicate their presence to rivals or potential or actual mates has to be confronted if they are to survive.

The Madrid ornithologist Diego Gil realised that the sudden surge of noise at the city's airport, starting just before dawn, in a rush hour designed to avoid aircraft flying over the city at night and to meet market demand from early morning commuters, would have a sharp impact on the dawn chorus. The aeroplanes are so loud that there is nothing a songbird can do to compete. Noise levels on the runway often reach more than 110 decibels, the equivalent of a speaker stack at a rock concert, and can last for most of the morning.

Gil found at Madrid, and later at Barcelona, Valencia, Malaga and Berlin Tegel, that the birds were shuffling their songs back into the dark and quiet of the night simply to allow themselves to be heard.

Every one of the ten birds he measured was pushed into night-time singing, the blackbirds an hour and twenty minutes before sunrise, the robin an hour and a half, all of them finishing their announcements to the world before the jet engines made aural signalling impossible.

'What does this behavioral change imply for birds living near airports?' Gil asked. The answer remains unclear. It does not mean that the birds sing for longer. They start earlier but they stop earlier and so the cost to the bird in energy expenditure is the same. Yet the jet roars push later birds earlier and so compress the singing time of different species into a narrower window – a crowding of the acoustic space – and make it more difficult, for example, for females to pick out the strong-singing males with whom they need to breed. It could also be, Gil thinks, 'that the longer birds sing in darkness, the more vulnerable they may become to nocturnal predators'.

It is a pitiable thought when surrounded by the graded dawn chorus in a place like Perch Hill, where bird after bird joins in as their eyes allow them to see the day. Only thirty miles away at Gatwick, there will be blue tits, siskins and green- and goldfinches all crammed into a dark, overfilled space like aural refugees, bravely attempting to make themselves heard.

That picture may be out of date. The Madrid birds had adapted to the new dawn-thunder and there is no reason to imagine their Gatwick cousins have not done the same. The birds either learn the benefits of singing earlier before the first flights to Paris or Munich, or, as Gil thinks more likely, those that are genetically attuned to sing earlier are those that have bred and whose progeny has survived. Those that have been unable to adapt to the new regime have not been heard, have not bred and have died out. We have killed off the birds that didn't learn to sing when we allowed them to. The Anthropocene has shaped the dawn chorus to fit with airline schedules.

There are subtleties here. Acoustic space has always been crowded. Birds with high-pitched voices on the island of Barro Colorado off

Panama have to cope with the deafening song of the emerald cicadas that sing at the same frequencies. If the birds sang when the cicadas were in full voice, they would never be heard. Luckily enough, the insects prefer to sing at night and so these tropical birds, whose names are a cornucopia of richness – the white-flanked antwren, the great tinamou, the chestnut-backed antbird, the western slaty antshrike and the cocoa woodcreeper – wait until the cicadas fall silent with the coming of day and only then begin to sing themselves.

When Calandra Stanley from the University of Maryland played recordings of the cicada song after dawn, the birds fell silent. One can only imagine the thought processes of the antwrens and cocoa wood-creepers. Were the cicadas not meant to have fallen quiet by now? But the evidence is interesting: the birds do not start to sing through a kind of automatic clock that turns on with the dawn (or their eyes). They decide to sing when there is room for them in the acoustic space of the forest. Whether that decision is genetically determined (since only the birds that have learned to wait have survived) or made by birds that have the ability to act differently in different circumstances, nobody yet knows.

Finally, some evidence that has been published by Stuart Brooker, a doctoral student at Durham University, from a recording made at Highnam Wood in Gloucestershire in May 2015. The clip is only fifteen seconds long but the Cornell-devised spectrogram – admittedly a rather woolly and jagged image – seems to show a cluster of English woodland birds carefully subdividing between themselves the available acoustic space, both in time and in frequency. The result, and perhaps the intention, is that the signals they are making hardly overlap. The very analysis that Merlin relies on to pick out different bird songs from the mélange of the dawn chorus is the same mechanism that birds use to establish the separability of their songs.

Down at the bottom of the frequency chart, only just above zero kHz, where there is plenty of room in the acoustic space, continu-

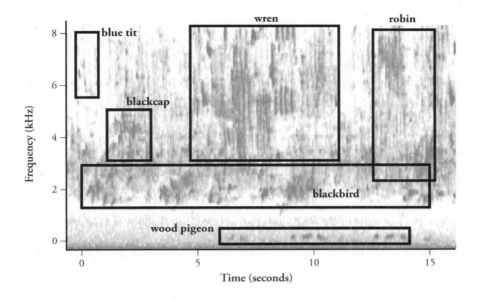

Adapted from Stuart Brooker's sonograph of birds in a
Gloucestershire wood singing and apparently accommodating each
other, either in frequency or in timing

ously strumming away, is the wood pigeon. Just above it, long-lasting and mellifluous, but with the relatively low-frequency tones that make me think it a contralto, is the blackbird, the constant undersong of the wood around 2 kHz. In the higher frequencies, separated by time perhaps because the size and narrow throats of these middling birds does not allow a greater separation by frequency and this space is more crowded, come in turn the chatter of the blue tit, at 6–8 kHz and for no more than a moment; the gleaming silvery song of the blackcap, like a blackbird that has brightened and lightened; the big multi-frequency and very loud song of the wren; and finally the high and deep, squeezed-out song of the robin, ranging from 3–8 kHz.

There is no better portrayal of the cool morning in the wood when the birds start to sing, turn by turn, niche by niche, as the light seeps downward, than this strange, muddy diagram of an aural ecology at work.

Why all this at dawn? Why this outpouring of song in the half-light before sunrise? Why do birds choose this particular time of day to announce themselves to their rivals and their mates or potential mates?

No one has a complete answer, but there are many suggestions, most of them overlapping. The first is mechanical. Like all vertebrates, birds have a daily rhythm, partly governed by the light-sensitive pineal gland nested deep in the brain between its two hemispheres. When darkness falls, the gland produces a hormone, melatonin, which makes the bird sleepy. With the coming of daylight, the melatonin level drops, the bird wakes up and starts to sing. A series of brutal experiments has shown that a pineal gland, when cut out of a chicken brain and kept in a glass container, continues to go through these sleep/activity rhythms for days afterwards.

Other biologists have shown that sparrows which have had the gland cut out cannot remember to behave differently by night or day. An equivalent and opposite effect appears when birds are exposed to constant bright light for twenty-four hours day after day: the pineal gland never produces the melatonin, the birds never stop singing and are soon exhausted. In these unconscionable ways we have come to know that birds and their lives are adjusted to the turning of the earth. They wake and sleep as the world wakes and sleeps.

Alongside that is a picture derived from economics: the birds might arrive at dawn with some spare energy from the reserves of fat they accumulated the day before. They store up more than they usually need, a reserve used to keep warm only if the night is unexpectedly cold. On most mornings, the extra energy goes into song and there is some evidence that if you give blackbirds a lot of food and make sure that they spend the night exceptionally well fed, they start singing earlier, go on for longer, both more loudly and more constantly, with

fewer pauses at either dusk or dawn. It may be that all of this is telling
the female blackbirds what they want to hear: their mate is in such fine
song because he is in such fine condition. When the blackbird pours
out his song into the half-dark, he is pouring out his beauty as a biological fact.

Or it may be a question of practicality. It is dangerous to sing in the
dark. The woods around the birdhouse are full of tawny owls, two in
High Wood, one in Leggett's, one in Kiln Shaw, two in Coombe Wood
and several over in Black Brooks. It would be suicidal for a songbird to
sing in the dark with all those unseen beaks and eyes waiting for their
chance. For security alone, a bird must wait until it can see the dangers
around it. But a world in which a predator could be spotted may not
be one light enough for the birds to find food themselves. It may be
that pre-sunrise dawn is light enough to sing but not light enough to
look for food. Dawn gets the necessary singing out of the way before
the daylight business of foraging can begin.

Or it may be that birds sing at dawn because the world then is more
receptive to song. We know that ourselves: the dawn's stillness, the
dewy silence of it and the feeling it engenders that we should talk
quietly then. The same recognition may induce in the birds a desire to
sing. What better time could there be if you want your song to be
heard? The air at dawn is less disturbed than it is at midday and
although it has been shown that sound does not travel further then,
birdsong is less degraded as it carries across the dawn wood than it
would be in the turbulent noon air. We know this too: there is a clarity
and precision to dawn song that is audible to us. Dawn birds have a
needle-sharp presence in the trees, as if none of them were that far
away. No time could be better suited to singing if dominance is what
you require. It is not that the song reaches further but that where it
reaches it remains clear. The benefit is a better definition of who it is
that is doing the singing. The fact that every other bird in the wood has
come to the same understanding does not seem to matter. The clear

expression of a bird's individuality outweighs the competition it has to face.

It may be a social statement, the cock bird advertising to its neighbours and to its mate that he is still alive and has survived the night. The song declares that the territory is still occupied and to the partner that he has come back to see her at the nest. Male tits at dawn sing near the entrance to the hen's roost. She hears him, emerges into the morning light and they leave together.

In some, such as the marsh tits that pair for life, the cock still sings in spring at dawn, even when he has no need to attract a mate. He can only be signalling to other cocks to keep away. As soon as his hen is incubating the eggs he can be sure of having fertilised himself, he stops singing. There is no longer any need.

Finally, there is the idea that it is even more directly about sex. For five years in March and April from 1998 to 2002, the bioacoustics specialist Angelika Poesel and her team listened to sixty-one male blue tits in a ninety-acre oak and beech wood in the hills a few miles west of Vienna. The wood is near the Konrad Lorenz Institute for Ethology and has long been studied, so is now peppered with about 250 nest boxes, many of them used by blue tits.

Poesel already knew from other studies that hen birds of many kinds preferred older cocks. But the older blue tits are at something of a disadvantage compared with other species. Birds that have wide and complex repertoires of song, such as the canary or the starling, can learn new song types as they age and the hens are able to detect an older mate by the show-off riffs he plays. Yet blue tits are not virtuosi. They sing the same old chatter-song with a touching dependability. How, then, do the females detect the older potential mates? Poesel found that it was all about the dawn. Blue tit cocks that were two years old or more began to sing on average 5.8 minutes earlier than one-year-old birds.

Starting early was sexy for blue tits. Those early starters had more partners and more progeny than those that came later. And this wasn't to do with the better survival of the sexiest birds. Blue tits get sexier the older they are and they demonstrate their prowess to potential lovers by their early dawn song. 'If females are the intended receivers at dawn and are attentive to dawn song,' Poesel wrote, 'it will pay a male to sing as early as possible.'

Her supposition was that female blue tits, already paired up, are sitting waiting in the dark of their nest boxes. Hearing that early song is a trigger for the hen to leave her nest and go looking for an adulterous partner. 'A male already singing while all his neighbours are still quiet may increase his success ... The average difference in the onset of singing between juvenile and adult males seems sufficient for females to leave the territory and attempt to copulate with an early singing male.'

The female tit cannot see the attractiveness of her new early partner but she can hear it. It is his dawn song that makes him beautiful. His earliness is his manliness. Blue tits that started singing earlier in the dawn cuckolded other males. And why don't all males start earlier? Perhaps because there is a metabolic cost to singing so early before it is light enough to have found any food. Such singing may be a sign that the cock is a good, strong one, in good enough shape to sing in the dark, with energy reserves to afford a little flamboyance first thing in the morning.

If that is generally true, the dawn chorus is what we believe it to be: the singing out of vitality itself to a wood world filled with careful, discriminating, listening ears.

5.

Robins

OCCUPYING

Until the last few years, it was thought that birdsong was largely a male phenomenon. Cock birds sang loud and long to compete for females, demonstrating their strength and fitness to possible mates and actual rivals. Hen birds were considered as little more than the recipients of and responders to male volubility.

In the last twenty years, as women ornithologists have entered the field, and as the net has been cast wider than the northern hemisphere, that assumption has been shown to be wrong. An old, male-dominated, northern bird-science had principally attended to the male song that could be heard outside the window. Only in 2014 was the first systematic worldwide survey made of birdsong, and it revealed female song to be common in all branches of the songbird tree. It is now known that male and female song was originally present in every songbird ancestor. More than 70 per cent of female birds are now recognised as singers, most of them in the tropics. And it is women who are making the discoveries: less than half of the lead authors in studies of general birdsong have been women; in papers on female birdsong, that proportion has risen to 68 per cent.

A question remains: why, in the northern hemisphere where most of the earlier science had been done, have the female birds largely given up singing? They are not entirely quiet: female swallows and blue tits, female dunnocks and their European relatives the accentors, several North American birds and the female European robin (at least in the winter) have all been heard to sing. They use song as the cock birds do – to summon their mates, to confirm a bond with that mate, to defend their territories, to communicate with their offspring. That said, northern female birds tend to be much quieter than the cocks, and are often silent, perhaps to conserve energy for migration. Singing is expensive and male robins that sing loud and long find it difficult to gain weight, probably because singing takes up time that would otherwise be spent foraging. The demands of laying eggs, hatching them, brooding and feeding the chicks, all in the short northern summer, plus the need to avoid telling predators where they and their nestlings are to be found, may militate against female singing. No northern female bird has been heard singing in the multiple-voiced sound-cloud of the dawn chorus.

The song-filled mornings in the temperate spring, whether you know it or not, are overwhelmingly male. This first bird music is the sound of male assertion and competition, as uncompromising as the bellowing of large, bearded athletes displaying at the shot-put or the hammer. A dawn wood may seem as tender as a piece of music by Debussy or Ravel; I may have loved the damp quiet of the early blue-grey skies; or watched in silence as a late moon or half-moon sailed first over Kiln Shaw, then Coombe Wood and finally into Black Brooks, but the underlying truth is different. This dawn song in Hollow Flemings or Long Field Shaw is the declaration of male demand and the woods a contested ring of male rivalry.

Each morning, the sheep lay on the grass of the Long Field where they had been all night. On that pasture, the wormcasts began the day crunchy underfoot like chocolate almonds. Every night the mole in the field extended his empire, another mound or two, a couple of yards.

The clay of the paths that my feet had worn through the wood was slick with rain, as the early spring moss brightened around the roots of the oaks.

Thrushes appeared with nesting material in their beaks like misplaced moustaches and then sang high in the leafless ashes as if someone were sharpening a blade on a strop, *Whop-whop*, followed by a piercing whistle, a schoolboy's halloo to his friend. The sun seemed to pour itself down their throats, so that the skin of their mouths glowed amber. Each morning they began their scratching, chattering and scratching again, sometimes with the atmosphere of a drunk losing it in a bar; or almost monkey-like, a howler monkey in an English wood, before resuming the *wwhhhhippps-wwwwhhhipps*, and always repeating each musical phrase twice. *Hear me say this, hear me say this: I am a thrush, I AM A THRUSH; read my lips, READ MY LIPS*. It was the doubleness that Robert Browning, away in northern Italy, remembered in his dreams of England:

> That's the wise thrush; he sings each song twice over,
> Lest you should think he never could recapture
> The first fine careless rapture!

The robins had been singing even in the snow. Early on a cold sunny morning one perched on a leafless oak branch outside the birdhouse, like a portrait of winter, its red never redder, its survival in harshness never more touching. I scattered some crumbs of a biscuit on the snow below it and the robin jumped down to find them, picking and looking, picking and looking. But the bird was far from alone. In the quiet of those December evenings, it seemed as if the wood were the scene of a kind of shouting match. I counted six robins singing there one night, each tinkling and brilliant, a multi-mouthed fountain in the cold. The voices were so sharp and strong I was expecting to see clouds of trumpeted breath emerging from their beaks. Each of them sounded as if the notes were squeezed from a bellows through the narrowest of mouths, all pressure, no outlet, as though the birds were fit to burst, the highest note first, and then eventually as the pressure broke, a warming of the tone, woodier, clarinetish, and the song trailing out at those lower frequencies, with no more form to it than the bubbles attached to a thought in a cartoon.

The robin's song moves up and down the scales, always beginning high and brilliant, even acidic, sharper than rapture, with none of the butter of the blackbird song or the madness of the thrush, but more, it seems, a song of undeniability and assertion than persuasion or seduction.

That gut-understanding of the ferocity of the cock robins is the truth. As David Lack, the twentieth-century ornithologist and author of the first modern monograph on the robin, once wrote, the robin's 'song is a war-cry and its red breast is war paint'.

One robin after another met me every morning as I walked down through the Long Field to the birdhouse, their music as clean and bright as spring water. They were singing at defined places, at the corners of woods, where a stretch of rough ground gave out, at a point where two fields joined, or hedges met in a T-junction, as if they were reading the map of the farm, singing its geography.

The singing stances were constant and I made a map of where I heard them – by now early spring, only just into March – and it could not have been clearer that what I was hearing was the setting out of territories: one stance in the far corner of Sarah's cutting garden by the hedge on to the lane; another at the opposite corner; a third just down from the polytunnels; and a fourth where the blackthorn thicket of a hedge dropped down to the stream that marks the parish boundary between Burwash to the north and Brightling to the south. A fifth was further along that boundary where it broadened into a little piece of hornbeam and hazelwood. Three more were in the edges of Long Field Shaw, a ninth right next to the birdhouse itself and a tenth at the foot of Hollow Flemings.

This was no chance pattern. The robins liked corners and places where open ground emerged from good cover and shelter. They sang high in oaks and hazels, each holding their own tiny barony, each proclaiming the uniqueness of their presence and tenancy. I thought of England and Europe parcelled out like this, one tiny robin-territory after another, some maybe two acres, many as small as half an acre, or even a stretch of dense, protective hedge, a place as subdivided as the parishes of a medieval city. The robin world was a mosaic of proclaimed ownership stretching from the Caucasus to Shetland and the High Atlas to Murmansk. It may have been particularly true here. Robins are much thicker on the ground in England than further east in Europe, where they are elusive and secretive and their forest territories can be roughly double the size of their English cousins'.

I tried to make out where the boundaries of our little prince-bishoprics might lie in the woods and fields below the farm but found it impossible. The robins do not all look the same: some are chubbier, some slighter, some browner and darker on their redbreast, some more orange, but in the quick turns and dives of their flight, pausing now

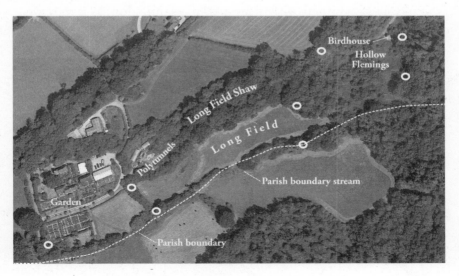

The singing spots of the robins, March 2022

and then to stand and flick their wings and tails, it was beyond me to identify individuals. Since the 1920s, professional ornithologists have captured robins and colour-ringed their legs to allow the birds to be identified one by one. But you need a licence to do that and so I was left unsure which of my ten robins was singing where.

Nevertheless, the territorial nature of what they were doing was unmistakable. It was clear from Lack's wonderful book, written at Dartington in Devon where he was a schoolmaster in the 1930s and revised at Oxford a decade later, that robins like to sing at the very corners of their territories. As I was witnessing. If each was singing at the boundary of his land, I could work out where those boundaries lay.

There is much that is uncertain here, but it is striking how much the robins seem to have responded to the form of the place itself. The fields are not part of any territory they claim. The birds like a full and even ragged bushiness around them. Robins pick their food off the ground, mostly insects but some seeds as well, and like damp shady areas, with good but not over-thick cover. Patches of open ground nearby seem to be important, with tall trees and bushes from which to sing.

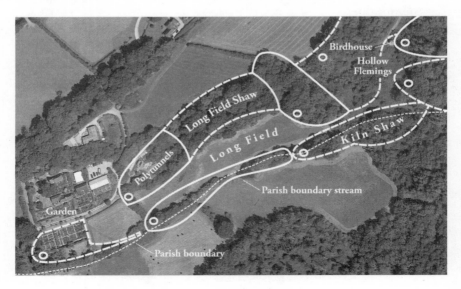

With some guesswork, I came up with a map of my robins' inter-locking, feudal world. The parish boundary has been a hedge for at least a thousand years and three or even four robins seem to have chosen it to mark the edge of their own lands. Sarah's garden hedges and the very distinct zone reserved for the polytunnels and cold frames seem to have been useful for one bird. Otherwise the margins of the woods have also provided clarifying boundary markers. An internal boundary within Long Field Shaw, where at some point over the last century the woodland was allowed to encroach over what had been open field, and where overgrown hedge oaks remain visible as a line within the wood, also seems to mark the border between two robin territories. Could that be a cultural memory, the inherited knowledge of what was once a more visible edge? I am not sure. Nearly three-quarters of all robins die in their first year and almost two-thirds of the survivors every year after that. The average lifespan of a robin is just over thirteen months. The field within the wood was abandoned about 140 years ago, after another landslip, and so some-thing like 120 generations of robins would have passed through here since the change occurred. Could the old landscape form have been that memorable?

David Lack was the first to understand that boundaries and territo-ries came and went, and that the size of each territory was elastic, usually depending on the fate of neighbouring birds. If a cock robin died, his neighbours or a wandering bird soon acquired what had been his. The map of territories and outlines was in constant movement. On average, though, Lack thought a robin territory to be some 1.5 acres, but with a wide variation from more than two acres to almost a fifth of that.

My guesses at the robin territories at Perch Hill fit the pattern, with an average of just under 1.4 acres.

Garden – 1.05
Polytunnel – 1.17
Boundary – 1.39
Kiln Shaw – 1.40
Long Field Shaw West – 1.76
Long Field Shaw East – 1.58
Hollow Flemings West – [Uncertain as its far edges are unknown]
Hollow Flemings East – [Uncertain as its far edges are unknown]
Hollow Flemings North-east – [Uncertain as its far edges are unknown]

What was happening? Why were the robins carving up their world with such care and precision? Why were they singing at the boundaries? And in what sense did they possess what they proclaimed as theirs?

The answer is that this is a map of song. A cock robin – and in spring it is only the cock that sings – rises to his tall singing perch and gives voice both to attract a mate and to warn other cocks that they are not welcome in the part of the wood where he and his hen will establish their nest and raise their brood. He is not protecting a food resource. Robins often get their food outside their own territory, skulking over the boundary so as not to arouse the ire of its owner. And conversely failing to spot an intrusion where a feeding neighbour creeps in. Food has nothing to do with either his territory or his song. The song is an advertisement of the robin's presence and splendour. That is why in late winter and very early spring the woods are alive with robin song. They are telling nearby hens that good-quality cocks are ready and waiting.

As soon as a hen robin is seduced by his marvellousness, he will stop singing. 'Silence,' Lack wrote characteristically, 'is either dead or married.' The robin has beckoned in his mate and, come March, she will build a nest in which she will lay the eggs he has fertilised. The nest will be secret and hidden in a hollow of a tree or under deep cover. Robin's nests are difficult to find. The wooing-singing stops but the cock does not stop patrolling his territory. Now above all, when the hen is in her most fertile and receptive mood, he must prevent other cocks swinging into his precious acres, finding his hen and secretly fertilising an egg of their own. Should that happen, all the effort he will put in to feeding the hen on the nest and the chicks when they hatch will be in the service of another cock's genes. It must be avoided at all costs and so the only songs that a robin sings after he has found his mate are those of an obstinate and uncompromising defender of land and trees and the air above and between them. It is then, especially, that one can hear what Thomas Coryat, the sparkling seventeenth-century walker-writer, called 'the redbreast's delectable resonancie'. The truth is that all the resonancie we might hear is intended to demonstrate his excluding power and territorial claim.

A cock with a hen on their nest will not leave his land. Lack tried to drive a spring robin from his territory but found it impossible: 'As the observer approaches, the bird retreats, but on reaching the edge of its territory it does not proceed further, and if chivvied it unexpectedly flies back over the observer's head to the middle of its ground.'

The duke is in his castle guarding his duchess and their heirs. Life is not easy. The hens will beg for food from their cocks throughout the breeding season by emitting loud and far-carrying 'seep' calls that sound like the begging calls of her fledglings. But there may be rather more to this than hunger.

Joe Tobias and Nathalie Seddon followed a population of robins in the Cambridge University Botanic Garden through two breeding seasons. The competition for the hen birds was fierce. About 20 per cent of all cocks failed to find a mate.

Tobias and Seddon wanted to find out why the hens were making their *seep* calls and for periods of no more than ninety minutes removed nine of the paired cocks from their territories and kept them in cloth bags, where they sat waiting for their release. How would the hens respond with the cocks away?

Not only did they call louder and longer but they flew closer to the territory boundary so that other cocks outside it would hear them calling. And they did so even more energetically in their most fertile phases. It seems unavoidable that the *seep* call was not just an honest statement of hunger from hen to cock, but an advertisement to the male neighbours of her own whereabouts and availability.

The neighbouring cocks could eavesdrop and with all this seep information, hop over the boundary to find the calling hen. But, as Tobias and Seddon speculated, it might also have been a form of blackmail. Feed me, husband, or the neighbours will pop in to take their chance. The louder I call and the nearer I fly to the boundary, the more inviting I will seem, particularly when I am fertile and ready to receive them. Only if you feed me and I stay in the middle of the territory and my calling rate subsides will the neighbours realise what a good mate I have. Be attentive or be betrayed.

These territories are overflooded with unattached birds waiting and wanting to occupy the breeding niches taken by those that are for the moment successful. A now-horrifying experiment was conducted by a pair of Cornell scientists, Robert Stewart and John Aldrich, in a spruce and fir forest in northern Maine in the summer of 1949. They wanted to know how effective the resident birds were at ridding the trees of a moth whose caterpillars, called the spruce budworm, fed on the spruce needles and often killed them.

Across a forty-acre tract of the forest the scientists tried to remove every living male bird. Once they had been shot, the spruce budworm population would be studied.

Before they began, Stewart and Aldrich counted 149 different males occupying territories in the wood. From the middle of June, they started killing them. The spring migration was over and the place was full of the most wonderful American birds: nuthatches, kinglets, wrens, flycatchers, vireos, finches, juncos and all sorts of warblers – Tennessee, Nashville, Parula, Magnolia, Cape May, Myrtle, the Black-throated Green, the Blackburnian, the Chestnut-sided and Bay-breasted.

The two men shot for three and a half weeks. 'Shells used were loaded with very fine (No. 12) shot so that birds would not be too mutilated for specimens. By using this method the total population on the area was greatly reduced, although the actual degree of reduction could not be readily appraised.'

If they were not quite sure of the effect they were having, they realised they could not keep up with the birds. Within a week or so the bird population was down by about 80 per cent but it remained obstinately at that level as neighbour birds flooded in to fill the territories and keep up the numbers.

Stewart and Aldrich continued with their task, shooting bird after bird as the tide rolled in against them. Until 8 July, when they stopped, the population maintained itself at about 20 per cent of pre-holocaust levels but by then the Cornell men had shot a total of 455 birds, more than three times the number of male birds that had been there when they arrived.

The Olive-backed Thrush was found to be a very difficult species to collect. It was much more wary and secretive than the other species and was seldom seen, although its songs and call-notes were evidence of its continual presence. Although a total of 18 adult Olive-backed Thrushes was taken during the collecting period, the rate of collection was so low and repopulation so fast that the resultant voids in the population were filled by new males almost as soon as the voids were produced. As a result, the population level for males of this species was reduced only slightly below (probably about 80 per cent of) the pre-collecting population.

It is the story, in microcosm, of human wrongness in relation to nature; and of a natural system's refusal to be bowed.

The experiment was repeated the following summer: there were 154 breeding males in the tract on 6 June 1950. Two weeks later that population had been shot down to 32 birds, a fifth of its previous number 'and held at this level by continuous collection of new arrivals'. Over the next three weeks another 406 birds were shot so that by 11 July a total of 528 adult birds had been killed.

> Combining the two seasons gives a grand total of 947 birds removed from the 40-acre tract during the two consecutive breeding seasons. A combined total of 49 collecting days was involved.

Not a single mention was made in the two papers of the effect this might have had on the welfare of the spruce budworm. Presumably the territories filled with more birds and the pressure on the moth and its caterpillars remained what it had been.

A robin territory exists only in time. As soon as the chicks are fledged, and both cock and hen go into their quiet, hidden summer moult, the idea of a territory drops away. The map of the Holy Roman Empire with its hyper-definitions and convoluted frontiers melts into a blur. The Bird School is on its long, quiet, summer break. But then, late in the autumn, something intriguing happens. Both cock and hen set up their own territories, independent of each other, and they hang on to them over the early winter. The territories are not permanent fixtures and their boundaries tend to drift with time, taking the form not of unitary states with policed frontiers, like the male territories in spring, but a few defended clumps of trees and bushes with urgent flyways between them. Nevertheless, these archipelago-like territories summon from their possessors – both cock and hen – the song that declares their ownership of them.

Winter female robins are unique among the birds of these woods in singing just as loudly and as long as the males. If you walk through here on a winter evening, you are as likely to hear a female robin as a male. It may be that the extra exposure in winter, after the leaves have dropped, makes the robins more vulnerable to sparrowhawks and that if the birds live separately, they are better able to find hiding places. In addition, independent territories are more likely to guarantee a food supply to each of the birds in a time of dearth.

The hen robins in winter behave like their tropical ancestors, competing for their patch on their own behalf, singing out their enemies, seeing off intruders of both sexes and sometimes even attacking them. To have control of their own winter territory probably also helps them start the breeding season in good condition. Only then, as the other demands imposed by breeding kick in, does the hen robin cease to sing, allying herself with the loud-singing cock while mothering the next generation in protective silence.

In her 2019 book *Habiter en Oiseau* – a title that crosses the boundary between living *in* a bird and living *as* a bird – the Belgian philosopher Vinciane Despret has proposed the idea that a bird's territory is not property as we understand it but an act of self-expression. For her, territory is not a possession but a performance in the theatre of the self.

I read her book in the birdhouse listening to a great spotted woodpecker at its manly, hollow-knock hammering in the dead and dying ashes to the north. I could hear it two hundred yards away, a noise as large and insistent as its own high-vis plumage, uncompromisingly unhidden and wanting to be seen. The rapid tom-tom of the woodpecker was audible over at least twenty acres of wood and field. In Despret's understanding, the bird itself was filling those twenty acres, the percussive song an extension of its body across the territory it wanted to claim, the hammering a powerful aural enlarging of itself.

Song extends the bird body across the performance-moment of territory and in that sense song, territory and bird are one. Hear a bird song and you are hearing the territory with which it is, for these few weeks, entirely identified. Despret quotes a description by the French novelist Maylis de Kerangal of a young man, Hocine, who traps and sells goldfinches in the markets of Algiers:

> He knew every species, its characteristics and metabolism, could tell from the way it sang the provenance of each bird, even the name of the forest where it was born … But the appeal of the goldfinch went beyond the musicality of its song and was linked, above all, to geography: its song was the manifestation of territory. Valley, city, mountain, forest, hill, stream. It brought a landscape to life, evoked a topography, gave the feeling of a soil and a climate. A piece of the planetary puzzle took form in its beak … the goldfinch sang something solid, scented, tactile and coloured. So it was that Hocine's eleven birds sang the cartography of a vast territory.

A bird's territory is not an object but a composition, an amalgam of bird, place, time and song. Its boundaries are where it meets the songs of other territories, where the bodies of the neighbouring birds, conceived not as warm-blooded feathered things weighing a couple of ounces, but as the extended and expressive song-body, the sound-envelope of song, comes into contact with another. Each performs its territory across the boundary, so that song is the meeting of geography and time, the performative expression of desire and competitiveness, the assertion of a local dominance across the space over which the voice carries.

It is a transforming vision of birdsong, recognising that to walk in the wood or along the ragged parish boundary stream is to find yourself inside the song-bodies of these creatures. It is as if you were snorkelling in a shallow sea, pushing your way through the fronds of bird-being and bird-life as if they were the kelp and wrack that brush up against and past you in a tidal sea. A singing bird becomes mysteriously vast. Birdsong actually enters you and reverberates within your skull, so that your own body also becomes part of the birds' song-body world.

Early one March morning I was in the birdhouse watching a dunnock, a hedge sparrow, singing in the sunlight on the little oak to the south-west. With the windows shut, I watched it opening and closing its mouth. The sunlight through the side of the mouth was making a kind of dull tawny orange in this grey brown bird, a bright signal of spring, the mouth lit, the body dark. I opened the window and heard its slightest of songs – *tip i tik tikee tik da* – but one cannot represent these things and it was good enough to watch it among the old bronzed leaves now gleaming in this spring light.

On the other side a gang of long-tailed tits had arrived in the little oaks beside the birdhouse. While I was watching them a robin fight

The dunnock sings

Long-tailed tits

erupted on the ground beneath them. It was a sudden and violent face-off. The long-tailed tits were soon away while the patch of bare earth below and to one side of the birdhouse began to take on the air of the dusty street in a Western.

By chance we had built the birdhouse right on the boundary of two robin territories and now the two robins claiming them were below, confronting each other and behaving in ways I had never seen birds behave before: one was standing stock still, staring ahead, the other wavering to and fro, with its head up, its neck feathers ruffled, its wings open and fluttering. Acute mutual antagonism filled the air. His redbreast was a hot red bulbous display of testosterone, so intense that the bird seemed almost agonised with it. Not for long, maybe thirty seconds, they confronted each other and then the displayer, its whole body looking unbirdlike as it stood there, as miniature-potent as a red-breasted totem, dropped low and chased the other hard across the bare ground.

Other birds kept away while the robin performed to his rival. He stood again, higher this time, his whole torso wavering like a leaf, with the head held high, the beak pointing skywards and his throat feathers exposed as a raging red flag to his enemy. All sense of scale disappeared. A male chaffinch came into the arena but scuttled away before the two robins also flew off into the wood, one in pursuit of the other.

A robin returned to the grains that had fallen to the ground under the bird feeders. The other soon came after it and the fight began again, as the first repeated his gurgle-throated, high-head, tail-cocked stance, with the strange slow wavering to left and right, but it was not enough to put off the rival, and for a moment both were up and fighting in mid-air, wings clashing, eight or ten inches off the ground, rising and falling as the fight came and went. And then it was over. Nothing was apparent except that one robin remained, high in the branches of one of the oaks, singing his territory song.

A few days later, it happened again but without such drama. A robin was standing below the birdhouse, pecking then looking, its tail half-down, half-up, when another flew up fast behind it and chased it away, leaving the aggressor/defender holding the ground, turning, jumping once to the left and then to the right as if he were the champion in the ring abandoned by all challengers. Shadows from the trees were falling across the ground he occupied and I saw not only that his redbreast glowed bright in the sunlight but that he seemed to choose the sunlight in which to pose, pausing there, spending only a moment in the shadows so that the redness his genes had given him could work its magic. Another robin crept in behind the leaves of a bramble but the champion seemed not to detect it.

A redpoll arrived, and even though the robin had ignored a chaffinch a minute earlier, it now faced off towards the redpoll, which lifted its wings to each side while the robin quivered away in response, doing the to-and-fro shoulder-shake with the big ruffles out on its neck feathers, as cockily demonstrative as a courtier suffused with anger at some offence to his honour, before driving the redpoll away and resuming its ferocious peck-and-peck, peck-and-look as if daring any other creature to come near.

It is a strange fact that one cannot see something until you know it is there to be seen. I had never before been aware of robins and their territories but now I can look out of the kitchen window in spring and see almost daily on the brick paths outside and on the hazel posts we use for staking in the garden the robins making their displays with all the expressiveness of a bird whose genes are intent on survival: sky-pointing with their tiny beaks (in just the way of gannets but at a twentieth of the scale), the chest almost painfully pushed out, his eye rolling in the back of his head (if I am not imagining that?) and all the ruffle-chesting, wing-flicking, hate-chasing, duchy-singing, world-dividing, song-asserting ferocity of marvellous and adamant life.

6.

Tawny Owls

HAUNTING

Every evening I listen out for the tawnies. On some dark winter days, they call late in the afternoon but usually they wait for dusk and their voice in my mind is inseparable from that subtle and lingering time of day. As the light drops, the stillness of the dark comes on, the trees acquire their night-time solidity, and the hooting of the owls begins. The night mist leaks in as the sun goes down. The dogs' breath starts smoking in the cold. A jet heads south and in the western sky Venus appears white and washed.

'A tawny owl calls from the wood's dark hornbeam heart,' J.A. Baker wrote of his Essex woods in *The Peregrine*.

He gives a vibrant groan; a long sensitive pause is held till almost unbearable; then he looses the strung bubbles of his tremulous hollow song.

I have spent many early evenings walking in the woods listening to that 'hollow voice floating like a sail in the dark', as Baker described it, trying to map their presence from the calls I can hear around me. It is not easy because the owls are always on the move and I cannot be sure

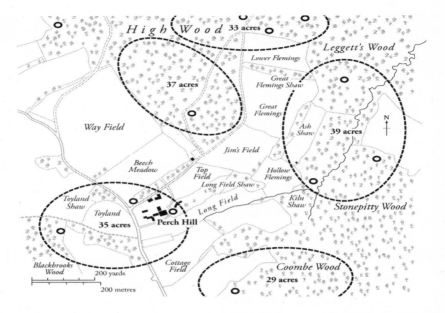

of the boundaries, but the farm is afloat in the owl world, wide pools of owl-life distributed around me in territories of between thirty and fifty acres each.

Never far from my mind is Olivier Messiaen's wonderful description of a tawny's voice: *'vocifération douloureuse et lugubre'*.

I look at the rough map I have drawn and see in it a country made of owls, as if the owls were as emergent here as the trees. The oak has long been called 'the Sussex weed', as saplings will spring from acorns wherever they are allowed space and time, and the tawny owl is something of the same. These are owl woods and always will be unless something is done to remove them. They are as present here as the night air.

My diary is full of attempts to distinguish one tawny voice from another.

5.58 in the morning and the tawny is still beating on in Stonepitty Wood. The old man of the night, the watchman not yet in bed.

Sometimes the owl in Lower Leggett's goes a little hesitant. His voice breathes before he means to say anything, like a cry muttered in sleep, a sigh-cry.

The dropping, distant tawny on the far side of Coombe Wood. Sounding as if it is saying 'Coombe Wood'. Half a mile away, too faint for Merlin.

So mournful the distant owl in Black Brooks. Northern, frosted.

In the half dark of High Wood, the owl hoots around my path. Calling three times, a hoot, a pause, then the shortest and quietest of interruptions, like a comma, very faint, and finally the long wavering, dropping pennant of song, trembling as it ends, with all the owl's commanding solemnity in it.

No one has ever described these duets between owl and dusk more richly than J.A. Baker in *The Hill of Summer*. In his account of an Essex owl evening, all senses seem to merge, and all distinction between animate and inanimate disappears. As the dark fills his wood, owl and dark become each other's intimates.

It was the stillness of the trees that made them so vividly alive. They were drawing together across the last remaining light, closing in, massing. The soft greyness of the wood was

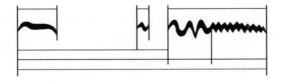

The hoot of the tawny owl: Hoot – *long pause* – hu – *short pause* – huoo-o-o-o-o-o

hardening to a unity of black … A smoke of sounds drifted from the distant village: the fraying bark of a dog, a dusk of voices.

The tawny owl's dark release of song quavered from the pine wood. The sleek dusk bristled with it, like the fur of a cat. I moved under the gloomy trees. The owl surfed out across the rising night. He could hear the turn of a dry leaf, the relaxing of a twig, the loud scamper of a soft-skinned mouse. To him the silence was a flare of sound, a brilliant day of noises dazzling through the veins of dusk.

Baker's synaesthesiac grasp of the tawny's song, in which its voice can ruffle the fur of night and in which silence is luminous, may be reflected in the neural structure of the owl's brain. As Jennifer Ackerman has described, the Dutch ecologist Kas Koenraads has found that 'part of the hearing nerve that goes to the brain, "branches off to the owl's optical centre … Owls may actually have a visual image of what they hear. It could be that if an owl hears something moving in the dark and forested environment, it gets some kind of visual information of where the audio cues are coming from."'

Koenraads could not be sure of this – how can one enter the mind of an owl and see what he hears? – but speculated that when an owl hears something at night, he may see 'an illuminated dot of light in the dark forest'.

It is as though the owl is inspecting its own internal oscilloscope screen. But if owls can see what they hear, the distinction between seeing and hearing may not in the end be significant. If we hear an owl, perhaps we are, in a sense the owl would understand, seeing it. Presence is aural in the dark. We see its voice; its body is its voice, so much that to see a tawny owl is uncanny. I remember coming down to the bird-house one summer night (it was 3 June) and seeing one sitting like a finial on the very peak of the building as I approached. As much as the wren coming to adopt the birdhouse as its own, this was another blurring of the boundaries. The tawny slipped silently away as soon as I saw him, off down towards the ash shaw, where after a while he hooted to me in the wood and with my wooden owl call I hooted back.

I have long treasured Edward Thomas's desolate, wartime poem written in 1915 before he joined up, on the summons made to a wider consciousness by the sadness of the tawny's voice. Thomas, not yet in the war but struggling with the thought that he should go to France, had been out all day and come into the warmth and comfort of an inn. Inside, with the door shut, he sat by the fire and

All of the night was quite barred out except
An owl's cry, a most melancholy cry

Shaken out long and clear upon the hill,
No merry note, nor cause of merriment,
But one telling me plain what I escaped
And others could not, that night, as in I went.

And salted was my food, and my repose,
Salted and sobered, too, by the bird's voice
Speaking for all who lay under the stars,
Soldiers and poor, unable to rejoice.

We all hear that distance and removal in what the owl says, its nakedness and reproach, a song in silence, but Thomas was also responding to something he knew well, the song with which Shakespeare had ended *Love's Labour's Lost*, tracing the story of love and desire through the year, and coming in the end to the winter when

nightly sings the staring owl,
'Tu-whit, tu-whoo!' – a merry note ...

To Thomas and us this sounds like the oddest of characterisations. We know the owl's call is far from merry; and most of us know that no owl ever said '*Tu-whit, tu-whoo*'. The *whit* and the *whoo* are from different owls. On a few nights here I have heard an upside-down version of the phrase '*Uh-hoo, ke-wick*'. It came from two owls, in all probability a male calling as he set off to hunt in the evening and his mate's response '*Uh-hoo, ke-wick*' is a double tawny owl statement of close pairing. True to his reputation as a naturalist, Shakespeare had transcribed a duet of love and partnership between two owls as part of a song of lust and merriment. His instinct was right: always to my own surprise, on the corner of Long Field Shaw, or buried in the depths of High Wood, on autumn evenings or in early summer, nothing sounds merrier than two long-paired, territory-sharing tawny owls greeting each other with '*Tu-whoo, Tu-whit*'.

We all have tawny owls in our lives. It is the commonest of all owls, perhaps twenty thousand pairs in Britain and a million in Europe. There is a famous pair in Kensington Gardens and they, like many others, hoot in the daytime. They can live for twenty years or so in the wild (the current record is one in Scotland found newly dead twenty-three years after it was first ringed) and they remain attached to their particular pieces of ground. That aged Scottish owl was found two miles from where it had been ringed nearly a quarter of a century before. They never migrate, their young only rarely travel far, and their familiarity with their own country becomes richer year by year.

All this pushes them into a different category from the robins and brings into question Vinciane Despret's distinction between territory as object and territory as performance. I have been on this farm for thirty years. It is likely that one or more of the tawny owls I hear around me has been here almost as long. The owl's territory is owned by it for all its adulthood. The same is largely true of Perch Hill and me. How then is our ownership of where we live any different from the birds'? We recognise at our saner moments that we do not own what we claim to own. I can name more than fifty human occupants of this place over the past centuries. Most if not quite all of those names are of men and each would have been surrounded by at least five or six others. In the 1841 census, fourteen people were living in the farmhouse, nine of them children, three servants. For hundreds of human beings this has been their territory. Our gardens and farms, our houses, porches, lean-tos, gazebos and birdhouses are statements of power and possession but also more than that. Are they not a performance and expression of who and what we are? Plant a line of roses up to the front door, or fill the flowerbeds around it with aromatic herbs, improve the grazing, build a shed, pasture the cattle and you are engaging with land and space not merely as an owned thing but as a kind of show, a demonstration of a certain kind of life and even belief. A birdhouse dedicated to permeability with the natural world around it is a statement of an ideal. Place may be its medium but it is framed in a way to make explicit a certain kind of attitude to the world.

For all their rootedness, the owls in these woods, along with every other living thing here, come from far to the south. The ice ages had driven them into refuges in Italy and Spain and in the Balkans, and it is thought that all the British tawnies probably came up from southeast Europe, spreading north and west as slowly as the forests that recolonised the warming continent. The owls would have moved as slowly as the oaks, helped by the jays carrying and hiding the acorns, easing north into the post-glacial grasslands at about three hundred to five hundred yards a year. They were known in early modern England as the wood owl and it has been calculated on the basis of the number of owls in those parts of Białowieża Forest in Poland that are relatively unchanged that in the Britain of 8,000 BC there would have been 160,000 pairs in the scarcely touched oak woods. Their numbers dropped only because their wood world has diminished and because Victorian gamekeepers liked to shoot them. Gamekeepers, defending their pheasants, still set traps for them, but it may be that here, surrounded by the woodlands of the Weald, we now have as many as there ever were.

They live bound to their place. In autumn and early winter, after the late summer moulting of their feathers and replacement with a new set, the owls both male and female sort out their territories, almost always with the same boundaries as the year before. He begins to feed his mate in late winter and by March their two or three eggs are laid. The male does all the hunting and brings his prey – young songbirds, voles, wood mice, earthworms and beetles – to the tree-hole nest where the female is sitting on the eggs. The young hatch in April, and he continues to feed them and their mother; they grow fast and by early June the chicks have left the nest.

This is far from the end of the story. For almost three months, the young owls are fed by both their parents and start slowly to learn the shape of the territory into which they have been born. Very few die when looked after in this extended infancy but they do nothing to feed themselves. For week after week the parents bring them food.

The adults do their hunting largely by ear. Their wings are both covered and outlined in fine soft down that does not rustle like other feathers and breaks up the noisy vortices that spin off the back of the harder-edged wings of daylight birds. The serrated leading edge of the wings, along with the opening fingers of feather at the tips, have a way of binding the passing air to the wing itself. The air flows unbroken through a layer that is half down, half air, a blurring of the boundary between owl and world. Turbulence is banished by softness. All eddies are absorbed in the down and as the owl follows the rides of the wood, the current of wind across it is laminar-sleek. The whoosh of turbulent air you can hear from other birds when they beat their wings is absent. Owls leave their trees in quiet. You hear nothing if you happen to disturb one on its hunting perch in the dusk. The shadow slips away in front of you. They float into the air and that buoyancy is not an illusion. Their wings are large for their bulk (a span of more than three feet for a female tawny of little over a pound in weight) and so they ease away in majestic, muffled slowness, a movement down the woodland ride that seems feather-like itself.

Unlike barn owls, which are birds of open country, and of which there is none here, these wood owls do not hunt on the wing. Their method in the dusk is to perch and pounce, sitting listening on the branch of a tree for the movement of prey beneath them. If I stand beside the birdhouse on a quiet evening I can hear what the owls hear, the fatal micro-rustlings of the wood mice or voles as they creep between the fallen leaves and brittle grass stems under and beside the brambles and bracken. The owls hear them and drop from their branches, spreading their talons for the biggest reach in the dark – it is like the expanding pattern of lead pellets from the barrel of a shotgun – to skewer a mouse or vole. With the body transferred to the bill, the owl returns to the nest.

It is the scene imagined by T.H. White in *The Once and Future King*. Merlin has turned Arthur into an owl and Archimedes, Merlin's pet owl, is attending to his welfare:

'Eat this,' said the owl, and handed him a dead mouse.

[Arthur] felt so strange that he took the furry atomy without protest, and popped it into his mouth without any feelings that it was going to be nasty. So he was not surprised when it turned out to be excellent, with a fruity taste like eating a peach with the skin on, though naturally the skin was not so nice as the mouse.

For two years in the late 1940s, the pioneering Oxford owl biologist H.N. Southern followed the lives of two broods of young tawny owls after they had fledged. The map he produced of their progress across the university's Wytham Woods outside the city is a chart of growing understanding. In mid-June the chicks were still clustered in a small spinney set away from the main bulk of the woods. By late June they had crossed over to a long narrow belt of woodland. In one direction was another owl territory and they didn't venture far there but to the east they gradually pushed onwards until they met the far boundary of their parents' territory. Southern could measure these enlarging frontiers because, like Lack's robins, the young owlets would bounce back into the middle of the woods they knew whenever he pushed them towards or over the edge of unfamiliar country.

By the middle of July, each brood (of two chicks) knew between fifteen and twenty-one acres of Wytham Woods. 'It becomes obvious,' Southern wrote, 'that the first purpose of this long dependent period is to teach a young owl its way around the territory in case it should inherit it.' Although the chicks had learned only about a quarter of their parents' territory in these first three months of flying life, this was

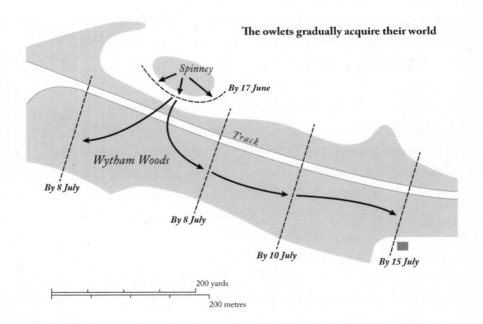

Adapted from H.N. Southern's map of a brood of tawny owlets' growing consciousness of their world

an intensive form of schooling for everything they might one day call their own.

At the same time, the adult birds are defensive of their chicks. In May 1937, the photographer Eric Hosking, then only twenty-seven, had made a hide perched on a twenty-foot-tall 'pylon' opposite a tawny owl's nest in the trunk of a tree at Doldowlod in central Wales. On the afternoon of 13 May he and a friend set up his camera and flashlight in the hide. The friend left him to wait a couple of hours for the birds to appear. But nothing happened and at about nine o'clock that evening Hosking signalled with his torch that he wanted to come down and return another day. The night was pitch-black so the two of them decided to leave the camera and flashlight in position in the hide.

> But as we walked across the field to the waiting car we imagined
> we heard voices coming from the direction of the hide.
> Poachers? If my flashlight apparatus were stolen that would be
> the end of owl photography for that season. Should we go back?
>   We retraced our steps. I felt my way up the pylon and
> fumbled with the fastening at the back of the hide.
>   There was no sound, not even the whisper of a wing. But out
> of the silent darkness a swift and heavy blow struck my face.
> There was an agonising stab in my left eye. I could see nothing.
> The owl, with its night-vision, had dive-bombed with deadly
> accuracy, sinking a claw deep into the centre of my eye.

He fell unconscious and could remember nothing until he woke up the next day in Moorfields Eye Hospital in London, having been driven there by his friend. A fortnight later, the surgeon told him the eye would have to be removed if he was not to lose the sight in the other. Hosking knew that unless he dared to return to the hide and the nest he would never regain the courage to photograph owls again.

I was there within twenty-four hours of being discharged, but my face was covered with a fencing mask. I found the hide just as it was left. As I entered it I trembled from head to toe and my hair literally stood on end. But the young owls had flown, the nest was empty.

The following year he returned and photographed the owl that had half-blinded him. The story, for all its terror and damage, set him up for life. The accident brought nationwide publicity and Hosking (soon to be the owner of a Rolls-Royce that he drove from lecture to lecture around the country) became one of the first professional photographers to make a living almost entirely from pictures of birds.

Eric Hosking's photograph taken in 1938 of the tawny owl that had destroyed one of his eyes the year before

The adult pairs stay together all their lives, faithful to each other and becoming, it seems, ever more expert in the art of being an owl. An owl's hearing, unlike that of mammals, which usually declines with age, is constantly renewed by the replacement of the fine ear-hairs that provide the sensitivity to sound. The one exception to an exclusive owl partnership is when a neighbouring male dies and the widow, looking for a new partner, usually favours not a young wanderer but the old settled male next door, which then annexes the territory and mate of the dead bird without resigning his own.

How does the widow female know that there is an old, experienced and suitable male next door? Because older males, with long-held territories and many progeny, emit hoots with longer notes and more often than less successful males. If you can hear an owl making extended, persistent, confident calls, it is more than likely you are hearing an old man proclaiming his worth.

This longevity comes at a desperate price for the young owls. More often than not a tawny pair will lay between two or three eggs. That is the number of chicks that will hatch and thrive on the long adolescence in the wood. But after the beginning of August, those carefully raised, fed and educated owls are left to their own devices. If it happens that an owl territory has become available, through the death of an adult, the young tawny will move in. But the owls' long life means that in most years there is no vacancy. A territory-holding male will disappear about one year in seven. With no territory, the young owls will struggle and so in late summer and early autumn most owl chicks will starve and die.

It is a ruthless system. You have to wonder why so much investment is poured into successive generations of chicks, when all the effort, in most years, goes to waste.

The answer is plain: it is the price exacted by the owl's choice to hunt in the dark. In part, the owl is suited to the night. The silence of its wing and its large forward-facing eyes, packed not with the cones that can distinguish pattern and colour but with the rods that respond to dim light and can detect movement, are adaptations for the dark. But physically the owl is not supremely capable in darkness.

Graham Martin, now emeritus professor in avian sensory science at the University of Birmingham, has described how the eyesight of a tawny owl may be a hundred times better than a wood pigeon's but is no better than ours. In the light levels you would usually find in a broad-leaved woodland at night, a darkish mouse walking across snow-covered ground would be invisible to an owl and to us if it was any more than ten feet away.

Almost certainly, an owl can see neither prey nor thin branches at night. Owls have been seen colliding with trees in the dark. Nor, unlike a bat, can it use its hearing to detect obstacles.

How, then, does a tawny owl manage in its complex, obstacle-strewn surroundings at night? Martin's answer is that it can only hunt, survive and breed through a detailed knowledge of its local world. A tawny must know the territory in all its minute and intimate particulars. It can only live and move at night by knowing the shape of the country it calls its own. Its vision will be able to detect the trunk of an oak tree but only its knowledge will recognise that a bough has come down in a previous storm and blocked what had been a passage through the wood. And so a tawny owl territory is not only a self-delimiting prov-ince of song; it is a knowledge realm, a part of the world in which for a quarter of a century or more a pair of owls establish themselves by understanding what it is.

Martin compared the behaviour of owls in their poorly lit world to human car drivers at night. 'People frequently, sometimes habitually, drive in a manner which is beyond the control of information immedi-ately available via their visual system.' Car crash statistics show that 'the driver is quite often operating beyond his visual or perceptual capabili-ties in a number of key driving situations, including overtaking, joining or crossing a high-speed road, and a number of nighttime situations'.

People drive not according to the information they are receiving but according to what they already know or think they know about what is going to happen. The reason there are not more accidents is the safety margin added by the driver, the adjustments by other road users and the designers of the roads.

Martin's suggestion is that the owls, like us, are driving blind or half-blind at night, not receiving information but relying on their knowledge and expectations. And for this to work, the owls have to know their territory. If they are to know it well enough, they have to stay there a long time and make sure no other owl is invading the estate into which they have poured so much effort to acquire the knowledge. They can only hunt from familiar perches. They nest in holes they know and they sleep, and even sunbathe, in old, familiar nooks.

Their entire lives are folded into and moulded into their place. The hooting of the tawny is the voice of the wood. It is the reason widowed females might choose an old hooter from next door over a young blade: the old familiar bird has over the years acquired the place that a young one has yet to know. And it explains the annual wastage of owlets in the autumn. Biologists have often found them lying dead in the territory where they were so carefully reared: not needed, not as valid a carrier of the genes as their old and learned parents. It is no coincidence that humanity over thousands of generations has understood that owls are both pitiless and wise.

7.

Ravens

THINKING

A year or so after finding the dead body on the Cretan mountain road, I met the living ravens on a summer morning at home in Sussex. I looked up and above me was a sight no one, for the last century or more, would have thought possible: five ravens, a pair and three others. Deep and resonant cries were running between them. Talking, sky-mastering creatures, in curious and constant conversation, acrobatic and variable. *Quork-quork, aark-aark.* In the three decades I have lived here, I had never seen one. More than a century ago, they had been exterminated by farmers and gamekeepers, some shot, most poisoned. Almost the last breeding pair inland in Sussex was spotted in 1878 just down the road in the oaks of Ashburnham Park. Some hung on a little longer tucked into the cliffs of the English Channel, but after 1895 they had all gone.

Now this. *Quork-quork, aark-aark*, a heavy two-syllabled statement of scale and reach. The ravens were back in Sussex only because people had stopped exterminating them. The five this morning seem to be on passage, heading south. One stays high, half a mile away from me, surveying the others that hold their course maybe four hundred feet above the woods. I see in the binoculars their bills opening and one or two seconds later hear their voices, runs of quick *quork-quork-quork-quork* as a pair of them drop together, one smaller than the other, the sound rippling down the dive along with the birds themselves. The two of them flick-twist, touching wingtip to wingtip, flipping into spirals and half-spirals, as the sun on their backs flares into sheenlight.

They cruise for a moment, their tails held narrowly behind them and then as they drop again to the pursuit, those tails spread like skirts. There is nothing fixed about this. They are pure fluidity, always changing places, the pursuer turning pursued and back again, swirls of life spiralling down a stream, and it is clear this is no struggle for resources or control but a moment of what is rarely seen in nature: *play*, birds toying with their connectedness, their sociability as aerial performance.

They move off, each raven becoming no more than a single pixel on the horizon. I watched one as it got beyond me making a single 360-degree pirouette, a rotation on a spindle, and then onwards. And I heard its soft warm light bark, almost puppyish, small and welcoming, nothing harsh but low and horizon-reaching.

Two or three mornings later they were back again, all five, and now I stood and listened as they crossed above me. They sounded as chatty as old friends in the pub. The voices were not quite a *honk*, but more complex than that, some of them croaking higher and longer, *haiink*, others deeper, a little brusque, pure guttural. One sounded almost as if it were laughing, or at least laughing in the way a comic might imitate a laugh. Between all five there seemed to be a web of companionship and even friendship, stretching and linking, parting and touching.

They talked as they went and, for all the aerobatics, that conversational expansiveness, the sense of a social and familiar life being conducted between them, seemed to be the core of what they were. It made them companionate, part of the same world in which I lived. They are here every day now and have become ordinary, not rare but part of the usual beauty. And as I look up I think, Who are you? What can I know of you? What is this bird life?

The meetings accumulated: the beautiful corpse on the Cretan mountainside; the birds above the farm at home in Sussex; a raven that croaked one morning in a tree beside our house as we were about to leave for the funeral of Sarah's brother who died young after a long illness, the bird there as if to sing his death; and to those I would add a fourth: the unforgettable boyhood encounter with the mountain ravens described by William Wordsworth in *The Prelude*.

Of all English poets, he had the most raven-like of souls. When out walking, day or night, he used to hang his head between his shoulders, staring down for hours as his boots made their marks on the dust of the road, step after step, and as line after line of poetry formed itself in his mind, with his shoulders up around him, adopting even in his late twenties a haunted and otherworldly darkness from which he gathered his visions of the world.

His grandest soul-adventures as a ten- and twelve-year-old were to climb among the early springtime cliffs in Yewdale near Hawkshead, looking for the nests from which he might take the young ravens – its eggs are laid before the end of winter and there are young ravens to be caught even as the first primroses are in flower.

He was, as he wrote twenty years later, with some pride and a dose of unfelt, false shame,

> a plunderer then
> In the high places, on the lonesome peaks
> Where'er, among the mountains and the winds,
> The Mother Bird had built her lodge. Though mean
> My object, and inglorious, yet the end
> Was not ignoble. Oh! when I have hung
> Above the raven's nest, by knots of grass

And half-inch fissures in the slippery rock
But ill sustain'd, and almost, as it seem'd,
Suspended by the blast which blew amain,
Shouldering the naked crag; Oh! at that time,
While on the perilous ridge I hung alone,
With what strange utterance did the loud dry wind
Blow through my ears! the sky seem'd not a sky
Of earth, and with what motion mov'd the clouds!

Not stated, but intended, is the recognition that Wordsworth was near-raven himself, held by the air, at home with his fingers in the cracks in the rock, in a 'loud dry wind' that seemed to speak to him of the aerial world to which he felt he might belong. Is this a young boy in Westmorland hunting for his few pennies' reward? Or more than that, the first elements springing up of a poet's mind, the emergence of an English shaman, ready to engage with a sense of reality that depended less on observation or analysis than on a kind of trance-like immersion in nature, an identification with it, a sense that he and the ravens were in some ways continuous?

These were among the first lines of the *Prelude* that he wrote in the winter that he and Dorothy spent alone in Germany in 1798–9. They are some of his deepest recollections of how he became a poet. That image of the boy hanging like a raven above the raven's nest is not a summons to watch birds or to examine them as interesting specimens, or even to understand them, but in a sense to join them, to get with them as co-actors on earth.

I wanted to find the place where Wordsworth had hunted on the crags as a boy. Chris Hind, the county recorder for birds in Cumbria, and Sue King, who has made a study of the ravens of the central Lake District, guided me to the most likely spot: the cliffs in Yewdale where from all the evidence it seems that the young boy – his friends called him 'Bill Wordsworth' – had gone adventuring:

My anxious visitation hurrying on
Among the lonely eughtrees & the crags
That looked upon me how my bosom beat
With expectation

Chris and Sue walked me out to the places that could be seen from
below, in particular the raw, dried-blood red rocks known as Raven
Crag above Yewdale Farm. After an hour or two, talking birds, chat-
ting about the little balls of tightly rolled up clingfilm Sue had found
in raven pellets, picked from the sandwich-wrappings discarded by
Lake District walkers, they left me to it, standing at the foot of the
cliffs among the oaks and ashes filled with singing redstarts and greenfinches.

We had seen some ravens together and although Sue has become
aware that their numbers in the central Lake District seem to be in
decline – perhaps because modern farming methods mean less carrion
left on the fells – a pair had on cue made their way along the cliff face
above us, straight through Wordsworth territory, the two of them flashing above the sour-milk white of the ghylls, beating into the wind.
When a third caught up with them it was greeted with a turn and a
twist from the others, a momentary gleam in the dark of their feathers
as the sunlight caught them.

Sue was clear there was no nest now on Raven Crag – it had probably been washed away by winter rains – but if I scrambled up there I
might find the overhung nook where the nest had once been. I began
on the big rounded haunches of rock, their surfaces a dark scab-brown
red. Foxgloves and heather had pushed themselves into the cracks. I
arrived now and then at welcome shelves of rock carpeted in a virulent
green moss. Below me the rushy, buttercup meadows of Yewdale
stretched out to Coniston Water and the air was filled with the white
noise of the becks running down towards it. Of course this was a place
that made a poet.

Yewdale from Raven Crag

It is not a famous dale, but a beautiful one, and these high, exposed shelves are the sort of refuge in which Wordsworth loved to rest on his pre-school walks, when

> among the hills I sate
> Alone, upon some jutting eminence
> At the first hour of morning, when the Vale
> Lay quiet in an utter solitude.

A redstart went ahead of me as I climbed through the ferns, hand over hand up the part-mossy, part-bouldered hill. The bird bounced away from me through the occasional yews and birches that sprouted from the rocks, calling from each of its stances. There were shallow gullies and grooves in the crag, and I was part-way up a long slanting rake that ran between two red lichened slabs before I felt alarmed at the exposure, looking down the way I had come, seeing how much more difficult it would be to descend than to climb. I stopped, not wanting to get crag-fast, as happened to a young and frightened friend of Bill Wordsworth on these very rocks in 1783.

I crept downwards, sat again for a long time on the damp moss shelves, looking out at the dale, waiting for a raven to come. None did. Instead, only Wordsworth as the great poet of sky and stillness, of 'sounds unfrequent as in desarts', of the loud, dry wind and at least the imagined presence of these great dark birds.

I have now attuned my ears to the ravens at home, listening out for the soft croak-barking as they drift across the sky. The calls do not grate or screech like a crow's; the raven's voice seems older and larger than that. It may be a function of size. Palaeontologists have seen in the form of the raven's throat and mouth something similar to those of the later dinosaurs from which all birds are descended. Some have speculated that in these beautiful, dark, serious statements we are hearing the sound of the Jurassic and the Cretaceous, a pre-mammalian voice more ancient than anything we know except the buzzing of the insects' wings.

I watch them as they go and see that, for all this chatter, they have no real need of the voice. As an instrument, the raven's body is even more expressive: black glossed, reckless, capable, turning up into steep-walled, stalling surges and then falling away into equally gravity-banking dives. Occasionally they achieve a sleek orchestral unity, four or five as one for an instant, each of their flight paths as twisted into the others as a braided rope, rippled, as quick as fish, then breaking apart, riffling into the distance.

Sometimes they glide. Or they can flick and turn above each other down the valley below the farm. Or come towards me in long, slow, waltzing swoops. I have watched them silently coming together and drifting apart as if describing the kind of long looping pen line that sometimes decorates the border of a charter or indenture. They can click at one moment from pure independence into synchronised flight, their wings beating together, eight or ten times, followed by what feels like a mid-air pause, with a *quork-quork* from one, only then for the mutualising, interlocking flight to start again. As they diverge, one tucks and dives, levelling for a moment and then tucking and diving again, as if a footballer were cavorting through air in the ecstasy of having scored. That does not seem like an insignificant comparison: as much as its voice, the raven's social instrument is its body.

I have taken to leaving out carrion – rabbits, squirrels, rats, a young deer I found dead in the wood which I dragged half a mile across the farm, its head scuffing along the track behind me – in the hope it would attract the ravens and even make them feel somehow welcome and at home. I have had no result yet but the provision has not been consistent and besides, ravens are notoriously bait-wary, applying a kind of canniness to anything that might look like a free gift. That said, a friend of mine brought home a roadkill badger and laid it out in the field behind his house. The next day he found a raven carving chunks off it with its bill and burying them in different places around the field.

They are scavengers. There is the long-inherited idea, shared by Wordsworth, that they are the killers of lambs, an accusation still widely believed (and for many years the source of persecution) but almost certainly either untrue or at least rarely true. Derek Ratcliffe, the twentieth-century protector and lover of the birds, called the raven 'in northern Europe a vulture substitute'. It will always find and focus on carrion, with a miraculous ability to detect dead meat. It will finish off a weak or dying animal but will rarely kill a living thing as large as a lamb.

In the absence of some giant dead beast, they are as omnivorous as we are. An analysis by the Northumbrian naturalist George Bolam, conducted one winter early in the twentieth century, picked apart the contents of 433 separate raven pellets he found lying beneath a roost somewhere near Llanuwchllyn in Snowdonia.

It sounds like the hungriest of shopping lists.

Fifty-one of the pellets contained parts of sheep, twenty-eight the hair and remains of cows; one seemed to be filled with bits of dog. Thirty-seven of the birds had eaten rabbit, forty-eight rat, and many contained the skeletons and skulls of mice, voles, moles, shrews and weasels. Two had managed to swallow a hedgehog each. One had eaten an enormous fish, another an entire grouse. The birds had been down to the sea and crunched their way through crabs, sea-urchins and winkles. Most of the pellets contained oats, wheat grains, beech mast and acorns. One bird had tried a cherry and another a hazelnut. One had swallowed a stick and several contained lumps of stone, chalk and cinders. By far the commonest of the minerals in these stomachs were lumps of glittering, crystalline white quartz that had drawn the ravens' wide and attentive eyes.

We might think of them as creatures that belong to the ultimate wild but it is striking how large a part is played in this list by a connection with human beings. For all our recent persecution of them, ravens have spent much of their lives in the outskirts of our own and when I now see them in the sky above me, I realise I am meeting our commensals, sharing the same table, in all likelihood co-evolving through our shared histories. Even in the relatively wild forest of Białowieża in Poland, the biggest raven roost nowadays is next to a municipal rubbish dump.

That connection may be among the oldest of all our intimacies with birds – or with animals of any kind. Beginnings often hold the answers and recent research in the Czech Republic by the palaeo-ecologist Chris Baumann has started to reveal the time-depth of our companionship with ravens.

Cats and rats first lived with us when we had settled into farming villages in the Near East about 9,500 years ago. The first cows, sheep and goats had joined us about five hundred years earlier. The first dogs became human companions in about 13,000 BC. But twice as long ago as that, about 28,000 years BC, as Baumann has revealed through analysis of the thousands of bones found in a series of palaeolithic sites in Moravia, ravens became our familiars. Listen now to the ravens quork-talking above you and you are hearing what people deep in the last Ice Age knew as their animal companions.

We were living then in a marginal world. To the north the snowfields stretched unbroken to the pole. To the south the Alpine glaciers were pushing ever further into the valleys. The world was reaching its glacial maximum and the grip of the cold was inexorable. People were subsisting in a kind of open parkland, if that is not too comfortable a term, that hovered for much of the year on the edge of frost. The river courses were lined with willows and alders – no nightingales or warblers sang in them for the truncated summers; they remained south, down in the damp birchwood of the Mediterranean – and the tundra-like grasslands were scattered with woods and copses of spruce, larch and pine. Those were the trees the ravens, then as now, preferred for their nests, some set high, 130 feet or more, surveying their surroundings. A commanding height is one of the fundamental aspects of a raven's world.

It is almost impossible to imagine how embedded in nature those people were. This is before 'the severing' – the deep disconnection from nature brought about by the invention of agriculture in Mesopotamia some ten thousand years ago. Even the conception of 'nature' as something different from us seems irrelevant to the lives of palaeolithic Europeans. They may have been among the first human artists and the first makers of effective hunting weaponry, but the overwhelming fact for this tiny cluster of ancient humanity was its vulnerability.

Abandon all sense of dominance. We were fewer than the wolves or bears, many fewer than the birds, surrounded by an all-powerful and increasingly hostile nature on which we had to rely. We perched in the world and were not distinct from it. We knew there were others like us at some barely comprehensible distance, months away, out in western Russia, in southern France or the north of Spain, but, for all that, we were alone, with no powerful boundary drawn between our own gatherings and those of other herds of large animals – the herbivores and their predators – that accompanied us in the forest and the night. We all both hunted and were hunted. We all both bred and died. Our houses like the animals' were semi-subterranean, half-burrows. We and the other creatures all spoke our different languages. We all had to listen out for the hints of threat and glimpses of opportunity. We were one among many. And the others, the carnivores and the great birds, seemed to have capacities we did not have.

The people of this Ice Age Gravettian culture – named after the site at La Gravette in the Dordogne where its fine-bladed spear- and arrow-points were first discovered – lived off the animals they hunted. The cold made fat valuable, and no animals had more or fattier meat than mammoths. Tons of mammoth bone have been found at their campsites. The lowest levels of their buildings – which were insulated and the walls up to a metre thick – were often made of those bones. Analysis of the human remains has revealed that 60 per cent of the protein they consumed consisted of mammoth meat. Hyenas, wolves, deer and reindeer, as well as hares and foxes, formed part of the diet but mammoth haunch was its foundation.

Among the other bones, the palaeontologists made an extraordinary discovery. There were many from black grouse, willow grouse, partridge and ptarmigan – meaty birds – but more than 40 per cent of all the bird bones belonged to the raven. Almost as much as a mammoth culture, this was a raven culture. Some of those raven bones were analysed for the nitrogen, carbon and sulphur they contained, elements that could reveal what the ravens had eaten. And here the picture cohered: like their human companions, these ravens fed mostly on the meat of large herbivores, usually mammoth.

It is a near-heraldic picture. Man, bird and beast interlock on the face of the shield. Chris Baumann and his team concluded that the ravens were probably attracted to the mammoth carcasses near human camps and killed while feeding on them. They may have been netted – the oldest evidence of knotted nets in the world comes from these sites – or perhaps shot with bow and arrow. Many of the surviving stone points, originally cut with care and precision, show the kind of percussive impact scars that come from an arrowhead colliding with a hard surface. The evidence provides another irony: many of the raven remains consist of their separated wing bones, with the implication that wings were cut or torn from the bodies and the ribbed, rigid feathers taken for arrow or spear fletching. The ravens provided the means by which they were hunted.

It was a real symbiosis. Ravens and their hunters were partners in a shared ecosystem to which they both contributed and from which both benefited. Despite the small scale of human life, this was already the Anthropocene. Nature was not untouched. The hunter-gatherers had altered the ecology around them, creating human-formed niches into which other organisms could fit and adapt. The ravens would have done well from all the mammoth carrion the hunters gave or left for them. Only when the human beings had killed the mammoths and opened up their hides could the birds gain access to the meat. In the absence of more powerful carrion feeders, ravens can get to the soft internal tissue only through the eyes, mouth or anus of the dead bodies. Cutting the hide open was a human service to them.

In turn, the hunters, like other carnivores, would have gained from the ravens' unequalled ability to find dead meat, perhaps a mammoth that had died of natural causes, which the hunters but not the ravens were able to cut into. And the men made use of the feathers they could take from the ravens that had guided them there.

The strange pleasure I get from hearing the ravens talk above me is simple enough. A wonderful wild creature is alive again here in Sussex. But there is also a vibrancy in the continuation of this long history. We have cattle, sheep, dogs, hens and, occasionally, pigs on this farm, all large, breathing vertebrate companions that bring life and vitality to the place. But they are all in their different ways our prisoners. Unlike them, the ravens, the old mammoth-pickers, the Ice Age arrow-birds, are here of their own accord.

Life scientists have tried to understand what ravens, which are after all songbirds, are saying but the attempts to translate their remarks into intelligible signals seem futile. The American biologist Richard Conner spent four years in the 1970s trying to learn raven from birds he followed around the oak and hickory forests of south-west Virginia. You have to feel for him. His report reads like a monoglot Englishman's attempt to hear what French means without knowing any French.

Conner came up with eighteen raven-words. Some were associated with aggression (a growl, with 'a pulsing quality' and a *kow*), courtship (a rattle and a bell-like call), alarm (a staccato *caw-caw-caw*) or distress (whining and clucking), but for Conner most of the 'behavioural contexts' for what the raven had to say, even after four years of his sitting watching, listening and recording in his hide, remained

'Unknown'. He listed the words the birds used: a sound like *cawl-up* – very loud and audible several miles away over the mountain ridges of Virginia – *Awk, Ku-uk-kuk, kow, ko-pick, ank-up, woo-oo-woo*, an 'uvular' sound – a reverberant gurgle like a French 'r' – *o-ot, puddle-puddle-puddle* and *ke-aw*: but all these barks and babblings, laughings and crowings emitted into the mountain air by the loquacious birds defied any meaning discernible to a human being.

Again and again the naturalists have tried to transcribe the raven's voice. In one scientific paper after another, they read like parodies of what science might be. Danish ravens say *krok-krok-krok*. In Russian that sounds like *kruk-kruk-kruk*. Americans prefer to say their ravens emit 'a hoarse, guttural, rolling *cr-r-r-r-cruck*'. Englishmen have heard a *tch-reep*, a *krack*, a *kow*, a *kronk* and a triple *toc-toc-toc*. In Alaska ravens are said to sound like a xylophone. Germans hear them say *rapp* or even *krapp*.

It may all be true but what can we know? A near-anarchic ability to flare and fluctuate from one state to another, to adopt and shift, seems to be embedded in the raven's voice as much as in its genes. Derek Ratcliffe once heard a raven say *gurgle-plop-clink*. George Bolam watched and listened to a raven in Wales

chewing and chuckling to himself for a long time, sometimes changing his perch a little, the variety of his repertoire being extraordinary; no sound uttered beyond a half-tone, but almost every voice of the mountain being imitated in turn, and some of the noises defying all similes. He yapped like dog, reproduced the call of a grouse, and a crow to perfection, bleated like a sheep or a goat, and made all sorts of metallic noises, from the click of a blacksmith's anvil to the creaking of a rusty hinge.

We do not know what they are saying. We remain apart. For all our connections, we occupy different thought-worlds. We are parallel co-occupants of the places we share.

The Austrian ethologist Konrad Lorenz made one step into this mirror-mystery. He named his pet raven Roah, after the call the bird made. It was Lorenz's close friend and used to go with him 'when he had nothing better to do, on long walks and even on skiing tours, or on motor boat excursions on the Danube'. When out in the wild, Lorenz would summon Roah by name and Roah would call 'Roah' in return. Only after a year or two did Lorenz realise that not only was 'Roah' Lorenz's name for the bird, it was the bird's name for Lorenz. Roah never made that call when addressing any other creature.

When the Ice Age hunters moved into new country, as they did each summer, their ravens would have kept up with them, cleaning up the food scraps left at the camps, continuing to remove the meat that might have drawn in the wolf packs. The people, like Lorenz, might have known individual ravens and developed a form of mutuality and intimacy with them. Roah would always remember places where he had been frightened or disturbed and never liked them. If he saw Lorenz lingering in such a place, he could not endure it but would 'bear down upon me from behind and, flying close over my head, he wobbled with his tail and then swept upwards again, at the same time looking backwards over his shoulder to see if I was following'. All the

time the raven called 'Roah, Roah' to his human friend, urging him away from danger.

I long for such a friend. There is one individual at home in Sussex that often flies above me and I wonder if it is seeking me out. Its left foot dangles below the wing in the relaxed, authoritative way of a man lying back on a sofa. I recognise him now as the Dangler, and imagine he must be some kind of risk-taker who somehow caught his leg in a fence or twist of wire and broke it to escape. Other birds don't like him. I have watched a buzzard chase him across the woods, flogging in his wake, the raven corkscrewing away.

Stone relief of the Gallo-Roman period from Moux, France, showing a man with birds perched on each of his shoulders and a dog at his feet. The man is probably a priest or druid and the birds have the appearance and attitude of ravens

Long Field Shaw

Hollow Flemings

The birdhouse

Bullfinch in the snow

A dunnock

Brambling

Robin

It is scarcely the closest of relationships but, as Konrad Lorenz knew with Roah, ravens can make beautiful, if unpredictable, pets. Ravens in the wild can live twenty-five years. One kept in the Tower of London lived until he was forty-four. Priests and shamans all across Siberia and Central Asia have made companions of them. Many deliberate raven burials have been found in Iron Age and Roman Europe, some of them whole birds, some the wings only. Many were old when they died, with arthritis and wounds to wing and claw that had mended when they were alive. Unlike most other animal remains, the ravens were not eaten. There are never any traces of butchery.

Rather more recently, Charles Dickens kept a series of pet ravens all called Grip. They were allowed to roam about the house, addressing its other inhabitants. 'Halloa, old girl,' one would say to anyone passing and steal interesting objects from the household: halfpennies and cheese, raw potatoes, brushes and a large hammer taken from a carpenter. This booty ended up buried in the garden.

The ravens are here above me today on the farm, not pets but undeniable after a mere blip of an absence that will be invisible to future historians. Raven is thriving in the Anthropocene, cruising in the Sussex sky. In the field-glasses I see him look down at me looking at him. He does not bother to look for long. His companions are a few hundred yards behind or to one side, some of them crooning as they leave me in their wake.

For a moment as I watch, they come across a flight of swallows heading south. It is the meeting of two opposite principles of life: the swallows are en route to South Africa but the ravens are from here. They are not migratory. These birds do now seem to belong to this Sussex valley. And so here the great residents encounter the great migrants, both of them masters of winged existence. As they cross, they twitch and quiver at each other, the swallows, no more present than the scraps of burnt paper that blow up from a bonfire on the smoke, tease-badgering the ravens, for part of a second, and then away; the ravens, almost guardsman-like against the little birds skittering around them, swipe at the swallows in return or flicker away themselves. Is it curiosity about the other that makes the swallows do this? Annoyance? Or the flying body version of a careless hello from a man on a racing bike as he slips past the Bentleys?

If we were birds, we would be ravens. Like them, we are both solitary and sociable, independent, clever, playful, fierce, territorial, loyal to our family and deceitful of others. It is a connection that has always been recognised. In the oldest myths of the ancient Siberian peoples and their relatives who moved over to the Americas, Raven is a high-powered version of us. Across those long-inhabited landmasses, story after story describes him as a non-human person of enormous potency, exhibiting all the human virtues and vices but with skills beyond our own. He is capable of anarchic selfishness and of creating the conditions in which people can survive. He was the inventor of the first human beings (when he was feeling bored), and of the reindeer, fish and other wild animals that became their food. Demonic forces had previously hoarded the sunlight, freshwater and salmon but Raven liberated them.

He repainted the other birds in all their colours, giving some of them tufts and others long beaks, and once he had finished, he said he would feast them and cooked a great deal of meat. He then ate it all himself.

The birds were angry at this breach of faith, and Robin began to growl at Raven. Then the others began to growl. Raven became angry, and took up a stick and threatened them with it. They all then ran away, and hid in different places. The ducks to the lakes, the grouse to the woods; some to the mountains, and some to the rivers. Thus they were scattered. Before this the birds had all been together. Raven said, 'It would not be well for all kinds of birds to be in one place. It will be better for people if the birds are scattered. Henceforth the birds shall be scattered throughout the country, and each kind shall live in a different locality.'

Although he had begun life pure white himself, a whole series of disasters turned him black.

In one North American version, Raven and Great Northern Diver or Common Loon, both birds that were created white, agreed to tattoo each other.

The loon was to be tattooed first and all the fine little patterns of its plumage [the little fire sparks or *kukualarniuit* in the Tlingit language of coastal Alaska] are the tattooings that the raven gave it. But then the raven became impatient and took a handful of ashes and threw them over the loon. That is why its head is black. The loon was furious and gathered the soot from its cooking pot and threw it all at the raven, with the result that its whole body turned black.

The Raven of the stories is the best and worst of us. He is both a clever trickster and an unstoppable glutton, often stupid and often wise about the nature of the world and our place in it. As the Oxford environmentalists and historians Tom and Patricia Thornton have written, Raven is the understander of change and mutability. In an unpredictable world, he improvises. In his sometimes chaotic power, he

> adapts, innovates, and transforms with Earth's changes, sometimes by relying upon his intimate knowledge of local species, sometimes by cunning and wiles, and sometimes by happenstance as a result of his ulterior manipulations, and, at times, buffoonery.

As a creature of appetite, he is our mirror and in many ways the mirror of the excess, the drive to more, of life itself. There is nothing complacent or settled about him. He is the careless acrobat, the bird of darkness that is also the bird of a vivid, flashing intensity of life. As the model of the accomplished overreacher, he has been in human minds for millennia.

'Raven's fate,' the Thorntons have written,

> is in many ways the human fate, one of constant appetites leading to confounding consequences and the need for continuous adaptation. Yet Raven is not human, and his fate is not exclusively the human fate, but rather the fate of all species that reach beyond their means, their limits, their territory, their niche.

He is both the creator of disaster and its survivor. The very qualities that make him unreliable – his ambition, his meddling, his egotism – give him flexibility, versatility and resilience. In one Alaskan version of his life, he outlasted the Great Flood by flying up to the mountains and becoming a large rock on which the destructive waters of the flood broke and dispersed. As the flood withdrew, he once again acquired his wings and flew out across a transformed world of which he was king. He taught human beings how to have children by making a girl sick, telling her that she would only get better if she went out of the village and sat down on something she found sticking out of the ground. He then hid himself under the moss, making sure his penis was standing out prominently above it. When the girl sat on him, he impregnated her and the first human baby was conceived.

Raven is filled with lust but not much love, Protean in his essence, exploitative, vengeful, homeless. He does not know who his father was, nor how he came into being. He can be gormless but never sweet. He once tried to tell the trees that they could eat the flesh of a bear he had brought them.

Raven discovers the first human beings hiding in a clam shell, by the Haida artist and sculptor Bill Reid

The trees and roots became angry, because they knew Raven was fooling them. Then a tree fell across the bear, covering it up, and nearly hitting Raven. Now Raven said, 'I have done wrong. I should not have done this. I should not fool people. People must not fool or joke to the trees or rocks, or game, or anything in nature, for these things will seek revenge.' This is why Indians are careful not to offend anything. If they make fun of a tree, they may get hurt by a tree; if they mock or fool with the water, they may be drowned; if they laugh at the snow, a snow-slide may kill them.

He is the great mediator-bird, the connector between wisdom and idiocy, life and death, this world and others, both gullible and amorous, not all-powerful but often anxious to please. He once considered long and hard how to find a way of providing food for all the people of the world but all his thinking did no good and, because he was finally unable to devise one, he, like us, quite often starves.

I have been watching a family all year. Layer on layer of meaning seems to accumulate around them. Almost every day, they tell me they are here.

They are symbols of resurgence and intelligence. They range from one horizon to the other, often visible in the far distance, tussling and playing with each other, or flogging from one destination to the next. They have added another layer to this place, as if a sheet of tissue has been laid across a landscape I already knew. They are the re-asserted voice of a natural world we had previously attempted to exclude, and so not the voice of the Anthropocene but of a successor age. Tom and Patricia Thornton have proposed a new term: the Ravencene, the time of necessary and clever adaptability. The raven has always seemed to understand that an inventive, many-winged readiness to change and live with change needs to be at the foundations of life. And so here now, despite the decades of poisoning, in which Raven pulled himself away for safety to the distant coasts and mountains, he has sprung back, and the deep *quork* above me is not the voice of the Jurassic but of the future.

The five I have seen over and over again are I think a parental pair, whose territory this valley now is, and their three offspring. They have been hacking to and fro all summer, I realise now, between the two nearest recycling centres, one seven miles to the west at Heathfield, one about seven miles to the east at Mountfield. No mammoth corpses but the detritus of our lives.

This is the parents' country, a big territory for now because ravens are still rare here. But unless they are shot or poisoned, I can be sure they will be here to stay. The parents will stay together for life. I will see Dangler for years to come, maybe for a decade or more, keeping to and defending the same territory of our valley, driving out intruding ravens, including his own offspring.

These five will not stay together. When winter comes, the family will disperse and any sense of solidarity between them will dissolve. The young, if they survive, will join a marauding pack of territory-less juveniles. It may be that they will eventually return to set up territories nearby, but that is far from certain. Ravens do not pair up until they are at least three and as much as ten years old, when they are capable of finding a mate for life. Many other bird species, to one degree or another, abandon their spouses. Among house martins for example the annual divorce rate approaches 100 per cent. But in the ravens, as in many seabirds, divorce is almost unheard of. And so we now have Dangler and his wife as a permanent aspect of where we live. This is their country, and they will know, as much as I know this, that there is at least one human being below them who will always look up when they call.

One of the few tracking experiments on settled ravens was conducted over two years in the Olympic peninsula in Washington State. A breeding female provided the researchers with a brief biography. They named her Q6 and she and her mate held a territory over the big gravelly meanders near the mouth of the Quillayute river that drain the Olympic Mountains.

Their territory was some two miles across, about two thousand acres, in tall, dense second-growth forest, which Q6 and her mate used as their hunting ground and home range from when she was caught and ringed in April 2005 until June 2006. Raven territories vary in size, but in the wild forests of north-east Poland, the only place in Europe where something approaching primeval woodland survives, that is the extent of the territory of a breeding pair. In the best conditions, it is also the scale across which a raven's voice can be heard. Evolution over millions

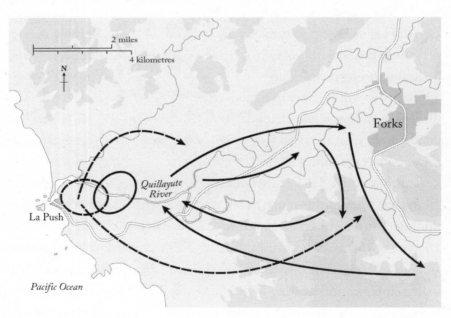

Eighteen months in the life of an Olympic raven, spring 2005 to autumn 2006. Solid oval: her original territory until the death of her mate in June 2006. Solid arrows: her wandering in search of a new mate June–August 2006. Dashed oval: Her new territory with new mate after August 2006. Dashed arrows: visits to cow carcasses, autumn 2006

of generations has managed a kind of fit: a raven's voice fills the landscape it patrols and calls its own. The voice addresses the audience it can command. No part of a raven's estate will remain ignorant of its presence. If ravens are anywhere, they will let you know.

Then in June 2006, catastrophe: Q6's mate was shot dead, triggering a complete change in her behaviour. Where before she had stayed close to her own lands, that summer she wandered far outside the old home territory, up to twelve or fifteen miles, over some 35,000 acres of forest, far inland away from the river she knew, up the valley of the Sol Duc, out to the suburbs of the city of Forks. The resources of her old territory had not changed. There was no need to travel that far for sustenance. The GPS tracks look in effect like a map of grief and loneliness. She was wandering and searching in the months after the death of a life partner.

In August, she found a new mate – it is not clear where – and together they set up a new territory almost at the mouth of the Quillayute within touching distance of the beaches on Puget Sound. But the experience had changed her. Q6 had learned to travel and her life habits expanded. She now regularly flew to visit the carcasses of cows up to eight miles inland.

This territorial fixity is a key aspect of adult raven life, as of many birds, but what of the young? The instruction period lasts all their first summer. Ravens breed early and so perhaps from March to September the young can learn some of the complexities of adult life from their parents. That is what I see as they dance in the sky above the farm. It is as much education as play. They too are at Bird School. But with the first autumn, the young are driven away, and the years that follow are hard and exploratory.

Modern trackers attached to young ravens in the Austrian Alps have revealed their roaming lifestyle, the gangs of juvenile ravens like young Vikings travelling their world to encounter it. The three young birds I had seen romping and playing with their parents in the summer sky would soon be off on their own long, perhaps international journeys.

The vagrant gangs are looking for giant bonanzas. In the Alps they have been recorded flying far and fast, up to twenty-five miles in an hour, more than a hundred miles a day and over the twenty months they were tracked covering almost seven thousand miles. These are not steady migratory journeys but like kids on motorbikes, fast crowd-rushes to the modern equivalents of mammoth kills where the birds will gorge for many days.

The roosts in which these large flocks gather to spend the night – often with as many as 1,500 birds – work as information exchange centres. Ravens, including those that don't know where the food is, arrive in the evening at the chosen forest trees, as singles, in pairs or small groups, over a period of up to an hour. It seems important for the birds to advertise their behaviour far and wide, especially if they are

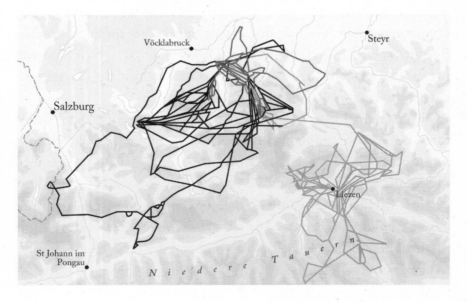

The journeys of four vagrant ravens in the Austrian Alps over three months, September–November 2018. The image is about ninety miles across

about to move their roost to somewhere near a newly discovered food source, and so, as the Washington University bird scientist John Marzluff described,

> large groups of soaring birds occasionally formed and flew
> lengthy circuits around the roost site (travelling several
> kilometres from the roost) before returning to settle in the roost
> as a group ... Individual ravens were attracted from a distance of
> at least 10 km to those that were soaring.

This knowledge tower of soaring ravens, like a spiralling bird thermal, communicates possibility and opportunity to all other ravens over some 75,000 acres of forest.

At dawn, in a highly synchronised way, with no more than seven minutes between the first bird leaving and the last, the roost departs en masse, the whole group 'giving a few noisy *kaws*, followed by *honking*', as Marzluff put it, heading to the known food bonanza, led by the ravens that had visited it in the days before.

Deer, elk and salmon carcasses are good but better and more reliable is what we provide for them: roadside rubbish, roadkill and the guts of gralloched carcasses. Ravens need us and in landfills, sewage plants, fish hatcheries, prisons and livestock farms, we give them what they want, the 'super-abundant, permanently renewed, spatially fixed resources' that ravens have been looking for since the Ice Age.

Nothing is better in winter than a ski resort. Snow cover limits access to natural food but that problem is countered by the Alpine huts scattered across the slopes whose skiers leave behind their odds and ends of würstchen and schnitzel, chips and baguettes for the birds to feast on. There are often resident pairs of breeding adult ravens in these high territories but here as elsewhere they are outcompeted for food by the hordes of roaming juveniles, muscling in, clustering around the benches and tables.

The sight of such a group on a half-eaten deer carcass is unsettling. All raven grace and wisdom seems absent. The body of the dead animal has been torn open, perhaps by a fox, or perhaps the skin has begun to rot. When the mob arrives, sometimes en masse, sometimes singly or in pairs, a riot develops. Although the adult residents peck away at the heads and bodies of the incoming juveniles, the schoolyard mêlée soon develops around them.

The violence is unforgiving. For many years the biologist Bernd Heinrich watched the ravens in the snow-bound winter woods of western Maine, leaving out large amounts of meat for them in clearings, wallowing up to his hips in snow to deliver it and waiting hidden to see how the birds behaved. They liked to yell as they arrived, summoning others so that the residents would be outnumbered. (The mustering yell is heard by Austrians as *Haa*.) They begin by digging through the snow to find the cache and then the fighting turns fierce. These gangs are not fixed. Individual ravens swap between different groups. At first, the resident adults try to attack them and sometimes juveniles roll over on their side in appeasement, particularly if the vagrant gang is not yet large, but in the end sheer numbers count.

Heinrich quotes a letter he had from Kathy Bricker, a Michigan photographer who had been watching her own ravens:

14 ravens at 11 am. A lot of fighting ensued – no friendly play that. They jab viciously at one another's head – I saw one grab hold of another's leg with his feet; the two thus joined stood with their beaks open, facing one another, and finally disengaged and flew off chasing each other. When they rush at each other with wings flapping, they throw out their feet with those sharp talons. I saw one knocked to his side by the blow; instantly he was surrounded by other ravens who had been nearby. Apparently there is nothing quite so exciting as a fight,

or perhaps quite so tasty as raven meat. The meal in question righted itself and quickly flew off.

What was going on? In one, economic sense it is clear. A piece of land can only hold a certain number of raven territories. Those are occupied by the present adults. The young wanderers are a reservoir from which new breeding adults can be recruited when a resident dies. And they will compete with each other until they graduate to their own breeding status.

There is more to their life than those everyday facts of getting and spending. The wild ravens above the farm, even half a mile away, exude an intelligence and sociability, an alert, multivalent consciousness that is somehow able to communicate itself across the air, and which was recognised in the raven stories of the ancient cultures. People have always detected from the birds flying above them their communicativeness, their mutual response, the way in which antagonism seems to dance around the edges of their sociability, as human beings also josh each other as a sign of warmth and connectedness, even of trust, and at the same time of competitiveness and challenge. Beneath that understanding is the sense that an intelligent social life brings with it a calculation of individual interest. Sociability and deceit are each other's companions.

Aspects of the raven that are implicit, or only hinted at, in the birds you might glimpse in the wild have been made explicit in a series of experiments conducted in the Vienna laboratory of the Austrian animal psychologist Thomas Bugnyar and his team. Over many years, they have repeatedly shown that ravens are clever and mendacious, canny operators and almost infinitely adaptable. They defend territory, aggressively claiming it from others, are fond of their families – at least up to a point – slow to mature, able to experience what the biologists call 'contagious emotion', capable of imagining what is in the minds of others and of playing subtle politics to achieve their ends.

This social consciousness begins in the vagrant bands of juveniles. Those contentious scenes at the carcasses or the ski resort huts are the first dramas of social education. Each raven has memories that last for years, like Roah's, and can distinguish up to two hundred different individual ravens, remembering their own ranking in relation to others and, more strikingly, the difference in rankings between those others. These juvenile mobs are organised in complex social networks, with different birds constantly leaving and arriving, and each recognised for its part in the hierarchy: males (which are bigger) usually above females, old and experienced above young and naive, those that have a strong bond with another raven above the loners. This mobile fission-fusion social structure is part-physical and part-social. Bigger birds will dominate, as will those that have more experience of life, but so will those that know they are not alone in the world.

These bonded birds, which are not yet breeders but are usually a male-female pair, often siblings, look after each other's well-being. If a raven gets involved in a fight, her partner will either jump in and help out, attacking the other bird, or provide help by standing by and looking supportive. He is more likely to get involved if his friend started the fight. If she is under attack, he will probably wait on the side, not wanting to risk being attacked himself.

Stranger ravens hardly ever reconciliate after a fight – the risk of the tussle starting again is too high – but pairs, if they squabble, will make up. And after the fight with a stranger is over, bonded ravens will console their partners, the bystander preening the victim's feathers, standing close, touching body to body or even holding a leg or a wingtip with their bill. The purpose is to relieve their partner's distress. She will often ask for it, nudging him into closeness.

This sense of togetherness is not unique to ravens – if a greylag goose sees his partner or a sibling in a fight, his heart rate goes up in sympathy – but ravens, like other crows, rooks and jays, are attuned to what their partner is feeling. The fiercer the fight, the longer and more careful the emotional repair afterwards. Nor is it only a question of soothing the anxiety. If one of a bonded pair starts to play with a new toy – ravens are always wary of strange new things – it is much more likely that his partner will play too. It seems that playfulness is contagious and that, I now realise, is what I have seen morning after morning at home: the family group is heading somewhere or other, doggedly making its way across the valley, often separated by a hundred yards or more, but all going in the same direction, when one of them approaches another, flicks a wing at him, a full-bodied wink, their primaries touching, and the other responds with a twist, or stamps on the brakes into a sudden stall, or falls into a dive, and for a moment or two all of them are playing or tease-taunting one another, body-jokes, an aerial way of pulling someone's leg, before resuming their course, as if a stream of laughter had convulsed the family on a long car journey.

At the end of the season young ravens often move on to other partners, in trial relationships for what might in the end become lifelong loyalty as breeding birds. Not that all ravens find these everlasting partners. Many adults remain single, living their entire lives with the vagabond gangs.

Alongside solidarity comes competitiveness and the necessity of deceit. Young ravens need to hang out in mobile groups that will take them to scattered food sources that are often difficult to discover. But once there, each must look to his own. These may be temporary bonanzas and because the surplus must be hidden for later, each raven has the habit of taking food and hiding it from the others. Individual birds can remember up to twenty-five different caches, which they will revisit and consume within a few hours or even days.

It is all-important that other ravens don't know where the food is hidden and so tactics develop. The hiding place can be a long way off, or out of sight behind a rock. Or if other ravens look like they are on the scent, the hider will come back and recover the cache or defend it.

They will only do this when the stash is approached by birds that were watching when the food was hidden. Ravens that arrived after the cache was made (and so don't know where it is) can be ignored.

At the same time, other ravens stalk around the area, looking disengaged but in fact watching where the caches are being made. As soon as the coast is clear and the original hider has disappeared, the observers jump in and pilfer the food. Or at least they will if they see that other ravens are still around who also watched as the cache was made. If they are surrounded only by later arrivals, who don't know about it, they will refrain from plundering it. And if the original hider returns, the pilferer just as quickly pretends to be about something else, digging in random places in the soil or playing with sticks or pebbles.

These deceitful corners of the raven mind grow subtler still. If a raven knows that a rival witnessed the burying of one cache but not another, that is the cache he will dig up, ignoring the other. He knows not only which bird he saw when he was hiding the food but what the other raven saw at the same time. He knows, in other words, what another raven is thinking. And when scientists played the role of intermittently present observer, the ravens also understood which cache to open and which to ignore. There may well be no bird that is more like us.

8.

Buzzards

FLYING

From the windows of the birdhouse, I can almost touch the nearest birds. I have to be still when looking at them. They scare at any movement. But if I put myself behind one of the mullions of the windows and manage not to move – the necessary stillness of the predator – it is like looking into an aquarium of birds. The little copse is stirring, not in the wind but with the reverberations of these arriving and departing creatures, each transmitting a quiver to the branch, so that the hanging raindrops shimmer like the water in a fishtank that moves with the animals it contains.

Great tit, blue tit, marsh tit, coal tit, chaffinch, goldfinch, a dunnock on the clayey ground below them, a blackbird beside it, a robin. They swim and hang in the green air. Everywhere the wide slight sense of spring. The orange disc around the blackbird's eye glows like a headlight. The chest of the male chaffinch is both a brighter and a deeper red than in the grey of winter. A female chaffinch a yard beyond him is picking at the hazel bark, her coat a muted, fusing range of browns and greys.

These birds are quicks. Their governing term is 'quick'. Quickness and smallness is what they are. They are living in a cloud of rapidity and self-absorption, unaware of my presence. Existence as a flicker, the Brownian motion of molecules in a glazed chamber, bright, agile, fragile, seemingly undirected, with a restlessness and a lack of pause – all the volatile aspects of life that sitting here, looking down at them like this, seems to remove from my own.

It is strange how much happiness it brings. I can hardly tear myself away. I am learning nothing. I am seeing life in action and it has all the pleasures of listening again and again to the same song, the confirming familiarity of those repetitions. I do not need to dominate the birds or think of them as mine but day after day their close co-presence brings a heartfelt, life-opening sense of well-being. There is no narrative, no crisis, no revelatory transforming of anyone's fate or hopes. The birds are acting out the drama of continuousness, the theatre of things happening. It feels as good as when in a dinghy and the sails are set, the world can seem for a moment to be in dynamic and coherent balance, the rig taut, the bow-wave streaming past, the wake running behind you, or the uncomplicated sensation of walking and pausing in a hay meadow in full summer flower or diving on a fish-rich reef and becoming aware of the multiplicity of life around you. Perhaps this is the most banal of thoughts – the miracle that these things exist – but it is encompassing. In the grip of it, nothing matters more: not *how* things are, but *that* they are.

One of the big named storms blows through. There is a roaring in the tops. High above the wood, the buzzards are kicked and bullied by the wind. The great tits cling to the branches. They don't seem to mind the sudden mobility of everything around them. Even in the unreliability and unlocatedness of branch and stem the birds hop and leap from spot to spot as if they know every place on which to land. The wind is so inconstant and blustery that the trees respond to it like horses on a halter, jerking upwards with head and neck, a thrashing downwards, an abrupt shocked pull the other way. A blue tit is turned upside down by the wind as it leaves a branch but swings back upright.

In the gusts, reaching sixty miles per hour, the birdhouse shudders and gives as the green oak sways under the pressure, rippling down into its stiff oak bones. Branches are being blown off the trees in the ash shaw and as they fall they knock like scaffold boards dropped in a builder's yard. All the time the birds continue with their usual industrious busyness, at home in the wood even as the wind is doing its best to trash it.

Then the wind strengthens. In the strongest gusts, the small birds are blown off and fly hard upwind to regain their perches. The feeders are swinging about like lanterns in a storm, while the small birds are pushed off into the air like children thrown into a swimming pool, scrabbling for the edge.

A flock of goldfinches is blown here and there as if they were a clutch of leaves torn from the hornbeams. And, as I watch, that gust of finches, swirled in on itself, is for a moment caught up with a blow of leaves from those very trees, each golden fleck a leaf or bird, it is not easy to tell which, billowing away downstream in the westerly gale.

There is a marsh tit among the oak trees. If you saw the bird briefly and from some distance – or heard its *pichou* call – you would think it the neatest and most precious of creatures. From a distance its black cap and grey flank look tailored, not a feather out of place, and different from the rather roughly turned out coal tit. But the bird here is not that careful, coutured figure. Seen close-up, these wrongly named birds, which are of the woodland and not the marsh, seem more like individual survivors than their images in the books. He is wind-tousled around his neck. This storm has ruffled his breast and wing feathers, which have not folded back properly. The sheeny black cap is smooth only in the way human hair can be half-smooth when brushed back across the scalp. His eyes look bulbous, large in his head, supremely alert, and capable of holding me in their stark binocular stare.

He is not alone. Wherever he goes within the lattice-work of the trees, he is accompanied by another marsh tit, his mate. They are gentle birds, often sitting on the same branch and usually following each

A marsh tit

other from tree to tree. But their modesty matches their place in the wood hierarchy; they are near or at the bottom of any pecking order that develops here.

The buzzards and the sparrowhawks are the terror tyrants far above them. Buzzards can fly through high mature woodland and often hunt across the woodland floor and understorey, watching the ground, searching for voles and nesting birds. But they are too big to manoeuvre neatly between young trees. Much more easily they can look down from their cruise in the open air above the wood or perch in the topmost branches, where they like to sit warming themselves on cold mornings. If a buzzard floats overhead, the small birds plunge for the undergrowth, sinking into the skin of trees, where they disappear and take many minutes to return.

The sparrowhawk is different, more duplicitous, an ambush predator. He can be seen sometimes waiting hidden among the lower leafy branches from which he departs for his raid unseen. If the hawk is spotted before it makes its dash, the songbirds flurry away from it in a Protean escape-burst, spreading out like the spokes of a fan, or the jets of water from a garden spray.

The tits are not always so passive. When they spot a hawk as they are foraging in a flock together in the wood, they will mob it, making their high, sharp alarm calls. If a hawk is seen flying over towards them, their calls rise in pitch and urgency, summoning two different responses: the birds either freeze motionless, their feathers sleeked down, staying immobile for five minutes or more, hoping they haven't been targeted; or, if they think the hawk is after them, diving straight down from the trees and into cover near the ground where they can hide until the danger is past. Studies of different tit populations seem to show that they have evolved to think it is better to be safe than sorry, and that to give large numbers of false alarms is wiser than failing to raise the alarm even once too often.

The blackbird alarm call – a high and desperate shriek – alerts all others to the danger. But usually the hawk gives no warning and you will know of its attack only as it happens – a detonation of leaves and panic, a missile strike into the little rivalries and enmities you had been witnessing a second before. And afterwards again many minutes of silence and absence.

From time to time, a magpie sits coolly in those trees, supervising, calm and patient, displaying the emerald-and-teal glamour of its tail and back, waiting for a songbird to make itself vulnerable.

I have never seen a rook, crow or raven attacking these birds, but the dominators are stacked in many layers below the high and famous predators. First the woodpeckers, which are capable of doing extraordinary violence to the nest boxes, axing openings in their timber façades like Jack Nicholson's maniac in *The Shining*. Even in midwinter they are hungry for any egg or chick the box might contain. No songbird lingers nearby when a woodpecker arrives.

The nuthatches respect the woodpeckers but overawe the robins. The robins overawe the finches, but the goldfinches in particular, arriving as a gang of eight or nine, expel the others, squawk-squabbling with the siskins, their near rivals, which like the goldfinches arrive mob-handed and fight among themselves. I have seen one goldfinch skewer another on the clay ground beneath the birdhouse, where it quivered for a few seconds, shook itself and flew away.

It is a landscape of fear in which each bird has its role. The goldfinches are brazen and aggressive. The nuthatches more careful, approaching with circumspection. The great tit is perplexing. It looks big-shouldered and big-bellied, with a substantial body, as if muscled around the bull-like shoulders but, for all that bulk, I have seen one great tit shooed away by a male chaffinch and the goldfinches always see them off. They usually dominate the blue tits, brushing them from their places on the branch, but the blue tits then dominate the coal tits. If a coal tit is waiting somewhere on the edge of the trees for its moment to grab a seed, blue tits will fly past it at head height, not quite touching it with a wing. The coal tits duck and cower at the bullying and continue to wait their turn.

Somewhere in the same rank, the most modest of all, the marsh tits in their pairs behave as if scarcely welcome at the party, skulking low down among the brambles, retreating into the further recesses of the wood, or poking at ground level as the large competitive cavalcade revolves above them.

There is little that is heavyweight about these interactions. They pass in an instant and my camera exposure has to be set at a thousandth of a second or less to still their movements. The aquarium never settles and, even when the birds are sitting still, the motions never cease. I made a short film of a blue tit sitting on a branch, its chest facing towards me, and for the half-minute, the bird shifted its attention thirty-three times, a neural flick from view to view, left, right, down, up, forward, back up, in no smooth panoramic survey, but a restless check-

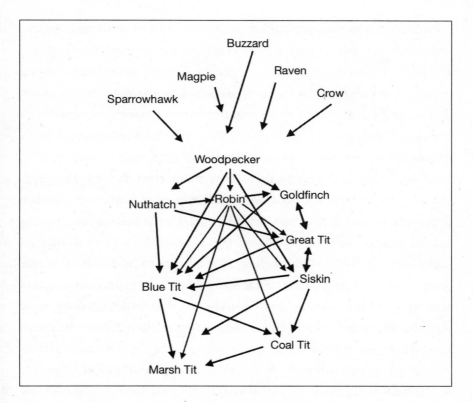

Dominance hierarchy at the birdhouse

ing, like a man in the airport repeatedly reminding himself where he put his keys, passport, wallet and phone. From the human distance, the life of the blue tit looks pathologically anxious.

There is something to be said about the artificiality of this situation. The bird feeders force these different species and individuals to interact in a small area at the feeder ports. Normally they would be among the branches of the surrounding trees, interacting far less, and able to avoid each other in space and time. The effect of the feeders is to heighten stress and conflict, demanding high-energy responses from the birds in which certain species will thrive and others suffer.

I made a second film, this one four and a half seconds long, of a goldfinch flying a yard or so between branches of the oak trees outside the window, and then watched it again at a tenth of its original speed. The goldfinch performed like an athlete, thirty-two actions in 4.5 seconds, nearly half of which was spent sitting on a branch. If you subtract that interval, the bird was making a movement nearly thirteen times a second. Nor were these minor gestures. That repeated scimitar flash of the golden wing went through at least 180 degrees at each beat, so that at their full upward extension the wingtips crossed and clashed.

Nearly all of this is invisible to us without the help of technology. We see a bird fly from branch to branch and think little of it but that difference between what we perceive and what the birds perceive is central to any understanding we might have of them. They are essentially quick. Their metabolisms run hard and fast. Their blood temperature is hotter than ours at 41 degrees Celsius and you can feel that heat when you hold a bird, caught in a room and needing to be released. For a few moments its little warm feathered body pulses in your hand.

Compared with other animals, a bird's heart is large and heavy for its size and pumps fast. The smaller the bird, the faster it goes. At rest and untroubled, a macaw's heart runs at 127 beats a minute, a vulture's at 132, a crow at 224, a starling at 335, a wren at 450, a chickadee – the North American cousin of the tits – at 480, a hummingbird at 615 and a willow warbler at 647. When alarmed or in trouble, these pulse rates among small birds can double. When the heavy whooper swan makes the effort to take off, its heart rate more than quadruples to over 400 beats a minute. Even that looks lackadaisical next to the pigeon's rate in full flight of 600 beats a minute or a hummingbird hovering at over 1,200. If you want a comparison, the heart of a Galápagos tortoise has a pulse of six beats a minute.

Some counterintuitive calibration has to be made when trying to imagine the birds' experience of life. Because their metabolisms run fast, their sensations and perceptions also run fast. Birds can distinguish the passage of time at a more closely resolved scale than we can.

If they are trained to react differently according to whether they are shown a steady or a flashing light – food given under a steady beam, denied if flashing – it becomes possible to know at what stage the flashes come so quickly that they seem to be from a constant beam. In human beings that horizon is at sixty flashes a second. Above that, the light seems steady to us. Other animals are worse: eels think a flashing light is an unbroken beam at fourteen flashes a second, a salamander at thirty, a rat at thirty-nine. Birds – pigeons, starlings and domestic hens have all been tested – continue to see an intermittent light up to one hundred flashes a second. Given that the metabolisms of small birds run faster, it is likely that their time resolution is even finer than this. You can expect a tit or finch to recognise time divisions down to at least 120th of a second.

In a perceptual world more close-grained than we can imagine, time comes in these minutely subdivided packages. My slo-mo film of the goldfinch is something like the perception the goldfinch itself has of its own flight. It can feel, think and manoeuvre in its own steady time, so that the experience of a second or two for a bird can seem like half a minute for us. What we see and hear as too fast to comprehend in their flight and song is clear and overt to them. Just as a Galápagos tortoise must look at the human beings around it and wonder at the frenetic rapidity of our lives, we need to make a conceptual leap and see that a bird's quickness can only be its own normality.

It is possible to slow down birdsong to hear it much as they hear it. A great tit might only repeat to us *Teacher, teacher, teacher*, but at a quarter of the speed each word becomes complex and contoured. What we hear as the first syllable, *Teach-*, is in fact a double piped note, first lower and then higher, as if blown the length of a long and echoing steel tube; and the second, the *-er*, is a reverberating pluck like a twanged string, rippling out as it fades to its end. The burst of high-pressure and insistent robin song becomes at quarter-speed a beautiful cascading staircase of music, undulating and riffling across the wood as if tobogganing down the stepped slopes of its territory. The quarter-speed song thrush plays descants to his own melody, running both hands up and down the keyboard, sometimes barking back at his song, at others surfing through the heights and depths of the frequencies within the same short phrase. When slowed down like this, the most striking parts of the thrush's song are the pauses. He declares himself in some kind of ecstasy and then waits, declares and waits again, just as an actor in command of his audience knows that authority lies in the silences.

There is an evolutionary question in here. Why are these birds so quick? What is the connection between their warm-bloodedness, their fast metabolisms, their short lifespans and their smallness? Is it their life in the wood? Or their dependence on flight? Or a combination of those conditions, the particular demands of flight in a wood?

For all the immediacy of their presence, a deep time-structure is in play. These are ancient creatures. Their ancestors were dinosaurs. How the birds are descended from them remains uncertain but at a whole series of levels, the inheritance is clear. Dinosaur elements appear in every part of what they are. Feathers, warm-bloodedness and a fast metabolism; their wishbones – the flexible, yoke-shaped structure at the top of the chest, familiar from the carved chicken, which in the living bird stores and releases wing-beating energy at each stroke; a shoulder and arm that can allow the hands to fold against the body; the making of nests and brooding of eggs; the young growing fast and maturing soon; the ability to stand and run on two legs; thin-walled,

Top: A flying dinosaur, Zhenyuanlong suni, *not an ancestor of the birds, from 130–120 million years ago in Liaoning Province, China. Centre: Reconstruction of* Anchiornis huxleyi, *a 160-million-year-old dinosaur bird-ancestor, with wing feathers on all four limbs. Bottom: A magpie, with the same melanin-strengthened tips to the primary wing feathers*

hollowed bones in limbs and skull that can be filled with air from the lungs; the three-fingered hands forming the outer part of every bird wing: all these – in effect every aspect of the bird body and its habits – are dinosaur legacies.

The story nowadays begins with the discovery in China from the late 1990s onwards of thousands of fossils of ground-dwelling, meat-eating dinosaurs of the group known as theropods – the word means 'wild-foot' – whose bodies were covered in feathers. The remains of an ancient half-bird, half-reptile, the *Archaeopteryx*, had been found in Germany in 1860, but its fossils were rare and its role in the ancestry of birds uncertain. These large numbers of feathered Chinese dinosaurs changed the argument. There are now too many for the bird–dinosaur connection to be denied.

Their early feathers began not as aids to flight but as insulation for the warm-blooded animals and as a means of display. The first proto-feathers were no more than a thread-like fringe along the animals' backs but they soon developed into something we could recognise today. Those on one four-winged Jurassic dinosaur from about 160 million years ago, *Anchiornis huxleyi*, have been minutely examined. Most of the crow-sized body was covered in grey and black feathers. A big proclamatory crest on the top and back of the head was rusty red and brown, surrounded by a grey base, with a cockatoo-style lick on the forehead. The face was mottled with reddish speckles against a black ground. Both front and back wings were largely white with black tips, like the outer wings of a gull or magpie, where the melanin helps to strengthen the feather tips and reduce wear. The short feathers covering the bases of the long primaries on the wings, the coverts, were also gull-like, grey with black speckles.

It seems unlikely that this glamorous creature could fly. It was too heavy for the size of its wings. Only later, as the ratio of the drag of the bird's weight and the lift of its wings was brought more into balance, by a shrinking of the torso so that the wings became larger in proportion, were feathers co-opted as the ideal structures for wings in flight. They might have helped *Anchiornis* run or scamper up steep slopes. As in birds now, the metatarsals in these dinosaurs' feet – the long bones between ankle and toe – were held off the ground, so that unlike us but like dogs or horses they could skip along on their toes, running fast with long strides in pursuit or escape.

Piece by piece, in generation after generation, the bird recipe was assembled. The dinosaur body began to shrink and the appearance of many little Jurassic dinosaurs, if we met them today, would be indistinguishable from birds: pigeon-sized, big-breasted, with a deep-keeled breastbone to which the flying muscles were attached, no long bony tail and the all-important discovery of the beak, a lightweight multitool for manipulating the dinosaurs' world while leaving the fore-limbs free for flight.

Just as dogs carry into adulthood the domed skull and short snout of wolf puppies – a repeated phenomenon known in biology as neotony – birds developed by continuing into adulthood aspects of dinosaur embryos. Once a dinosaur had come into existence that was small enough, compact enough and quick enough to fly, life's tendency to evolve new forms was given a wide new niche. In the Cretaceous (145 million to 66 million years ago), the capacity for powered flight released a spike of evolutionary change and any number of new flying dinosaurs appeared. Where giant scale and ferocity may have served reptiles well for more than a hundred million years, it was quickness and lightness that filled the largely tropical woodlands of the Cretaceous world. Many of the flying creatures were feathered birds, others were tiny flying dinosaurs or pterosaurs, some as small as thrushes.

This enriched world came to a violent end 66.5 million years ago. A six-mile-wide asteroid hit the Yucatán Peninsula in Mexico at thirty thousand miles an hour in an impact equivalent in destructiveness to ten thousand times the entire modern global nuclear arsenal, levelling trees for a thousand miles in all directions. Debris was blown halfway to the moon before falling back to earth as a burning meteor shower that in three days set fire to and destroyed the forests of the earth. Smoke and dust darkened the sky, probably for years, and in those global fires and the following lightless year-round winters 75 per cent of all life died. It may have taken a hundred years, or as many as ten thousand, for the forests to regrow.

While the early birds were decimated alongside their close dinosaur relatives, the catastrophe created a new world for those that survived. Fungi, ferns and other 'disaster flora' began to fill the devastated forests.

With the occupants of niche after niche in the world's woods destroyed, untold ecological openings were there for the taking. Birds exploded into the varieties on offer. Life had been left in ruins, but here was the chance to become a kingfisher or a crow, a penguin or a pigeon, a blue tit, a rook, a warbler or a cuckoo. Many of the niches were filled in the first surge of speciation after the meteor, many more in a second wave some thirty million years later following a long and worldwide series of ice ages had once again cut down the variety of life.

Because of the cataclysm, the family tree of modern birds does not stretch back into the complex and many-limbed history of dinosaur experimentation in the Cretaceous. The narrowest of bottlenecks was applied to birdlife so that the bird family tree consists not of a steadily branching oak-like structure, stretching back almost two hundred million years, but of more like a coral head on a reef, with a wide post-apocalyptic bloom of 11,000-odd species balanced on a wine-glass-thin stem. It is the reason biologists can still not produce an agreed set of relationships between different modern bird families: their beginnings emerged very nearly at the same time, over something between two and eight million years, from a tightly defined, if not quite single root. Those few lineages that passed through the asteroid catastrophe and became the ancestors of modern birds were probably ground-living, not dependent on trees nor at risk when the forests were destroyed. Among them may have been a shorebird of some kind;

perhaps some pelicans and petrels; a parrot; the ancestor of the ostriches and kiwis; and, in another line, of the pheasants, hens, ducks and geese. Giant terror-bird predators, the now extinct *Phorusrhacidae*, up to ten feet tall and capable of running at thirty miles an hour, may have stalked and preyed among them. All the woodland birds and bird-like dinosaurs from before the apocalypse had died with the trees among which they lived.

Nearly all modern bird families formed within fifteen million years of the extinction. To begin with, biodiversity was low. There were the survivors from before the apocalypse, but none can be unambiguously identified, and most are known only from some half-abraded mandible or disconnected scapula. Others, like a cast of characters strolling into the book of creation, soon arrived. By about forty-seven million years ago, the world's coasts, wetlands and woods were filled with gannets, flamingos, swifts, nightjars and hummingbirds – these last three originally nocturnal, hiding from the mammalian predators then also spreading through a world freed of dinosaurs. In the tropical forests of Australia the first ancestral songbirds emerged, all with their first toe pointing backwards, the other three forwards, giving them the firm grip on the branches they still hold.

About twenty-seven million years ago, on the heels of a period of deep global cooling, when the ice sheets of Antarctica first appeared and the tropical forests had shrunk and suffered, bird species multiplied again. Almost as many new families appeared as in the post-asteroid radiation. With the return of the warmth, the perching songbirds that had begun life in Australia now colonised Asia and Europe. Alongside them came the gulls and woodpeckers. And in that way, across these lengths of time that seem unapproachable to us but represent no more than a hundredth of the earth's existence, the birds came to be in these Sussex woods. They arrived much as they are now, most of the changes having occurred before they pushed up into Asia and Europe.

There may be another aspect to this. Just as every one of the songbirds in this English wood, including the crows, rooks and ravens, all
the finches, tits and warblers, had an ancestor in the Australian jungles,
their enemies the woodpeckers, the hawks, buzzards and owls may
have begun their global career in Africa, as did the kingfishers now in
the valley of the River Dudwell below us. By the same theory, the
falcons, of which we see nowadays a kestrel and a rare and wandering
peregrine, originated in South America.

The evidence is thin – but there is no avoiding the realisation that in
some form or other the world's birds have met and mingled in this
wood. We are surrounded by the global. There is no such thing as an
English native.

Every wood is a bird cosmopolis. Every blink of life outside the
birdhouse windows is a planetary phenomenon. Just as much as the
atmosphere and ocean, the life of birds is a single, interlinked, all-world
presence, in which these tits and finches, for all their local adaptations
and variety, belong to the planet as a whole.

No one knows how flight began. Did ground-living animals climb
trees and from there benefit by gliding down with feathered wings? Or
did the wings help those animals that had stayed on the ground with
running and jumping? Did flight start from below or above?

Here now there are birds that live most of their lives on the ground.
The robins, blackbirds, dunnocks and thrushes peck at the earth for
seeds and invertebrates as their ancestors would have done. A pheasant
I disturb on the edge of the wood does not fly but runs away from me.
One of our hens leaps on to a gate and then down the other side, rising
almost entirely through a spring of its legs, but using two or three
wingbeats to help with the lift and again to brake as it jumps down. In
all these habits, ancientness is here.

Above the groundrunners, in the shadows of the wood and seen
usually only in the grey of dusk, is the treecreeper. It too seems to live
like an ancient inhabitant, arriving covertly and appearing at the foot

A treecreeper climbing one of the birdhouse oaks

of the oaks like a little mouse, darting up from place to place on the bark, its stark white breast held close to the tree. I have wondered if that whiteness is a form of illumination, reflecting light into the cracks of the bark to allow the prey to be seen. Sometimes the bird sways back and away to get a better look, while its dark brown and black plumage coats it in a sheltering mantle that is almost like lichened bark itself.

Once it has examined a whole trunk it drops to the ground like a tick off a deer, down to the foot of the neighbouring tree, where it begins again, up and up, as if on a ratchet, a constant bright curiosity, identifying hollows, almost wren-like as it moves from spot to spot in its solitary way. That vertical switchback from tree to tree may have been how birds first exploited the earliest woods of our era, the curved beaks pushing in like the treecreeper's gouge or awl to find the prey in the bark.

Flight is not the first option within the branches. Nearly every bird hops there. The blackbirds can leap from branch to branch with scarcely a movement of the wings. The blue tits, redpolls and long-tailed tits hop-dance from twig to twig. The nuthatch springs up on to an oak stem and then to a branch within the tree, before jump-twisting again to a higher spot, and once again to twist and turn downhill, from where it looks at me sideways, before turning up again the other way. Every one of these gymnast movements is made without using the wing.

When a bird does decide to fly, most of the initial flight velocity, the necessary take-off speed, is provided by a thrust of their legs. The smaller the bird, the less thrust it needs, so that a hummingbird, which weighs a tenth of an ounce, can take off at less than two miles per hour. A wild American turkey (which weighs a stone) needs to be travelling at nearly fourteen miles per hour before it can fly. The turkey requires a run-up; the little birds of the wood can get airborne with a jump.

Large and lumpen as we are, with a low power-to-weight ratio, we think of take-off as difficult. It is different for small birds. The power-per-ounce in them is large. Compared with our own expectations their experience can only be an almost miraculous sense of aptitude, with mobility and manoeuvrability effortlessly at their wingtips. I try to imagine it as something like the sensation we have when we first get on to a highly geared racing bike, or sit at the oars of a racing scull boat. Suddenly movement is ours. We are powerful in relation to our world. We can accelerate and freewheel at will. No effort is needed to leave here for there or to become the sort of quick, weightless being we are in our dreams.

Once airborne with that thrust, the first option is the glide. You can watch it in the buzzards when you come on them on the edge of the wood. They choose to perch high in trees that give them a clear and easy path out over open ground. From there they saunter into flight, a slow and elegant departure, little more than a dropping away from their stance as they slip into their gliding turns.

With the pale, milk-chocolate-coloured extended wings, they can begin to soar, making the cry that Messiaen thought 'otherworldly and

A buzzard turning above Hollow Flemings, February 2023

feminine … *un cri étrange – cri de femme*', bodies occasionally flexing down into a shallow V with the ripples of the wind, as if their weight were slung in their extended hammock, as the bird forms repeated silk-lined circles above you. In the breeding season, crows will attack a passing buzzard, which flops arrogantly away.

In part the buzzards are ground-birds too. I have seen one picking its way slowly across the grasshopper-thick summer sward in Great Flemings, looking like one of the ancient giant Cuban owls, magnificent flightless birds, four feet tall, that lived by pouncing on vulnerable prey. That is how the buzzard also behaved, slowly moving foot by foot across the field, its eyes fixed downwards, its talons ready.

More often, though, they float above me, sliding away down the clearing, 150 feet up, turning with little apparent hurry or concern. That perception is not true, though. You only have to watch them to see how much they are observing the world beneath them, you included.

The path they follow is looped like a line that lashes a sail to the boom, so that each turn overlaps the next. This is not a casual cruise but a ground-covering, resource-inspecting strategy, mesmeric to watch in binoculars: the buzzard's wings flash pale and dark as they catch the sunlight and are shadowed in it.

The form of the feathered wing reveals the dynamics at work. Its leading edge curves downwards so that the air is guided up and over it, reducing the pressure on that upper side. The pressure difference between the two surfaces lifts the bird, so that buzzards rise into the low-pressure hollow the camber of their wing has made. You would only have to blow a current of air across a buzzard's extended wing and it would start to float up and away. The trailing edges are sharp (as they are on aeroplane wings) to prevent pressure from beneath the wing leaking upwards and diminishing the lift, while the wing itself is long and wide to sustain the bird even as it flies slowly above the field. At their tips, the wings are slotted to break up the turbulent vortices that would form there on a blunt-ended wing, causing drag. Those primaries can be folded in for speed, splayed for slow-motion control.

The whole ensemble is a form of perfection. The two wings together cover about five square feet, sustaining a bird that weighs about 1.5 lbs for the males, a little more for females. That is about thirty-five square inches of wing for each ounce of buzzard. No wonder they seem to float above you, a life sprung on air.

One of the secrets, apart from the form of the wing, is the nature of the feather: mouldable and yet rigid, an insulating undercoat and a

A magpie in flight completes its upstroke with folded wing, straightens the wing at the top and beats down in a single movement, flaring and separating the wingtip feathers as they descend to add thrust to the lift provided by the inner or 'arm' part of the wing

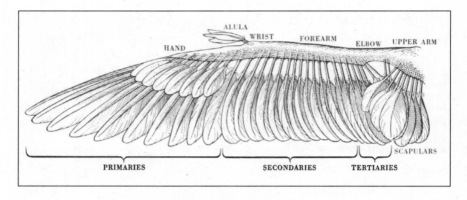

ALULA
WRIST   FOREARM   ELBOW   UPPER ARM
HAND

SCAPULARS

PRIMARIES   SECONDARIES   TERTIARIES

The inner half of the wing, from the shoulder to the wrist,
provides lift; the outer half, wingtip, is adapted for control
and propulsion

weather-resistant outer, light because strong, made of a stronger version
of the keratin that forms our fingernails and hair. The feather's rigid
shafts sprout barbs and the barbs the smaller interlocking barbules of
the vane itself. Stroke the vane of a fallen feather and you will understand the fundamental principle: each barbule is coated in micro-hooks
that join it to its neighbour but not rigidly. Rigidity and elasticity meet
in its construction.

One summer morning in the birdhouse, with the window open and
a light breeze coming in from the south, a small buzzard feather I had
picked up – it had fallen, I think, from its chest – was lying on the
desk. The breeze collected it and it hung for a moment, as if suspended
on strings, in the way I saw a harrier once pausing and hanging over
the grasses and sea lavender of a Norfolk marsh. The feather was pure
buoyancy but it hesitated and then, carried by the breeze, took up its
course and floated past me to the far side of the birdhouse where it
stopped again, circled and then dropped in a slow zigzag, east and
west, to the dust of the floor. It had flown there as if it were a living
thing, but this was physics at work, an object in which air resistance
and weight are so matched that it can move on the breeze from one

side of a room to the other. Imagine your body were made of such things.

Powered flight is a step beyond the feathered glide. It involves movements and a set of calculations no one except a qualified engineer could hope to understand in any detail. Unless stilled in a photograph, the variable geometry of the wing remains almost invisible to us. Only when caught in a very fast exposure can one see the convolutions the birds go through several times a second.

The nature of this movement is worth pursuing if only to grasp – or to attempt to grasp – something of the reality of bird life. The wing is not unlike the human arm, with flexible joints at the shoulder, elbow and wrist, but in different proportions to us. Two-thirds of the wing is made up of the hand. On the downbeat, which takes up about 60 per cent of the whole cycle, all those wing joints are held straight and in that form the wing produces both lift and forward thrust. On the quicker upbeat, the wing bends at both wrist and elbow so that the large 'hand' hangs downwards for minimum wind resistance. The feathers are opened to lessen drag and only as the wing comes to the end of the upbeat, above the bird's back, does the hand flick out again, so that the wing is fully extended and ready for the next downbeat. It is not unlike the movements we make when swimming breaststroke.

The birds' energy consumption is prodigious. For manoeuvrability, the wings of small woodland birds are short. Unlike the high-floating buzzards, any glide of more than a few inches is out of the question. In the very smallest birds, the wrens and goldcrests, which have to navigate through the meshwork of stems inside a bramble or rose thicket, their wings are so short they can fly only by continuous flapping, and only for short stretches. The wren burrs with a constant whirring of its wings like a mini-drone. If you see a goldcrest hurrying away from you, the impression is of a tiny animal rising from a standing start and levitating over a bush or wall as if defying gravity. In this way, environments sculpt the birds: large, weight-sustaining wings for the buzzards

Top: The sparrowhawk has a fearsome reputation, but is neat in scale and proportion. No bigger hawk could thrive among the trees. Above: Its flight feathers are furnished on the lower side with a wide vane for lift and a short one on the leading side, creating the rounded edge to drive air over the upper surface of the wing

in the uninterrupted air above the woods; tiny, never-still wings for the wrens among the undergrowth.

The faster you fly, the greater the lift produced by the wings, and so speed itself for a small bird might look like the answer. But flying fast with short wings is exhausting and also produces drag on the body, and so the most efficient pace for a wing-beating bird is to fly quite but not very fast – about twenty-two miles per hour or ten metres a second for the budgerigars and cockatiels on which these measurements have been made in a wind tunnel, seventeen miles per hour for a blue tit and thirty-seven for a pigeon. These small birds do not dawdle between the branches.

The hawk's claws are both narrow and deep, slipping between the obstacles of the wood and deeply penetrating the flesh of the prey

As a way of conserving energy, the larger finches, tits, nuthatches and woodpeckers have adopted a different tactic. Despite our expectations, it soon becomes clear that these birds do not fly with a continuous and energy-draining flapping of the wings.

Instead, they flap-bound from place to place. This intermittent flight alternates a powered sweep of the wings, giving forward thrust, with a tucked passage through the air in which the wings are brought tightly next to the body. The body itself has some aerodynamic qualities, as the airflow across it creates some lift, and so the bird can air-cruise for a moment with wings closed between flaps like a feathered bullet.

Larger birds might glide between wingbeats, as the pigeons do, but the wings of these finches and tits are too small for much effective gliding. They save energy by bounding, as do the woodpeckers, each beat of the wing giving a lift, each bound involving a drop, and so the woodpecker, once it is done with knocking its hollow coconuts into the ash tees, leaps into the air across Hollow Flemings and flap-bounds to the alders on the far side. It conducts its bouncing, kangaroo-hopping flight across the clearing, on a dipping course, in which each wingbeat sounds both full and hollow, like the clop of a horse-hoof, as the air compresses and decompresses beneath the bird, or as if a slightly cupped hand were quietly applauding its progress.

Intermittent bounding like this can save up to half the energy that would have been used in constant flapping. The scooped rise-and-fall of the flight path is evidence of the dynamics: adding gravitational energy with the wing flap, at which the bird rises, and using that energy on the bound, as it drops. Again and again, the bird invests and cashes in. It was a sight loved by John Clare when a boy, 'wandering about the fields watching the habits of birds to see the woodpecker sweeing away in its ups and downs'. This is so central a part of the songbird's life strategy that it is the exceptions – the constant helicopter whirr of the wren and goldcrest, the ground-level, torpedo-like escape flight of the alarmed blackbird, fired from the foot of a shrub as if escaping under-water – that seem like anomalies.

Pulsed flight increases a bird's endurance and allows it regular rests from flapping, but there may be another factor in play: the pauses probably increase the bird's ability to comprehend the world around it. 'The graceful – even sedate – impression we have of bird flight,' Douglas Warrick, a zoologist at Oregon State University, has said, 'belies a violent physical reality.' The impression of calm, he adds, is 'largely a product of our own poor sampling rate'.

Birds' swervings and turnings, all the quickness, the sudden leaps and rolls, make it harder for them to understand what is around them. Try looking at your own hand while shaking your head: it is unseeable. The eyes of a bird rapidly beating its own wings would be full of what Warrick calls that 'sensory clutter' if it had not developed adaptations to cope. Bounding flight may be one – moments of still and blessed comprehension within the visual jarring of powered flight. Another, derived early in their evolution, is in the structure of birds' necks. They have between thirteen and twenty-five cervical vertebrae (we have seven) with highly moveable joints between them. Whatever the violent and often extreme movements of the bird's body made necessary by flight, the line through the air taken by the head and eyes can be independent of them.

A pigeon can roll its body through 270 degrees while keeping its head and eyes on the horizontal. In a wind tunnel lined with mattresses, Professor Warrick fitted pigeons with collars that prevented them isolating their heads when their bodies moved in flight. It was a disaster. A third of those fitted with the collars were unable to stay in control and crashed to the padded floor.

Once they had been launched, they quickly lost balance. 'They continued to flap powerfully, frequently pitching up dramatically and tumbling end over end until they tumbled to the ground. In all cases, after the birds landed, they regained their equilibrium, and took off normally from the mattress and flew straight to the perch.'

It remains astonishing that something so difficult is allied to such quickness. It is as if these birds were assembling the inner workings of a watch while racing a sports car around a city. If I follow a pair of coal tits or great tits in spring, weaving in and out of the young oak trees in front of me, I can just about trace the line of their flight. The idea of performing it is inconceivable. I imagine – although how one would prove this I don't know – that this chasing flight might be a form of test between potential partners. If you can follow me on my Ariadne's path through the trees, it may well be that you are the mate for me.

We are left only with the questions. How can we ever know what allows the wood pigeon to lift and breast the air in the matronly way it does, before slipping away and gliding in a slowed and perfect dive, flying like an Edwardian launch on the Thames? What is it about the raven that means it can keep its wits about it while displaying a full-body 360-degree spin? What guides the blue tit as it slide-slips between the trees? Or spring-loads its shoulder joints so that a gust is accommodated and the bird stays level in a billowing world? How is it, as Ted Hughes saw, that the hawk 'Effortlessly at height hangs his still eye'?

9.

Tits

BREEDING

It is late in a wet, modern winter and everyone has been waiting too long for spring. The fields are sodden and the world of the farm is grizzled.

Those who work outside are sunk into the hoods of their waterproofs. The cattle have stomped their bedding into a mush in the barn and every day the farm manager Colin Pilbeam puts in new straw so that the cows are now standing on the accumulated layers three feet above the chalk floor on which they began in November. They have to lower their heads to look out beyond the eaves.

We wait a week and then another and then one day it arrives, at least in part. A lit pale-blue sky at 7 a.m. and the song thrush appears, singing in the willows on the edge of Black Brooks. A robin struts and observes on the garden fence. A blackbird is silent, but his bill is a brilliant orange. He stands high on the hawthorns by the farm gate and emits six or seven bubbles of song. Another crouches, hunched over to make an effective poncho of his feathers on the ridge of the old byre. A fog slips in and the first blackbird drops into the garden squawk-crying as he goes, fast and low.

Even in the fog the song thrush now grows loud and inventive. He is alive with his own cheerfulness, like a teenage engineer cavorting up and down the frequencies on his newly acquired synthesiser. In every phrase he changes not only note and pattern but harmonics; the knobs he turns can do raw and rough, slick and smooth, bar-room and ball-room, growl and seduction. Sometimes the thrush cries almost like a kitten mewing, sometimes like a market trader, sometimes like Andy Williams or even Shirley Temple, trilling in the way of an old-fashioned telephone whose ringing burbles in dancing, spring-like gaiety across the garden.

The rain drips from the stems of the willows but still the thrush continues. The blackbird walks past with a bunch of black worms in its face as if it had just buried its bill in a plate of spaghetti *al nero di seppia*. But, as birds don't like being looked at, it rockets away.

The path in the wood is covered with the skidmarks of my boots where I have slipped all winter. But the signs of change are here. A badger in the top of Long Field Shaw has re-excavated part of a sett and a mound of broken clay and lumps of sandstone have been thrown out below the entrance. The stringy fibrous strop of the honeysuckle growing up into the hornbeams is dry until the point about thirty feet above me where the leaf buds have found the light.

On the ground, the purple blotched arums have emerged. Still it rains. Between the hanging raindrops the birch leaves are just coming out in fresh primary-school green. The oaks are covered in pink buds so that from a distance every one seems to blush away from brown, some far advanced, others lagging behind. The old oak leaves beside the new buds look now as if decades of polish had been applied to them. The buds of the pussy willow are cucumber green, the goat willow warmer, just yellower than lemon. The torn trunks of the ashes from the winter storms are darkening as the wood oxidises. The old brambles are the dullest, the municipal green applied to a shed in the 1940s.

The song of earth is never dead and Merlin is still my friend and tutor. A wren makes his repeated call. A stock dove is mooing away in the ash shaw, the song or call rising and falling in a simple sequence of ten or so notes, a slow climb up and a slow climb down. On the edge of Great Flemings the sheep's wool caught on the brambles is wet with rain. The leaves on the wild cherries are prodding into air.

It all feels like something of a beginning, the way a new term opens by shrugging off everything that has gone before. The white, almost-laboratory light of spring pushes down into the naked depths of the wood, penetrating through all floors, revealing the first, tissue-wrapped garlic flowers in bud and the first bluebells emerging grey-blue-green. We start to feel it too, this investigating light, as the melatonin levels under which we have been labouring all winter, the sluggish and sleepy hormone, are suppressed by spring's arrival. The levels of serotonin, the neurotransmitter that is linked to contented-ness and happiness, rise in the sunlight. If my summer brain were to be cut open and examined, it would contain more serotonin than in the winter. I am not sure if this is self-delusion but I feel I know it viscerally: more light is better and lack of light generates a hunger for it.

Many months ago, at the end of summer and in the early autumn, the birds acquired their new plumage, dropping the old feathers one by one, worn out from a year's use, and growing their replacements in the annual moult. It is only now, in the renewal of spring light, that the plumage comes into its own. They seem to dazzle with brightness and freshness. But if a brilliant feather coat is required in spring, why moult in late summer, when it must last all winter, wearing and abrading before coming into its own?

The answer is that feathers perform many tasks. Before they can be the springtime display coat they must work all winter as insulation and weather-proofing and above all as the means by which the bird can escape its predators. Effective wings need undamaged feathers and when everything is taken into account, the late summer moult is the better trade-off.

Hidden processes are at work. The colours of birds' feathers, beaks, eye ornaments, feet and legs are produced partly through the birds consuming the orange carotenoids present in seeds and prey. These chemicals make up the green, yellow, orange and red of the birds' plumage. The blacks and greys and the reddy-browns come from forms of melanin generated within the bird's own body. The third kind of colour, to which birds' eyes are more sensitive than ours, is produced by minute structures in the feathers that create interference patterns in the ultraviolet part of the spectrum.

Although the feathers themselves are new in the autumn, their colours brighten and deepen towards the end of winter, reaching a peak in early spring just as they are needed for sexual display. Partly, this is to do with the consumption of the orange-rich food and partly with the birds generating their own melanins. To us, male and female blue tits look the same but to blue tits they are strikingly different. All the parts that to us seem blue – the crowns on their skulls, the patches on wing and tail – shine in ultraviolet light more brilliantly on the males than on the females, especially in spring.

In the summer of 2006, before the birds had moulted, Mark Roberts and his colleagues at the Max Planck Institute in southern Germany near the Swiss border implanted small soluble tablets of testosterone in the backs of about twenty young male blue tits. When the birds acquired their new feathers, there was no discernible difference between those blue tits and an equivalent group that had been given a placebo.

The birds seemed to be unaffected, except one that started to behave oddly with 'extreme extrovert behavior', would not leave the scientists alone and had to be excluded from the experiment. Come the spring, though, as the need for attractiveness in males reached its peak, differences suddenly became apparent. The crowns, wings and tails of the

Male great tits (top) and females (above) can be told apart by the thickness of the black stripe down their chests, the yellowness of the breast feathers and, in certain lights, the gleam of the male's crown which is shinier than the female's. Top-quality males with brilliant caps, wide stripes and well-yellowed chests always attract more mates, are better parents and bring more chicks to fledging

testosteroned-up blue tits began to gleam far more brightly than those of the others.

Dr Roberts' suggestion is that the glamorous sheen is not a biochemical effect. The birds with increased testosterone were much more careful and attentive in preening themselves, repeatedly coiffuring the feathers to remove any dirt or waxy accretions and so maximise the attractiveness. Extra testosterone makes shinier birds because those more manly birds take the trouble to shine.

Once you know this, you see it and can start to distinguish the gleam-headed males from the females they are wanting to attract. In certain lights and at certain angles, the heads of male marsh tits and great tits also shine in the same way. Beside that, the great tits have their own bold sexually distinguishing marks, a broad black stripe down the middle of the males' chests, a sign of the melanin-rich hormonal system the bird has maintained, a much lesser one on the females, often thin or broken in outline. On either side of the stripe, the males display a rich, warm yellow in their breast feathers, more towards the red end of the spectrum than in the relatively grey-yellowed females. Both male and female great tits that have grown up and wintered in the impoverished conditions of urban gardens are greyer than their rural cousins. The yellowness, which shows that the bird has consumed plenty of the carotenoid antioxidants, combined with the blackness of the stripe, is an advertising hoarding for the male great tit's healthy, fertile, breeding-ready condition.

And so the springtime show can begin. I had put up some nest boxes on the oaks and hornbeams in the woods and Nick Walsh had fitted out the birdhouse with ten more, including a variety of entrance holes for different birds and none of them in the full sun on the south side of the birdhouse, where they would get too hot. Those for blue tits had entrances an inch wide; others had openings big enough for great tits; and some, intended for sparrows or nuthatches, were the widest, with holes 1.25 inches across. In the end neither sparrows nor nuthatches made use of them. A pair of nest boxes with big-mouthed holes – half the outside wall of the box – were designed for robins but they too never came. All the boxes were nine inches high, about eight deep and six across, made of rough sawn Douglas Fir a quarter of an inch thick, with a sloping roof and no alighting perch outside, as that is thought to make life easier for predators. Small birds can land on the lip of the entrance hole itself. All had glass walls inside the birdhouse, covered by little oak doors to preserve the darkness the birds needed. None had drainage holes in the floor, as the draught can chill the chicks. Thus equipped by late January, I awaited the arrival of the birds, scarcely thinking they would come.

Within a day of the birdhouse being finished, a bird had entered, not when I was there but during the night. In the morning I found one of the great tit boxes with a few droppings on the floor. It was a winter tit, roosting away from the cold and wet.

All through January and February, the droppings accumulated in three of the boxes. I went for a walk around the wood with my near neighbour Dr Martyn Stenning, the world's great expert on blue tits, who lives just down the road and for many years was part of the life sciences team at Sussex University. He has the modest and gentle carefulness of many bird people and is happily and laughingly obsessed with what he calls 'these enigmatic little birds'. Didn't I also, he asked me, love the way they were dressed in 'most of the colours of the planet, the colours the astronauts saw from space'? He told me with some relish the blue tit's scientific name, *Cyanistes caeruleus obscurus*, Linnaean Latin for 'the heavenly hidden blue one', as if each were some version of a minor Chinese god.

Martyn was not sure the bird boxes were quite right: the timber looked too thin and would be too easily damaged by the woodpeckers. In his own wood, one year, woodpeckers had done terrible damage. Over the course of nine days in May 1990, great spotted woodpeckers had smashed their way into twenty-four of the blue tit boxes he had put up and killed at least 132 nestlings. The contents of one nest could probably feed a single woodpecker family for a day and so this devastation may have been no more than the operation of one pair of woodpeckers feeding their brood.

Martyn advised me to put metal guards over the nest box openings, as he had after his disaster, to prevent the woodpeckers smashing their way in. Better in future would be to make the boxes out of marine-grade plywood, as the woodpeckers find it difficult to punch through the layers in the ply where the grain runs in opposite directions.

Apart from that, Martyn was encouragement itself. The droppings in the boxes had been left by blue tit males, he was sure, claiming them as their own, ready for when the spring arrived and they could usher in a blue tit hen if she could be persuaded to come.

A small dark feather appeared among the droppings. Outside, the birds were courting, the male blue tits displaying their colours in the

Woodpecker vandalism

Tit killer

patches of sunshine, singing their quick high-running songs in the young oaks beyond the windows. Martyn claimed I would only have to find a blue tit singing in these trees to see alongside him 'a female spending almost as much time sceptically watching him'. A sceptical blue tit? 'Yes,' Martyn said. 'And the male will be quite obviously singing in hope.'

Through early March, the blue tits were chasing from one tree to the next, half tangling in mid-air and then landing on different branches. Marsh tits and great tits sat among the hazel catkins. I sat in my own box, thinking it like my own nest. Or a classroom. Or a yacht that went nowhere, whose method was not to voyage but to let things come.

On the sunny morning of 20 March one of two blue tits on the branches of the young oak next to me flew up to the birdhouse, to the entrance hole of one of the boxes and went in. For a minute I held my

breath as it ticked and scratched inside. Co-occupancy! What a condition to reach, to be so thrilled by this arrival of the most usual of birds!
I felt like St Kevin, the Dark Age Irish monk, in whose upturned
palm, as he was praying, a blackbird had landed and settled to make
its nest.

> Kevin feels the warm eggs, the small breast, the tucked
> Neat head and claws and, finding himself linked
> Into the network of eternal life,
>
> Is moved to pity …

Perhaps it was a measure of the effort I had put into this birdhouse and
to this corner of ordinary country that this little cerulean songbird
scratching and tinkering in its box beside me felt significant. 'Why is
the cuckoo's melody preferred/And nightingale's rich song so fondly
praised/In poets' rhymes?' John Clare had asked in his poem to the
wren. 'Is there no other bird/Of nature's minstrelsy that oft hath raised/
One's heart to ecstasy and mirth as well?' That was my thought as I
heard the blue tit's wings scuffing at the timber two feet away.

That first tit was the hen which the cock had courted and introduced to his nesting cavity. She had accepted his invitation and within
a day, she had started to sort it out. Early in the mornings, with the
geese flying low overhead on their springtime journey north, and when
the wren had escaped through the top louvre after greeting me with its
sharp alarm cry, I could listen to the blue tit knocking and tapping on
its box. This wonderful process, known to old birders as 'putting up the
shelves', is the sound of the hen tit checking that the nest-cavity the
male has chosen is in good structural shape. Knock-knock-knock,
tap-tap-tap-tap, as if endless little tacks are being nailed in. She was
testing wall, floor and roof for soundness before deciding whether to
invest in nest and eggs, which is her work alone.

In this first box, in one other in the birdhouse, as well as three of those I had put up in the wood, the knocking continued for a day or two. Once they were sure the place was safe, the hen tits started to clear out the droppings and other rubbish the males had deposited there during the winter. They carry it in their throats and bills, spitting it out when they are away from the nest, or they shuffle it out attached to their wings and breast feathers which, once beyond the box, can be shuddered and rubbed clean. I knew not to open the doors to watch at this point as the birds can be so disturbed that they will leave. But I could listen. Click-scratch. Tempting to look. Busyness. Scraping. How stiff the feathers sound against the timber. The nest box like a sounding box. Careful housekeeping.

Spring was underway when, on 29 March, I opened the door to one of the boxes that I had checked was quiet and found a single long sprig of moss laid out as if by some theatre designer, a feather boa tossed across the floor of the stage.

I stuck Do Not Disturb notices on the doors of the boxes, addressed to me. The spring was cold, 4°C/39°F in the early mornings, and I lit the fire. The goldfinches were making a cool, liquid music from the high oaks outside, a filigreed wallpaper of sound. As I listened, a tiny lacewing, quarter of an inch across, with four translucent, iridescent wings and a lime-green body, landed on the iron lid of the wood-burner and stuck there. Its body smoked for a second in wisps, like the smoke wandering up from a crematorium chimney, and it died, its wings still perfect but shifted into the golden end of the spectrum, its body turned dun and caramel, its eyes black, the antennae burned away to stubs.

For about two weeks, the nest building continued. The entrance holes to the boxes acquired grubby feet marks where birds landed before going in. My mornings were filled with their flickering arrivals and departures and their little scratchy life inside, their tiny private rituals.

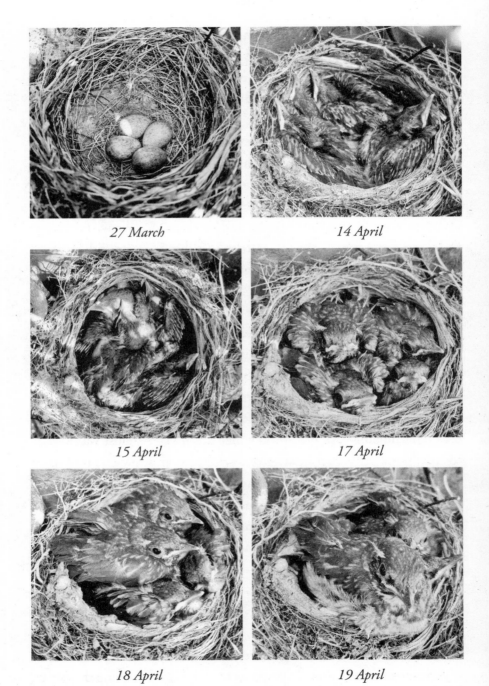

27 March

14 April

15 April

17 April

18 April

19 April

April blackbirds

I also had set up a small remote camera in a thick climber next to the barn and through April it watched parallel lives unfolding as a blackbird laid its four blue, brown-speckled eggs in a dried grass nest, concreted with mud, and in three weeks raised its first brood of the year.

The young birds gradually outgrew the space that had been made for them, their primary wing quills sprouting first from their blind nakedness, their first plumage shifting from dark grey to dark brown, their beaks trending upwards to implore food from the parents, dominance erupting between the four siblings and one of them always managing to be more prominent than the others. And then quite suddenly the nest was no longer fitted to their lives and they were out everywhere in the garden and yard, still crying to the parents for more, more, more.

In the birdhouse I ignored my own instructions not to look and watched as the moss piled up into early April, sometimes quite clearly dumped there in too much of a hurry, a landslip of it just inside the entrance, pushed in like a bundle of blankets and eiderdowns in the attic, and grass stems sticking out too.

In other boxes, the edges had been lined with a rim of moss but the centre of the floor left plain. In one, the bright-green moss was packed to a depth of 1.5 inches up against the glass, with straw-coloured grass stems in it. Martyn had told me to look for honeysuckle bark but I could find none. I went to clear out one of the nest boxes in the wood, thinking I could help the blue tits, but as I put my hand into the jumble of old leaves and moss in there, a dormouse leaped out through the entrance hole and so I left it. On another, I opened the lid, saw those old leaves just stirring like the surface of a pot of porridge on the stove and quickly closed it. Although dormice are some of the great predators of blue tit nests, consuming entire broods at one sitting, I was just as happy to provide dormouse housing as anything for the birds.

Spring was in full flood. I could feel the accelerator going down and the year rushing away. The blackthorn was so white it made the flowers of the goat willow below it look muddy. Even in the course of a morning, the green leaves of the birches unfurled and spread their green light into the birdhouse windows. Blue tits were arriving with their mouths so stuffed with dried grasses they looked like straw men in a cartoon.

To the moss and grass, now two inches deep, the birds added feathers. Some had come from the hen tit herself, which like most female birds, and some males, develops a brood patch during the breeding season. Changes in hormone levels during the nesting season start the process. Down feathers on the bird's stomach suddenly come loose. In some species, the feathers simply fall out. In others, the hen bird pulls them out. Ducks pull them out while building the nest and use them to make it soft and warm. Songbirds have one brood patch under which her blood heat can warm the eggs. Some of the feathers were larger and not from the tits.

These (which blue tits specialise in; there are many fewer in great and coal tit nests, and almost none in marsh tits') were – or so it is guessed – placed there by the female tit as a kind of decor.

They also add the leaves of aromatic herbs such as ground ivy and red deadnettle. We found some of the mint in the garden with torn leaves where the blue tits had taken the tips for their nests. The volatile compounds given off by these leaves control bacteria in chicks and potentially the mites that afflict adult birds. Some nests have been found with used cigarette butts incorporated in them and it is thought the nicotine they contain might work as another form of disinfectant.

By the end of April, the nests were coming clear structurally. Grasses and wisps of sheep wool, with both deer hair and cattle hair, had been wound into the mix. A blue tit – this was the hen – appeared on an oak sprig with a huge bundle of sheep's wool in her face from the remains of last summer's shearing. She sat hesitant, anxious, her head turning this way and that for almost a minute and then jumped into a nest box, where I heard her scratching, before she was out and away. She was

29 April: Persephone's bower in the birdhouse

back in three minutes, bringing deer fluff. Beside her a coal tit was trying to pick off the ragged ends of a piece of synthetic string dangling from a wire.

In first one nest box and then the other, next to the glass, the hen tits made deep cups, almost the size of a ping-pong ball, padded and fitted in feathers and deer hair, pressed out by their turning their own bodies inside the mattresses of moss and softness they had already made. Those inner cups are wonderful things, each one a feathered nest, a breast-moulded life-receptacle. One day in late April, the afternoon sun came in through one of the nest box holes and its beam lit up the cup, illuminating it as if it were Persephone's bower.

Now the moment. The new oak leaves outside are as soft as skin. Each frond droops in the mornings like the fingers of a hand, strengthening and coming up level over the course of the day. The trees look like enormous lettuces. I listen outside the wooden doors of the nest boxes as if outside a bedroom for any sign of life or activity within and then very quietly open the door, letting a peep of light into the safety of that dark.

Once only did I disturb a hen on the nest. The bird escaping in shock seemed too big, sideways on to the exit hole, and it panicked and scratched to get out until it finally turned and flew away, leaving me feeling big, clumsy and destructive. Not again.

By the beginning of May, they had started to lay their eggs and I held back. The doors stayed closed but Martyn Stenning knew what was happening behind them. Once laying has begun, early each morn-

Cock blue tits, the tails gleaming and crowns flamboyantly raised,
bring morning morsels to their hens in the nest box

Juvenile great spotted woodpecker, distinguished by its bright red cap

Blue tit and chick

Blue tit with caterpillar

Great tit

Long-tailed tit

Chaffinch

House sparrow chick

Goldcrest

ing, before dawn, with what Martyn described as 'heroic exertion', the ten-gram hen lays an egg that weighs about one gram, the equivalent of an eight-stone woman giving birth to an eleven-pound child. Martyn had watched the process under a blackout blind at his university lab: 'The enormous amount of effort and energy makes her beak open, her eyes close and her body pant.' Cock and hen will have mated the day before and the laying of eggs now continues at the rate of one new egg a day for between three and thirteen days.

Almost as soon as she has laid, a morning ritual follows: the cock visits her with a morsel of food, probably one of the moth caterpillars that are now proliferating on the nearby oaks. He gives it to her, she eats it and leaves the nest. He then inspects the egg she has laid. It is tiny, as small as a baked bean, white or very pale grey and scattered with rusty red-brown spots. He looks carefully because, as has been found by the French biologist Marie-Jeanne Holveck in a wood near Montpellier, blue tit eggs can convey important information to him. Those eggs that have large and closely clustered spots at the fatter end have yolks with higher concentrations of antibodies that will boost the immune system of the chicks. Each eggshell is a map of the hen's own health on the day she laid it. Healthier hens, which have recently absorbed plenty of antibodies in their diet, can transfer those advantages to yolk, embryo and chick.

Although the colouring of eggs in many species often deteriorates by the last egg, which can be almost spotless, all the signs of health run together: densely spotted eggs go along with nutritious yolks, producing in the end larger chicks with yellower feathers. A hen that is suffering from poor health or is in poor condition that day will fall down on those scores.

The cock on his morning inspection will be able to tell and so adjust his effort for the brood accordingly. If the hen is giving him healthy chicks, he will try hard to look after her. If not, he might keep some energy in reserve.

Marie-Jeanne Holveck's comparison of blue tit eggs. Male blue tits can read the signs: there is no significance in the whiteness or greyness of the underlying colour but the denser and larger the brown spots near the blunt end, the healthier the hen that laid them

Once he has made his inspection, the hen will cover the eggs with a wad of the soft nest material she has collected in such abundance. She is out feeding during the day and for a while the eggs will lie cold and dormant but at night will be warmed by her returning to roost on top of the clutch.

As the number of eggs accumulates, she will start to incubate them for longer each day, first in the afternoons and nights, gradually increasing the time she spends on the nest.

By 8 May, waiting until well on into the morning, we thought it possible at last to have a look in the nests. In one there was nothing. A woodpecker had hammered it earlier in the spring and the tits must have been sufficiently alarmed not to occupy it. In another, a great tit sat bright and alert amid her bedding. Two others in Long Field Shaw and Stonepitty had blue tits also sitting tight, tucked against the back of the boxes, while another in Long Field Shaw had a mere three eggs, partly tucked under the felted covering the hen had pushed over them that morning. She was still halfway through her laying time. In the two occupied nest boxes in the birdhouse, the hens were temporarily away and the eggs lay open to view, six in one, seven in another, cupped in down and deer hair. The brown spotting on the eggs was variable, some lightly sprinkled, some almost entirely white, a mark of the day-to-day variations in the well-being of the mothers.

One of the birdhouse nests: seven blue tit eggs. The brown spots on the eggs are noticeably variable in size and distribution on the different eggs, a measure of the daily variability in the hens' metabolisms. The nest box has an inner shelf to make predation more difficult

We closed all doors and lids and allowed them to get on with the most demanding time of their lives. It felt magnificent, those blue tit mothers beside me on their eggs, patiently exuding their warmth. Occasionally one in the box moved and the tail feathers brushed against the timber board. It was like having a sick child asleep in the bedroom upstairs. I crept about. I worried how she was doing. I wanted to see her but not disturb her. Even unzipping a zip or opening a velcro strip felt intolerably loud.

The world had never seemed more beautiful. The beech trees were dressed like bridesmaids. A crab apple tree on the edge of Great Flemings was pink in flower. The cattle were out and lying on the grass. The bluebells filled the underwood like the lighting in a nightclub. I looked in on one nest and the hen was lying down with her head in the tufted cavity above the eggs. I thought she might be dead but as I watched she moved in her bed like a sleeper, dozing away the afternoon.

I spent days in the birdhouse listening to the silences around me, that incubating nurture of body warmth making its way into the little laboratories of the eggs. There was no more than a single scratch now and then as the mother moved tail or wing, as if the tip of a quill had been scraped along a hollow board.

One great tit nest in the birdhouse, which had been smashed open by a woodpecker and I had repaired with a steel guard, was raided again by the woodpecker, using its long prehensile tongue to drag one of the eggs from the nest cup to near the entrance. The eggs were more heavily spotted than the blue tit eggs but I thought that would be the end of this particular nest. Amazingly, the great tit still did not abandon it and sat in there day after day, incubating her brood.

After fourteen days or so, with the summer rushing by and the blue-bells quite suddenly looking shot, collapsed and drowned as if in a flood, the time for hatching arrived.

The wood is full of arms races and this is the critical moment in many of them. Oak trees will need to wait until the last of the frosts because a late frost will kill their leaves and flowers. Any later replacement crop will be thinner and produce fewer acorns and so the rule for the oak must be to come into leaf as early as possible after the frosts. The caterpillars that feed on those leaves time their own emergence from the eggs laid on the branches to maximise their ability to strip the young oak of its new leaves. Because early-leafing and late-leafing can cheat those caterpillars, evolution has worked on the oaks and even within a single wood there can be as much as thirty days' variation in the date leaves emerge. In an everlasting timetable tussle, the caterpillars for their part need to follow their own local oak's habits.

It is these caterpillars – mostly the flightless winter moth and the oak leaf roller – that the blue tits need to feed their young. And so the birds have to time the hatching of their chicks to coincide with the peak of caterpillar abundance. How they do this is something of a mystery, as the timetable is set when incubation begins. Martyn thinks that blue tits may be able to estimate, some three weeks ahead, just when the caterpillar abundance will peak and so delay the start of incubation until the time is right, but no one is sure how. Once the caterpillars are out, the arms race continues.

22 May (top) and a week later (above)

The leaf-eating caterpillars are bright green, camouflaged against the new leaves they are consuming. Martyn suggests the blue tits' habit of hanging upside down from branches allows them to see a caterpillar in dark silhouette on the other side of the leaf.

The chicks crack their way out of the eggs, the hen eats or removes the shell fragments and demand kicks off. Each chick has to be fed about seventy morsels of caterpillar or other invertebrate daily, on a steep growth curve that enlarges them from one gram to eleven grams (three hundredths of an ounce to a little less than two-fifths of an ounce) in as many days.

They emerge almost naked, with small tufts of down on head and back, and a huge yellow imploring mouth attached to a scrotal body. Those mouths close like Donald Duck's into flat-lipped envelopes but open like the hopper at the head of a gutter, origami mouths, a bucket to receive the parents' latest offering. They soon begin to feather up with their wing quills but are still downy on their backs. The parents start to look worn and ragged and some to lose so much condition that the feathers are almost rubbed away from their heads, which become scrofulous and vulturine under the strain. The pitiable birds look like crones before their time.

Meal after meal is delivered to the nestlings in the dark of the nests, the parents arriving on the oaks outside with caterpillars in their mouths, pausing for a moment on a branch, quivering with the physical urgency of the demand. The nest boxes are never quiet, animated by the arrival and departure of the birds, their feet landing on the steel plate at the entrance and the timber acting as a kind of sounding box like the body of a guitar or violin.

The significance of the cocks' gleaming blue crests may be invisible to us but it remains important for the birds even through this demanding phase of their lives. A group of scientists at the Max Planck Institute at Seewiesen in Bavaria have made an intriguing discovery. Although the gleam fades with the wear and tear of the weeks of breeding and provisioning, the glow of their mate's crown continues to matter for the females well into early summer.

The Norwegian biologist Arild Johnsen and his partners decided to increase the attractiveness of some blue tits and diminish others by using T-shirt marker pens to create two distinct male types: one (more attractive) with an increased shine in the ultraviolet on their crowns and one (less attractive) with their crown colours shifted towards the human-visible part of the spectrum.

How would the females respond? A longstanding theory holds that when a female bird knows it has mated with an attractive male, she should be willing to pay the costs of investing more in the chicks they have together. He is, after all, providing her with high-quality offspring. Johnsen found that, particularly if the females were young, they fed their chicks more if the male's crown feathers had been upped in shine by the T-shirt marker. A top-quality husband was worth the extra work. Those UV+ males, for their part, did not respond in kind, nor trouble to feed their chicks as often as those whose father had his UV count reduced.

To test a related response, Johnsen put a rubber snake on the roof of the nest box and recorded the effort the birds put into defending the nest against the predator. Females with reduced-UV mates took less trouble to defend their offspring than those with UV+ mates. It was clear to Johnsen that the female blue tits were responding to what they saw in their mates' crowns. If the cock could keep his UV count up even during the stressful period of breeding and feeding, it was worth investing time and effort in the welfare of the chicks they had together. If he was fading away under the pressure of parenthood, she might be better off not working quite so hard. The calculations made by the cock when inspecting the spots on the eggs to see what kind of spouse he had settled in with had their equivalent in the hen's careful examination of his crown.

The work continued. The parents carried out the faecal sacs deposited by the ever-enlarging chicks, keeping the nest clean for them. The young birds began to bulge within the nest cup, flattening out what had become a globe of wool, feather and hair into a one-level mattress.

On a sunny warm day early in June, the first nestlings leave. Others are much later, some scarcely feathered or downed up, still largely consisting of vast yellow mouths with an attendant body.

It was not long before they too were ready for departure – just under three weeks between hatching and fledging – gathering below the exit hole of each nest box. A pathetic and perplexing scene developed in one of them. One morning I found all but one nestling, six out of the seven, had gone. The straggler was small and had lagged behind the others. The parents were not to be seen. That one little blue tit was left in there, mouthing and crying at me through the glass, opening its wide yellow lips before pausing, looking at me, closing its eyes, falling back in exhaustion and beginning again. I could not know what had happened, nor why it was crying to me.

It is a common situation. Many blue tit nests have one or two runts, usually the last to hatch, starting at a disadvantage and never catching up. If they survive, they are often not ready to fledge with the others and so are abandoned in the nest. If they try to follow, they don't get far and end up on the ground near the nest, where they quickly die.

This one had been outcompeted by its siblings and the food supply provided by the parents had been diverted into those other mouths. It is a genetic understanding that responding to the demands of the strong young birds is a way of guaranteeing viable successors. Feeding a few well is better than many poorly.

I could not think what to do. Because we had designed the nest boxes to be predator resistant, I could get no access to the chick without dismantling its box. I could only watch as the natural processes took their course. These birds live in a kind of warzone and the following day I found the chick dead in the middle of the deserted nest. I took the box apart, removed the remains from it and burned them all in the fire, including the sad and fragile final occupant.

Looking back on it now, I wonder if that is the right thing to have done. It was a way of honouring the pitiable nestling but burning everything deprives many other animals of the resources in the nest, including the little corpse. Many invertebrate species of moths and beetles rely on tit nests for their life cycle. Small corpses feed the flies that feed the swallows.

The birds had gone. There was an almost tangible sense of emptiness in the birdhouse. I never thought I would suffer empty nest syndrome but this was it. Blue tits have only one brood each year and so here, for the time being, was the end of the birdhouse-as-nursery.

I went out into the wood, and there the stream of life was still running at full throttle. The nest boxes were filled with restless, beautiful, big-eyed young birds, shuffling and scuffling to emerge into the light.

Blue tits not far from fledging

If I sat down near a nest box, the blue tits did not like it. The parents angrily and anxiously flew above me, rattle-chirring in their most aggressive voices, so that I knew I should withdraw. I thought that as soon as I was twenty yards from them the intensity would drop but it didn't, even when I hid. The same thing happened the following day and so with my binoculars I went to twice the distance, sat down in the shadow of a big oak and watched.

The blue tit still knew I was there and was adamant that she would not have her five nestlings threatened. Bees dozed in and out of the finger holes of the foxgloves. Green and black dragonflies cruised in the sunlight. A gaggle of long-tailed tits flew across my eyeline, each with no more weight than the bows on the tail of a kite.

The blue tit began clucking outside the box. She was summoning her chicks. It was time to leave. Nothing happened. She returned with a caterpillar but was reluctant to go in and hopped-flew to a hornbeam about twenty yards away before flying briefly above me, making her rattle-chatter alarm.

An air of acute and urgent anxiety filled this summer morning. She returned four or five times to the box, each time just putting her head in the entrance and then back out into the wood to find food. I thought she might be dumping the caterpillars in the mouth of the box to draw the nestlings towards it, but Martyn Stenning was clear. The most assertive and imploring chicks were already there waiting at the mouth. She was feeding the most demanding.

I had never seen a bird so busy about the wood, swinging on a narrow frond of a hornbeam above the nest, clinging to the mossy branch of an oak beside it, off to a field maple and then again to the hornbeam, back to the lid of the box, then to cling to its lower corner, to the top again, looking over at me and flying back to the hornbeam, *chuck-chuck-chucking*, into the box and out again, squeezing out of the hole and away to the rest of the wood. In the June sunshine, which was lighting the wood like a stage in pools and patches, everything looked calm and at ease, but in the blue tit I could see nothing but harassment and crisis.

Then I understood: the first little fledgling put its face to the hole. A beak, an eye, a yellow head. The mother was on the branch beside it squeaking to her offspring. And so they emerged, one by one, clumsying over to the near oak branch, crash-landing on the moss, sitting there somehow agog, their little wings quivering above their backs, as if the blood was filling them in the way it fills a butterfly's opening wings.

The wood was full of fledglings shouting for food. One blue tit fledgling came in through the open window of the birdhouse and perching on one of the taut strings that support the desks squeaked at me, not the jackhammer alarm call of the parent but its own high-pitch request.

Outside, young great tits, nuthatches, siskins and blue tits all began their noisy, vulnerable, fluttering acquisition of life, their one consistent habit keeping their mouths open.

A fledgling nuthatch

If one is used to the sheer capability in birds, their mastery of their own lives, the foolishness of fledglings is a surprise. They blunder on to branches without quite knowing where they are, confront adults as if the adult would pay any attention to them or their needs, and above all move so slowly that you fear at any moment for their lives. Midsummer, awash with fledglings, must be the bonanza time for magpies, jays, crows, sparrowhawks and weasels, filled as it is with edible young birds that are as naked and clumsy as calves. Nothing could be more obvious that to be a bird is in part a learned experience. None of them emerge into the world, as it were, fully fledged.

The rest of the wood is beginning to show its age. The oak leaves are already darkening and turning leathery. The thistles are in flower. Spring for the plant world seems a long way back but for the birds this is the soft time, filled with vulnerability. Fledglings are little but their own uncertainty. They are patently unfamiliar with the world into which they have been born and spend their time looking around for some kind of support.

A great tit fledgling fresh out of the box

A blue tit fledgling flew into the barn door. It collapsed on the oak boards at my feet, stunned and inert. I picked it up and held its tiny warmth in my hand where I could feel its quick heartbeat. Its eyes were closed. As I walked with it down into the wood, one bright liquid eye opened. I held it until a few minutes later when I set it on the ground in the shelter of an elder bush on the edge of the wood, laying it on a small flat piece of sandstone. It could not stand but fell over to one side and, when lying like that, its legs reached for the air as it spread one wing, opening it to the full extent, and with it began to shuffle its body in a wounded circle. I set it upright again but it fell again and started to turn again. I tried one more time but then I saw that, while its right eye and wing were intact, the whole of its left side was broken. The left eye was closed and the left wing was unable to open. It may have been paralysed by the collision. I held it for few minutes in case the effect was transitory and then set it back on the stone. Again it turned in its pathetic circle. For another few minutes I watched and saw no change and so I held the little body in my left hand until it died. I put the body in the damp ground under the fallen maple leaves from the autumn before.

One shouldn't mind. Blue tits are abundant. There are 3.4 million breeding territories in Britain, a number that with some small fluctuations is almost stable, apart from a very slow and so-far-unexplained decline in the last two decades. Thirty million blue tit chicks are born in Britain each year.

They are spread across Europe as far as the Urals and the Caspian, if not as densely as in Britain and the nearer parts of western Europe. Our mass bird feeding, the milder winters, all the nest boxes we put up and the elimination of major predators such as pine martens have enormously increased their numbers.

The bird has been in our lives since the Anglo-Saxons and the breeding blue tits that made the birdhouse their own for one spring were as likely to do so again for another two or even three. It is true that many of them die. Six out of ten fledglings will not survive to breed the following year and five out of ten adults will breed once and once only. The cocks have a 10 per cent better life expectancy than their mates, partly because they are dominant over females when feeding and partly because the hens are so vulnerable to a weasel or woodpecker when in the nests, incubating the eggs or brooding the chicks.

None of this can be about individual life or death. Perhaps it is better to see these bright little beings in the way we see flowers. They are born, emerge, live and die, many of them passing their genes on to the next generation. It is a brief, coherent, systematic and beautiful existence. Nothing is more tragic about it than anything in the life of a primrose or a cornflower.

But that may be imposing too much of a distance between us and them. We are part of that same world. We live a little longer than a blue tit, just as deep ocean sponges and clams live a little longer than us. 'As for the generation of leaves, so is the generation of men,' the Lycian warrior Glaucus tells his enemy Diomedes in the *Iliad*.

The wind scatters some on the earth, but then,
in spring, the forest blooms and new leaves grow.
One generation of men comes and another goes.

Martyn told me that just as the blue tits timed their breeding season to synchronise with the emergence of the caterpillars and the caterpillars timed theirs to coincide with the emergence of the oak leaves, sparrow-hawks timed the emergence of their chicks to overlap with the fledging of the blue tits. 'One family of sparrowhawks,' he said with the gentle, half-melancholy, half-smiling air of the true birdman, 'needs between ten and forty blue tits a day. Or their equivalent anyway. A whole wood pigeon would be just as good.'

10.

Blackbirds

SINGING

If you want to listen to a blackbird in spring, to hear more from it than its full and rounded promise of summer, or all the delicious roll of its harmonics, there is no better guide than Joan Hall-Craggs. She was a shy woman who used to draw the curtains of the room in which she played the piano in case strangers looked in, but when she died in 2006 she left behind her one supremely valuable document.

For more than ninety days between 8 March and 9 June 1957 Hall-Craggs recorded and analysed the song of one 'handsome jet black bird' – 'Blackbird A' was the name she gave it – that sang every morning from the gable of her bungalow at the western end of the Chilterns in south Oxfordshire.

Hall-Craggs had been a brilliant and successful concert pianist, winning strings of medals and prizes, dazzling audiences in piano duets with her friend Pearl Akerman, and so brought to the blackbird's song a musician's ear. From the Chilterns, she reported her findings to the Cambridge Sub-department of Animal Behaviour (sub- because it was subsidiary to the Department of Zoology) where the pioneer of bird sonograms, William Thorpe, recognised her expertise and lent her the laboratory's Kay Sona-Graph. This American sound spectrograph, the distant ancestor of Merlin, had been invented in Missouri a few years before, and was designed to analyse speech patterns and signals intelligence. Thorpe and Hall-Craggs were among the first to apply it to birdsong.

She wanted to know what happened to the blackbird's song as it changed and developed through 'the singing season'. Bird A soon got to know her, did not mind being watched and would even come when called for food. In the way of all great biologists, she became involved in his life, seeing him as something more than a mechanism for claiming territory or self-assertion. Hall-Craggs's account of A's effusive 1950s singing season in her paper on 'The development of song in the blackbird' is, apart from anything else, a record of sheer life-energy, the again-and-again pouring out of a bird's meaning into the world.

It is difficult not to see in her attention to its ambitious and enlarging concert performance something of her own story. Stumble on a blackbird and it will fluster away with its loud high-pitched police-siren of an alarm call, scootling off into the privacy of another part of the wood, curtains drawn, its selfhood preserved. Or if you tread more carefully, it will also know you are there and issue its warnings quietly *chook-chook, chook-chook, watch-out, watch-out*, a statement of aural modesty and self-concealment, to tell other blackbirds that something nearby is unfriendly.

But allow the blackbird its high platform – one at Perch Hill always chooses each spring the lichened branches of a thorn tree on the edges of garden and wood – let it stand there with its tail cocked up and its bill spring-bright, and there on its performance platform, alert and more visible than any other bird or creature, with the audience ready beneath it, it will sing and sing.

Hall-Craggs first established that every note the blackbird would use in the whole year was sung by him in the very first recordings made in early March. These basic phrases, with several simple variants, would remain his material for weeks to come. She recorded them on magnetic tape and played them back at a sixteenth of the original speed. The slow listen allowed her to hear more complexity within the phrase than the human ear could detect at full speed. Even after she had listened to the slowed-down song and transcribed what she heard, she was unable to hear all the notes the blackbird sang when she played it again at natural speed. The detail of a blackbird's song is inaudible to us not because we don't know it but because we are unable to perceive it.

To the twenty-six basic phrases and twenty-four basic variants that Hall-Craggs found in the first week, Bird A began by adding what she called 'terminal decorations', flourishes applied after a microscopic pause that followed the fragment of song. Listen to a blackbird in March and it is easy enough to hear this pattern: a moment of tunefulness and then a twittery, quick terminal flourish.

Hall-Craggs listened as morning after morning Bird A practised by repeating the basic phrases and adding different terminals to them. Once this elaboration was underway, he moved on and started to create compound versions of the basic phrases, in which two or more of them were linked together. Sometimes a phrase tended to be put in front of

A blackbird phrase as heard naturally by human beings

The same phrase when transcribed from listening to it at a sixteenth of natural speed and transposed to the original pitches

the others, sometimes added to the end. Once Hall-Craggs had alerted me, I could hear the blackbirds in the April wood doing this, playing with song fragments as if they were Lego blocks, or lengths of track in a wooden railway.

Hall-Craggs had been a music teacher during the war and she felt that development in Bird A was good and quick. By the end of the second week, he was starting to sound something like a mature bird, with one or two complex phrases already linked together. And so the editing process continued. By week three, he was pushing extracts from some phrases into the middle of others. Many of these new, evolved multi-source expressions were experimented with and rejected. Sometimes he would toy with a suggestion for four or five days and then abandon it. One phrase was altered and moulded for twelve weeks until finally dismissed as unsatisfactory.

It would be difficult to keep up with this process in real time, but Hall-Craggs made her recordings and analysed them over several years. Her paper was not published until 1962, five years after Bird A had sung, but through that analysis she found that he continued all spring to attend to the shape of his song. Individual notes were selected and added into the middle of existing sequences. Something like a grace-note – a rapidly flipped-through note preceding a central element of a

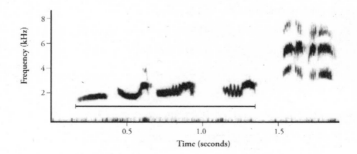

A spectrogram of the classic blackbird phrase: the tuneful motif, a microscopic pause and then the higher, scratchier 'terminal decoration'

tune – was here and there added to the contour of sound like a cornice on a façade or an adverb in a phrase. Sometimes Bird A contributed a trill or a soft and more musical version of the alarm shriek at the very end of a sequence as a concluding flourish. I have heard one of our blackbirds do that, a playful form of mock alarm, as if he were twiddling with the valves on a trumpet.

If you wandered down to the wood early on a May morning and heard as if for the first time a blackbird singing, what would reach you is not, as you might imagine, a plain instinctive song that has emerged unbidden from the bird as if from an automaton but something more deliberate, sifted and refined, a composition that has been considered, selected, buffed, burnished and chosen as the song which that blackbird, in that particular spring, felt it needed.

Bird A was not always on form. First thing in the morning, he would sometimes leave off his final flourishes, or when feeling threatened by another bird invading his territory he would be less demonstrative. In what Hall-Craggs called 'the desultory afternoon song' he would sing as if bored or his patience exhausted. Sometimes phrases were contracted and their rhythm syncopated, perhaps also out of sheer tiredness.

At the same time as developing this repertoire, A began to organise the phrases both new and old into recurring series. By late April, his song was no longer an anarchic sequence of random elements. Hear one phrase then and you could begin to predict what might come next. By May, he had developed long chains of song, never stereotyped, and always with some variation between them, but a resolved performance piece that the blackbird could sing with all the confidence of a bird that knew what it had to say. Song in March and early April had been filled with gaps and silences but not in May, when the pauses shrank away and continuity filled the air. The blackbird had come into his own and for as much as eighteen unbroken seconds, Bird A could ripple through his lines and half-lines like a tenor enjoying his triumph at the Met.

The Maytime blackbird sings to his world. Nothing is clipped. He has the voice of unalloyed authority proclaiming self and life without cavil. It is true that towards the end of the season Hall-Craggs realised that some rarely sung phrases were being abandoned and some of the more highly organised series were also let go, but by then the summer was deepening and the time had come to recognise that the bird, for this year, had done with his performances.

The process had begun the year before. By the time a blackbird is seven weeks old, he has learned from his father and from neighbouring blackbirds what it is to sing. The adults might have two or even three broods in the course of a summer and birds that are born late, after the father has stopped singing for that year, don't get the chance to learn. But they will learn the following spring as their father or other adult birds start to sing again around them. By the spring of 1958, Bird A had given phrases to ten of his neighbouring blackbirds, who went on singing them around the Hall-Craggs garden all year and on through 1959, 1960 and 1961. His carefully constructed compound songs that he had taken such trouble to create in the spring of 1957 were being imitated (rather badly, Joan thought) by his neighbours, who habitually dropped off the last three notes of each composition.

A blue tit nesting in a box near the bungalow gable in 1957 had not liked the blackbird song and repeatedly gave it a rough and angry *churrr* from a nearby lilac bush whenever Bird A embarked on his recital. A was not going to put up with that and took to scolding the blue tit in return, mimicking its voice, in a way that Joan considered a parody, although how she could have even guessed that is not clear.

She asked, finally, the most difficult question: 'To what end does [the blackbird] apparently strive to improve upon and enlarge the content of the whole basic song?' What was the point? Why does he make what we can recognise as 'a coherent sound structure'? Her answer, out of deep empathy with the bird, was aesthetic. The developed, mature song of the blackbird has better rhythmic balance and

The shapeliness of the fully developed blackbird song is visible in the staves of Joan Hall-Craggs's transcription, interrupted as it is by Louis-Armstrong, Satchmo-style chuckles

sense of symmetry than the early versions. To judge by its song and its long editorial process, Blackbird A had 'a feeling for completeness', a sense of form that strived after 'the shapeliness of the melodic line'. In search of it, A made 'a voluntary effort to cultivate the song as a whole'. What we and Joan Hall-Craggs love about blackbird song, its unmatched musicality, is, she thought, what a blackbird loves about it too.

Can that be true? How can we tell if it is true? Some seven decades later, it is no longer a fashionable answer. How, one might ask, can the blackbird, with its origins deep in the south-east Asian and Australian past, come to conform to the ideas of beauty in classical music developed in western Europe in the last few hundred years? (Unless, of course, that musical tradition took its cue from the singing birds …) Or is Joan Hall-Craggs's vision of the exquisite performer perched on her bungalow gable nothing but an act of wish-fulfilment?

Since her pioneering study, other more Darwinian questions have been addressed. It seems that a big repertoire is often a sign to female blackbirds of the excellence of the singing bird. The length of time he sings performs the same function. The breadth and length of his singing is intimidating to intruding males, not daring to enter the territory of a bird with such capacity. Certainly Joan Hall-Craggs noticed that

Bird A had to put up with very few trespassers. And it may be, like the peacock's tail, that a long and complicated song is a deliberate demonstration of the bird's ability to carry a handicap, a signal, through its sheer costliness, of his own strength and fitness. How wonderful, the blackbird hen might think, to expend so much energy on the brilliant and useless ornament of song when others would have to reserve every ounce of energy to chase away their rivals. And it may also be, finally, a blackbird's way of keeping ahead of those rivals, devising such a permanently evolving and ever-complicating song that they have little chance of mimicking it and so stealing all the signs of his virtue.

Most of these factors may be in play but a hint that the last is important lies in the blackbird's amazing ability to copy other sounds. Not only can they sing like other birds – golden plover, greenfinch, blackcap, wood warbler, nuthatch, swallow, great tit, green woodpecker, goldfinch, magpie and a domestic cock have all been recorded – but non-bird sounds just as easily enter the repertoire. Joan Hall-Craggs herself later heard different blackbirds in the Channel Isles singing like a shag, a raven, a pheasant, a tom-cat and her 'trimphone'. 'Inspiration for one Cambridge blackbird', she was told, 'was found in the "Cross Now" signal at a pedestrian crossing.'

The sophistication should not surprise us. Some bullfinches have been taught to sing exact copies of a German folksong, forty-five notes in a row without a mistake, even singing it when set at a higher pitch, while others can alternate their parts with human singers, knowing when to stop and when to come in.

In a 1980s experiment, the psychologist-composer Debra Porter, then at Reed College in Portland, Oregon, played a variety of music to some pigeons: first a one-minute excerpt from J.S. Bach's *Prelude in C Minor* for flute, then a snatch from the *Sonata, Op. 25, No. 1* for viola by the German composer Paul Hindemith, a modernist who had been denounced by Goebbels as essentially Bolshevik and an 'atonal noisemaker'.

If the pigeons pecked a panel in front of them when Bach was play-ing, they were rewarded with grain, but during the Hindemith they were not rewarded even if they pecked. The pigeons gradually learned what to do, pecking for Bach, waiting for Hindemith to come to an end. Porter then moved on: a new set of pigeons was offered Bach's *Toccata and Fugue in D Minor* for organ and part of Stravinsky's *Rite of Spring*. The birds were given grain if they pecked on the right-hand button for Bach, on the left for Stravinsky. Again, they learned what to do, eventually reaching a 90 per cent success rate in identifying the composers.

In the most difficult test of all, they were played vaguely Bach-like pieces from the Danish baroque composer Dieterich Buxtehude, from Scarlatti and Vivaldi, followed by vaguely Stravinsky-like pieces by the modern Americans Elliott Carter and Walter Piston. The pigeons started slowly but ended up doing relatively well, discriminating between classical and modern, except in the case of the fast-running movement of a Vivaldi concerto for violin and orchestra. For reasons

Porter could not discern, the pigeons thought Vivaldi sounded more like Stravinsky than Bach.

There are riches in this open ground between bird and human. In a village in the North Hampshire downs, not a famous piece of southern England but beautiful, clarified, chalk country, there is a small garden with a pale marble bust of Beethoven placed in front of a yew hedge. On the edge of the garden, where it faces the village's triangular green, the box bushes have been cut into rows of cockerels, a treble clef, another of a bass clef and a third into a dark-eyed, large-hatted man, which may be the only topiary Beethoven in England.

This is the house of the pianist Sylvia Bowden and her husband who is responsible for the hedge-sculpture. 'It's a bit of a menagerie,' she said over the cake and cherries she gave me one June afternoon. 'I banned the elephants.'

Sylvia is a spiritual descendant of Joan Hall-Craggs. Like her, she was a star pianist in her youth at the Royal Academy of Music, winning all sorts of prizes and scholarships, and like Hall-Craggs is in love with the song of the blackbird.

'You have to listen, Adam,' she says. 'Nothing is more important than intense listening.' Her first professor at the Royal Academy, Max Pirani, had the word *Listen* stuck up on the wall of his studio in every language in the world. Sylvia now teaches music at the University of Southampton and plays the piano, Beethoven above all, in her music room looking out on this Hampshire garden. 'My best performances are always in the music room,' she says. In spring and summer, with the windows open, Beethoven billows across lawns and hedges as if his compositions were the rustling of the trees themselves.

She apologised for the quietness of her blackbirds for our June tea. 'They have stopped singing by now because during the spring, they are a different animal. The equivalent in man would be to have testicles the size of melons and, poor things, they can't keep that up.'

It is the belting-out blackbirds that she loves. She likes to call them the 'melon balls' when the spring song is surging and spilling around them. 'They can go on and on, rhythmically and melodically, that melodic song and that wonderful *dolce* sound the blackbird makes.'

She quotes the remark by the great eighteenth-century essayist and connoisseur of civilisation Joseph Addison: 'I value my garden more for being full of blackbirds than of cherries, and very frankly give them fruit for their songs.' 'Those are the priorities,' she says. 'Music not commodity, delight not profit. You should put that up over the door to your Bird School. Come in, listen, hear what the world has to say.'

It became clear to Sylvia over several years that her blackbirds were not singing the usual phrases. Instead, when she made a close study of them in 2006 and 2007, she heard them singing two themes from the late Beethoven quartets, in particular from the difficult, wild and unleashed music of the *Grosse Fuge Op. 133*, first written by Beethoven in 1825. The fugue began life as the concluding part of a string quartet, but after being rejected and criticised by players and audiences as too crazy and too difficult, it was turned into a challenging and complex piece of its own.

In his mid- to late fifties by then, Beethoven had been losing his hearing for almost twenty-five years and been almost completely deaf for ten. The *Grosse Fuge*, which lasts about fifteen minutes, was in effect his final testament. 'When I first read the score,' Sylvia says, 'I thought I cannot read it. It is unrestful music. It's as if you are being ship-wrecked by music. To begin with, no one could play it. The publisher gave him a bit more money to write an easier movement, which he did, a light, Haydnesque thing and nowadays most people play that simpler replacement. But it's the real thing that grips me.'

She half-sings, half-taps the first theme. 'The opening – *de rm de rm de rm rum de d de dm* – that is the blackbird. Beethoven repeats it and turns it upside down and –' She pauses. The complexities of the fugue are so total that the music is not only all but unplayable, it is virtually indescribable.

'Late Beethoven is so different, more and more inside himself, with his deafness. It is the music of total isolation towards the end, but sublime, winged. It takes you to another place. He was so alone. Once, when he was walking in the streets of Vienna at night, he couldn't find his lodgings and he was locked up as a vagrant.'

Was he, I asked her, moving towards the condition in which a bird sings?

Maybe, she thought. 'Nature was so important to him. He was happy in nature. He walked every day for miles. And with his growing isolation he went back to something that came from nature. It's broken and fragmentary. It's not the music of sociability. It's wild. It began with the wild and came back to the wild.'

Sylvia wrote about this blackbird-Beethoven music in the *Musical Times*:

> The first of these motifs [*Grosse Fuge*] is particularly complex and is practised in sections by the younger, less-experienced birds. Although the rhythmic pattern can be plotted, due to the furious tempo and high pitch it is difficult to pinpoint the precise pitch and intervals of this phrase with the human ear.

So what happened? How did the blackbirds in Sylvia Bowden's Hampshire garden come to be singing phrases from a piece of music written in Vienna in 1825–7?

Beethoven was born in Bonn in December 1770, and as a child and young man, on his walks in the country outside the city, he always took a pocket sketchbook with him. Sylvia's term is that the natural world was his 'thematic playground'. When asked about the source of his ideas and his composing methods, he said he could not 'answer this with any certainty. They come unevoked, spontaneously or unspontaneously; I can grasp them with my hands in the open air, in the woods while walking.' As he wrote to his friend Count Brunswick:

> As for me, heavens above, my kingdom is in the air. As the wind
> so often does, harmonies whirl around me and, in the same way,
> things whirl in my soul.

It was the voice of permeation, a composer dwelling in the spongy boundary with the world, inviting what he heard around him to summon the music he knew he could write.

He would 'often stop with a sheet of music paper and a pencil-stump in his hands, as if listening, look up and down and then scribble notes on the paper'.

These notebooks were among his most precious possessions and when he moved to Vienna in 1792, he took them with him as his reservoir and inspiration. He liked to keep 'every musical idea that occurred to him on a bit of paper which he threw into a corner of his room ... After a while there was a considerable pile of the memoranda which the maid was not permitted to touch when cleaning the room. Now when Beethoven got into a mood for work he would hunt a new musical *motivi* out of his treasure-heap which he thought might serve as principal and secondary themes for the composition in contemplation.'

In that way, the motifs he had written down in the chaotic, barely legible script of the notebooks might lie dormant for years before he used them.

By the time he was forty he could no longer hear the birds. He took endless cures and had a series of extraordinary hearing trumpets made, several with an attached hairband that would leave both his hands free, but the condition was progressive and nothing could be done to stop the encroaching silence.

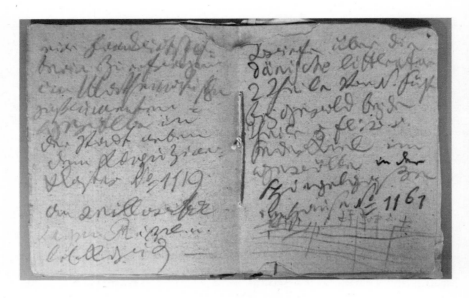

One of Beethoven's chaotic notebooks

He fell back on his memory and on the mountain of paper notes he had brought to Vienna. In that way the song of the Bonn blackbirds stayed with him for the rest of his life.

I went to Bonn to see if I could hear the blackbirds singing the phrases Beethoven had used much later in life. His house survived the British bombing of October 1944, which destroyed most of the old city and in one night alone killed three hundred people. While an incendiary had landed on the roof of Beethoven's house, the caretaker swept it into the yard and it was extinguished before too much damage was done. The rest of the old city was ruined and in the post-war years rebuilt on transformed lines. Little of Beethoven's world survives.

Yet just as epic poetry outlasts the destruction of the places in which it was sung, I wanted to find out if, amid the tragic memory of damage and ruination in Bonn, there might be any continuity in the city's blackbirds. Would I be able to hear what the young Beethoven heard?

Sylvia had seen in a correspondence in *The Times* that a man from Fife 'had heard several Scottish blackbirds sing the opening

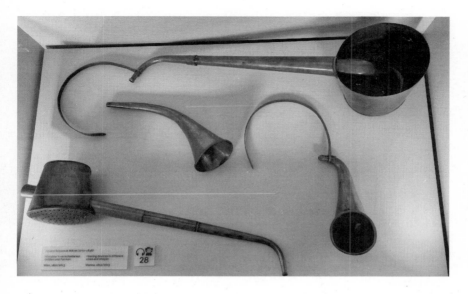

Beethoven's listening trumpets, some with hairbands, now in his house in Bonn

two bars from the finale of Beethoven's *Violin Concerto in D, Op. 61*. On a trip to Bonn in 1992 the same correspondent visited Beethoven's birthplace and he heard a blackbird singing the identical phrase.' So I was on the look-out for two blackbird expressions: one repeated from the *Grosse Fuge* in Sylvia's garden, one from the violin concerto in Fife.

In mid-April, sunrise in the Rhine Valley is at 6.30 but I slept with the window open and at 4.55 heard the first blackbird sing, more than an hour and a half before the sun came up, a sign that the morning city was a noisy place.

I got up to empty streets. On the Rhine, the sodium lights were throwing their glimmer across the river; the tourist boats were tied up at their quays. The apartment blocks were quiet and unlit, but it was a few days before the Bonn Marathon and forklift trucks were arranging the portaloos on the edge of the big royal park, the Hofgarten, beeping loudly as they manoeuvred them into place.

This is what Beethoven's blackbird-descendants were having to cope with, even before the sun was up. Yet the birds were singing and in a way that was so large and lavish, so rapturous and liberal, mounding up and broadcasting all the gatherings of their song, it was as if I had never heard a blackbird before. Up in the dark above me, just like the blackbird I had first listened to in the gateway at Perch Hill the summer before, a blackbird sang into my ear as if I were two hundred yards away. He could not have been more than a few feet from me, sitting on top of a carefully shaped yew, already practising his multiple phrases, his chuckles, his added *chook-chooks*, his repeated grace-notes and even for a moment an imitation of a great tit creaking away beside us on the banks of the river.

At first light, about 5.50, the giant industrial barges started to appear, sliding downriver towards Cologne and Holland, slipping their lengths between the piers of the bridges. I walked into the city. The first commuters were driving to work. The noise of the marathon preparations dropped away and in those rebuilt streets and alleys the blackbirds were the only life I could find. A sodium-lit silence around them. The rest of life completely muffled. A rat quietly making its way around the cleared stalls in the marketplace, beside the café where Beethoven used to drink coffee with the Bonn intellectuals.

Everywhere I walked, the blackbirds came with me. Or if one was not to hand, I was drawn to the sound of its singing, echoing between the houses in the little squares and back alleys. Florid, oratorical, reverberating music. By the church of St Remigius, where Beethoven played the organ, one was singing in the flowering chestnut outside the east windows. Another in the Turkish hazel tree beyond it. The hard surfaces of the buildings in the empty streets gave the songs a rolling and resonant echo, bell-like in their repetitions.

No other birds were singing in the dark. The blackbird by St Remigius was less experimental than his brother or cousin by the Rhine, merely playing and repeating three or four notes. Another in

Friedrichstrasse was singing in a Japanese cherry. A third was in the old back gardens beyond them, now a car park filled with song.

A little later at about ten past six the sparrows in those tree-filled yards quite suddenly turned chirrupingly loud, a gathering of piccolos, with the blackbird fluting in between them. And so the orchestra struck up and played, but by eight or so, it was over. The birds had largely fallen silent as the city started to boom around them.

Beethoven was an absorber and borrower of the birds' ordinary themes, which he transmuted into great music. I had Sylvia's words in my mind. 'I don't suppose Beethoven ever thought he had *taken* bird-song,' she had said. 'It was just out with the notebook, write it down and then it was his. It wasn't theirs any more. His talent was never in melody. He had to steal someone else's. But superb, supreme improvisation was what he was about. He could take a rest, a silence, and do something unequalled with it.'

Blackbird, Sylvia and Beethoven all fused in the dark of a cold Bonn morning. 'With the repetition in music and song we can feel it,' she had said. 'We are in it, we can own it, we are there with it, we can recognise it … With repetition and so with recognition, you are bonded to the music.'

I emailed Sylvia my recordings. It seemed to her that the blackbirds of modern Bonn were indeed singing in ways that contained 'the contours of the arpeggio motif in the violin concerto, and the swung rhythm in the theme of the *Grosse Fuge*'. That was not everything, but it was success enough: something of the motifs and rhythms Beethoven heard had survived in the city where he heard them.

And what of the blackbirds in Sylvia's own garden? 'Oh no,' she said. 'There have been plenty of new generations of blackbirds since 2006 and they have been highlighting their own creativity and preferences, so no, they have not copied these phrases. But they have developed new motifs from all these themes.'

*   *   *

Biologists have asked another question: how much of birdsong comes untutored from the genes of the bird itself? Experiments in pursuit of an answer lack every aspect of Sylvia Bowden's gracefulness and have been cruel, often enclosing newborn or five-day-old birds in sound-proof boxes to be fed and watered but raised in an envelope of silence. These so-called Kaspar Hauser experiments, named after the poor boy from early nineteenth-century Nuremberg who was kept all his life in a darkened cell before emerging semi-articulate into the streets of the city, were intended to reveal the innate structure of a bird's song but their findings have been no more than what one might expect.

The scientists, including Joan Hall-Craggs's mentor William Thorpe and his Cambridge pupils, often chose a chaffinch because its songs are clear and easy to describe, a repeating *tick* before finishing with a buzzing, high-intensity flourish. One seventeenth-century treatise considered the chaffinch 'fitter for the Spit than a Cage, having but one short plain Song'.

Thorpe found the Kaspar Hauser chaffinches to be predictably diminished even from this modest condition. They mumbled like the boy they were named after, singing songs in which phrases slurred into each other, without the smart, expressive syllables of a properly educated bird and often without a clear phrase with which to end. But if a group of those sound-deprived young chaffinches were housed together, they started to develop their own unique language. Like William Golding's boys in *Lord of the Flies*, they began to build their own social world with its own rules out of their primitive, example-less, inborn propensity to sing, composing what Thorpe called 'complex but highly abnormal songs quite dissimilar from those of normal wild Chaffinches'.

It is a disturbing picture of creatures deprived of their culture, with nothing to be inherited from their elders, and forced to devise their own meanings from their own diminished resources. The finer and subtler aspects of the chaffinch song, those modulations discoverable when the tape is slowed, are not there; they are only added and learned as part of the culture that chaffinches, over millions of years, have devised between themselves and passed down to their offspring.

More troubling still has been the practice of deafening young birds to see how they cope. The surgery is delicate and microscopic, cutting into the tiny skulls and removing the cochlea, the core mechanism of the inner ear, leading to results that are similar to the Kaspar Hauser experiments: a partial song, with incomplete development, the phrases veering between both higher and lower frequencies than in wild birds, a lack of control in the voice and sometimes in the body, with more jagged fluctuations and fewer syllables. These damaged utterances were not unlike the natural song of the wild birds but lessened and blunted. Some deafened birds were made radically different, singing songs unlike their siblings' or parents', as if the deafening had removed all controls, but they were the exception. Most of the damaged birds attempted to stumble towards normality with no ability to hear or know either what they sang or what the other birds might have been singing around them.

There is no doubt that some aspects of song can be inherited, either genetically or through the key learning periods soon after the birds hatch or in the following spring. In that way birdsong can outlast time, transferred from father to son, and in the tropics through the many female bird-singers, for generation after generation. The wrens in Japan, for example, sing in a way that is identical to wrens both in France and in New York and Maine. They have not heard each other for millions of years but the thread of their song still connects them.

While European, Japanese and north-east American wrens sound the same as each other, the wrens in Oregon or British Columbia, which have larger repertoires and more complex songs, sound quite different. It is at least probable that over the eons, shaped by repeated glaciations, the north-west Americans were cut off in their mountain ranges and developed their own variegated song, while those from New

York and Maine were somehow able to spread west, colonising Asia and then Europe, probably via the Bering Strait, taking with them the simple song with which they had begun, distributing it droplet by droplet across the widths of three continents.

We know that birds can listen, learn, transmit, develop, polish, project, recognise, distinguish, reject and cherish many different aspects of their own and other birds' calls and songs. But to know what they mean by their songs is not easy.

The Danish biologist Torben Dabelsteen has been investigating bird signalling for almost fifty years. He is sure that a blackbird's song has social functions. Its opening motifs and concluding flourishes are always more than simple notes, modulated in both frequency and volume, and every ripple in the sound is a vehicle for meaning of some kind. Each bird has between six and thirty motifs and every one has its favourites that it sings all the time. Individuality is embedded in the identity of every blackbird and expressed many times a day.

We cannot read the blackbird's mind but we can see the effect of his song on other birds – whether they are rival males or receptive females. He is communicating his blackbirdness, his maleness, his presence, his quality as a mate, his relationship to that place, his breeding status, perhaps his ancestry and his potential for aggression. And so, if one could translate into English the notes you hear all spring and summer from the blackbirds around you, this is what they are saying.

> I am a blackbird.
> I am male.
> This is my place.
> My name is Hamlet (since I am Danish).
> I want a wife.
> In fact I have a wife.
> I heard my father say something like this.
> His father taught him.

This is also what the others like to say.
I don't like them.
But I prefer them to strangers.
I don't trust my uncle.
I like this new phrase I've learned,
With a hey, and a ho, and a hey nonino,
I can sing with the best of them.
I am proud, vengeful and ambitious.
I can sing on and on.
And I will say it again.
Don't mess with me.
I have wings as swift as thoughts of love.
Listen to this.
I am sure you can't match it.
I don't want you here.
But what a piece of work is a blackbird,
In action how like an angel,
The paragon of animals.
I am indeed the Prince of Denmark.

It is the song of self-assertion, desirability, latent ferocity, exclusive territoriality and displayed prominence but *how* does that song mean what it does?

Modern researchers have at least begun to unpick the fine detail. It turns out that, although the Hamlet statement is the perceived meaning, at least to judge from its reception by other blackbirds, what we hear of the song is not what the birds hear. The songs we know, all the songs that people through the ages have attempted to describe, are no more their meaning to the birds than the paper, ink and boards of a book are the essence of what it has to say. The large-scale structure of song and the physical book are the necessary vehicles by which the meaning is conveyed, but the meaning itself is carried by the much smaller signals, the forms of the print on the page, enabled by those large structures. For blackbirds, the medium is not the message.

In the late 1960s, the young biologist Stephen Emlen studied the sound world of the indigo bunting, an American, vocal wood-edge singer that learns its repetitive song, full of paired notes, early in life and sticks with it without much variation. It is a much easier subject to study than the virtuoso blackbird. Emlen wanted to identify the actual signals that conveyed a bird's species, sex or identity to another and the likelihood of another responding to those signals aggressively or amorously. How did birds mean what they meant?

Emlen recorded the buntings on tape and then manipulated them, cutting up the tapes and splicing them together in a different order. Where an invading bunting had actually sung notes in its usual paired way that could be written as 1 1 2 3 3 4 4 5 5 6 6, and had been attacked by the resident bunting for daring to invade his territory, Emlen played back those same notes as 1 2 3 4 5 6 1 3 4 5 6 – all the right notes but not necessarily in the right order. The resident buntings didn't notice the difference, displaying towards the tape recorder as if it were an invader singing a normal song. Emlen realised that buntings did not consider the large-scale structure of the song in any way important. It had always been thought that the pairing of notes was the identifying mark of an indigo bunting song but the birds themselves did not notice if a note was paired or unpaired. That was not where any meaning lay. One of Hamlet's speeches printed on handmade paper was no different to the same speech in a cheap paperback. Humanity had mistaken vehicle for content.

Further manipulations produced different responses. If Emlen spliced silences into a song, keeping the notes the same but altering the rhythm, the buntings realised they were different, did not recognise the songs as their own and ignored the tape recorder, much as they did the songs of other kinds of birds. And if Emlen kept the same notes in the same rhythm but flattened them, shrinking the wide range of frequencies buntings usually employ and cutting out the sudden zigzag changes in pitch – the sort of jazz-jerkiness we know from song thrushes – the buntings did not think the songs had anything to do with them either.

This revelatory set of findings suggested, without quite revealing, that somewhere within birdsong were meaning-structures of which the human ear was unaware.

Birds have a double voicebox, the syrinx, set in their chest above the lungs and at the foot of the windpipe. Airflow from the lungs makes the syrinx vibrate in its double channels. Each half can produce the same sound so that the song can be double in volume what it would otherwise be – historically, blackbirds were thought to be intolerable as cage birds because like the bagpipes they sounded impossibly loud when inside – or produce different notes, either at the same time or in rapid alternation. Starlings, for example, can be heard to sing in imitation of two different birds at the same time.

The sound coming from the syrinx emerges at a wide range of frequencies, which are filtered and selected as they pass through the bird's vocal tract and out via the beak. If you watch a bird singing, its beak is busy shaping the sound, not to add the consonants that our mouths and lips impose, but to clean and filter the overtones from its voice. Look at the trace of a human voice on Merlin, and it is clear how it operates at a wide range of frequencies nearly all the time, filling the screen from top to bottom. Even our attempts at a pure note are blurry with harmonics. That is why a human voice sounds thick and fleshy. Most birdsong tends not to be like that. Look at the sung motif of a blackbird on Merlin and the trace it leaves is quite narrow, restricted to precisely located frequencies. Birdsong tends to be fluty because it has cut out the non-fluty overtones emerging from the syrinx.

This mechanism is capable of detailed control. The muscles in the syrinx can generate more than two hundred acoustic variations a second, with intervals between them as short as 4.6 milliseconds. The muscles controlling these movements are the fastest-moving that have been found in any vertebrate. Only the swim-bladders in fish and the tail-shaker muscles in rattlesnakes come anywhere near. One can hear the difference. The tits, finches, wrens and thrushes have these super-fast muscles and their song vibrates in the ear at rates that are beyond our knowing. Others, the wood pigeons and stock doves, with their low, slow croonings, are not equipped in the same way and seem to speak to us on a level we can actually understand.

Precision is all. The songbirds' syringeal muscles are controlled by parts of the brain that enlarge in spring and shrink in autumn when the singing is no longer required. Brain scans of singing birds show spikes in those brain nuclei that match the vibrations in the songbox. From one song to the next birds will repeat individual phrases that are identical down to millisecond tolerances. Nothing is left to chance or approximation. It may well be that bird communication occurs in these millisecond details.

You have to think differently if you are to imagine that degree of precision in the wood. It is not an empty space. There is a universe of understanding here, behind every leaf, in every crook of a branch, a silent envelope of attentive listening, hundreds of creatures alert for the sounds of other life. Everything is governed by a refined and integrated sensory exactness so that a walk through a wood, seen like this, feels like taking a path through an exquisitely tuned mind. The whole place is sensory, as alert to itself as any poet could imagine. Nothing is passive, everything alive.

Birdsong is part of that precision information-system, played out by the birds not as we hear it but in a micro-music beyond the range of human perception. In 2002 Robert Dooling, who for decades has pioneered the study of fine structures in birdsong at the University of Maryland, published research in which he compared the ability of birds and people to distinguish sounds that differed only in their slightest of millisecond variations. The voluble Australian species, the zebra finch, canaries and budgerigars all did much better than people. Dooling did not know how, but the birds had superhuman hearing and were able to tell differences in the shape of sounds as short as a millisecond. People could not make out anything less than three to four times as long.

It became clear to Dooling that the birds and people were hearing different songs. If he reversed a single syllable but kept the order of syllables in the song intact, human listeners thought no change had been made. The birds were unable to recognise it as a song they knew. But if Dooling changed the rhythm of the song and doubled the silence between two notes, the birds thought the song was no different while people thought there was a glitch on the tape. To birds in general, apparently, a song played back-to-front sounded the same, whereas a song played at a different pitch, which we might easily recognise when someone sings Happy Birthday first as a treble and then as a bass, sounded to the birds like a different tune.

We live in different auditory worlds. Birds can both sing and listen at a resolution we know nothing of. We might hear a wren machine-gunning its repeated notes, but in all likelihood what we hear as repetition is full of variety and meaning. Unheard by us but filling the wood is what Adam Fishbein, a researcher who has worked with Professor Dooling, has called 'a rich trove of information about emotion, health, age, individual identity, and more'. We might think of the natural world as something of a void, a realm into which we can project our own ambitions and desires. The reality is a crowded and jostling space, full of claim and counter-claim, of assertion and ownership, in a network of which we are constantly unaware.

'What Cartesian nonsense to think of birdsong as pre-programmed cries uttered by birds to advertise their presence to the opposite sex,' J.M. Coetzee wrote in his *Diary of a Bad Year*.

Each bird-cry is a full-hearted release of the self into the air, accompanied by such joy as we can barely comprehend. I! says each cry: I! What a miracle! Singing liberates the voice, allows it to fly, expands the soul.

We have to admit our ignorance in hearing what the birds are saying, allow Coetzee his point and listen to the short movement called the *'Lever du jour'* that Maurice Ravel placed at the heart of *Daphnis and Chloé*, his ballet composed in 1912 for Diaghilev who was then taking Paris by storm.

In a piece of music as seductive as any ever written, Ravel puts his meticulous orchestration in service of a glittering unreality, an imagined dawn in which the sense of emergence itself is at the root of the beauty. Overlaid glissandos of flutes, harps and clarinets sweep through the air of the early wood. Beside and beneath them are the haunted notes of the metallic-percussion instrument called the Celesta, invented in the late nineteenth century and much loved by Debussy, Tchaikovsky and Ravel, echoing in the half-dark. The only sound, as Ravel's note on the score tells the performers, is 'the murmur of the rivulets of dew running from the rocks'. Everything is muted. The hero Daphnis lies in front of the grotto of the nymphs and into this summoned world comes the first birdsong with the high dancing of a piccolo, as much flight as song, followed by the flutes and three solo violins, each playing in different harmonies the repeated, interrupted and sudden polyphonics of the birds.

It is a miracle of recreation, not the sound of a wood at dawn as much as a sound portrait of the human experience of a wood at dawn. The sense of promise comes and goes. Nothing is on a single trend, everything appears and disappears in the emergence and slightness of life. The sun breaks through in a moment of large, whole-orchestra unison when the mutes are lifted and the air is filled with growth and enlargement, as a blooming of the day, before it recedes again, leaving

The three violins become the birds in Ravel's score of 'Lever du jour'

behind in the oboes and bassoons the solidity of the wood itself, the ground against which the birds come and go in the presence-half-presence of their song.

Our music and the birds' are not the same, but we do share some things. Like them, we can vary the pitch of our voices and have the ability to sing high or low. We can both sing quietly or loudly. Like them, we have a sense of rhythm, even if ours is more regular. Our pieces of music like theirs have a structure: the music evolves through each phrase or set of phrases. And we all repeat notes and phrases, toying with the sense of expectation, fulfilment and surprise that comes from the interplay of repetition and difference. We all play trills, the rapidly repeated flourishing of a note, often at the end of a phrase, and we both relish the timbre of a sound, the richness and variety that comes from the harmonics of a simple note, the difference in overtones and undertones between a blackbird or a thrush, a piccolo or a flute.

And yet, for all that sharedness and Ravel's ability to make it seem as if the wood in ancient Greece is alive around you, there are deep differences. Ravel has written this music, in effect as Messiaen said, not as the music of birds but of the world in which Ravel heard them.

There is another way to approach this. In January 1849, Robert Schumann wrote an extra movement for his series of piano pieces called *Waldszenen*, 'Forest Scenes'. The new, strange piece he added is called '*Vogel als Prophet*', 'Bird as Prophet'. Schumann allows his piano to mimic the voice of a single bird in the wood, removed from all human presence.

The music is full of birdlike leaps and alightings. Silences intervene between the unlinked phrases. Unexpectedness and inconclusiveness hang in every corner. There is no sweetness here; the bird does not know us, nor we it. Each meditative, distant phrase introduces only a questioning and near-absence.

And yet the bird-prophet has an astonishing reality, nearly a bird we know, perhaps in its simple melancholic repetitions a mistle thrush, and yet it isn't. Schumann's bird hovers half in the world he has transcribed, half in the world he has invented for it. It is in the end only the suggestion of a bird, speaking through these tiny, trilled, off-centre four- and five-note phrases, always waiting to pause or to spring into song, to lift away from us or just as suddenly arrive. Never has music been able to convey so exactly the repeated double-sensation of being-with and not-being-with a bird.

Holly Watkins, the New York musicologist, has written of this piece that it 'suggests the song of nothing human'. 'Vogel als Prophet' is, she says, a 'virtual wilderness' in which 'the call's off-kilter appoggiaturas [nearly discordant extra notes within a chord] invest it with a degree of otherness, as if the bird's utterances do not quite fit into the conceptual framework of the human perceiver'. The bird's singing is momentarily interrupted towards the end of the movement by a short and very

*Robert Schumann's opening to 'Vogel als Prophet', 'Bird as Prophet',
to be played 'slowly, very tenderly' in the rising and falling four- and
five-note phrases reminiscent of the mistle thrush*

conventional chorale, a version of all-too-human music, but Schumann only introduces that to abandon it and return to the half-understood strangeness of the bird itself, repeating the opening in the ending of his piece.

The beauty of birds is in their resistance to understanding. The almost-untranslatability of birdsong comes as a relief to pupils in Bird School. You are not alone in your perplexity. Rare exceptions aside, neither the scientists nor the composers nor the poets lead us to the birds.

Schumann in the late 1840s, with some of his own powers as a composer beginning to fail, could guess the truth of that. At the end of 'Vogel als Prophet', when he returns to the bird alone in the wood, it is a transition Holly Watkins has compared to Immanuel Kant's description of the 'beautiful soul' who, after spending too long in art galleries and concert halls, exchanges them for the fields and meadows, where he wants to discover 'a train of thought that he can never fully unravel'.

11.

Migrants

ARRIVING

As the world shuts down in autumn, the wood acquires another slice of the wild. The cherry trees have turned a Chinese lacquer-yellow. The leaves of the elders are rusted and mottled. The wood as a whole is as flecked and red-brown as the breast feathers of a young robin. The swallows and house martins, which for whatever reason do not nest with us, come past for a day or two, flying low over Jim's Field and Great Flemings, hunting for the daddy long-legs in the pastures, but on passage far to the south. They have a flight like none of the woodland birds I have come to know, sweeping across the fields in long diving ovals, or twisted figures-of-eight, coming to within an inch or two of the grass-tips, so that their entire life looks unlocated, their world all ocean. They have none of the scurry of the woodland birds, the urge to hide in the safety of the leaves. They are long-distance migrants, headed for southern Africa. The sky belongs to them and they are soon gone.

At the end of September or the beginning of October, the first northerners come late in the afternoon: bramblings, a sudden polychrome surprise in the trees outside the birdhouse. The name may sound like an ancient blackberry pudding but has nothing to do with that. 'Brambling' may be a blurring of a word that means branded or brindled, like the dark-barred juvenile salmon known as a brandling, since the brambling cocks share that colouring: ashy, speckled black heads and backs splashed with bands of burnt markings against the ochre and tangerine of breast and wings. The hens and the young birds are paler than the others, the cocks dark, as rich as syrup, or a fire, or a cloud-barred dawn.

There are never many of them, four or five resting on the increasingly leafless branches or picking at the ground beneath the birdhouse, where I scatter beech mast, their favoured winter food. They have spent all summer high in the Russian Arctic or in the dales of the Norwegian and Swedish mountains, and have now come south and west, to that part of Europe that is kept warmer by the influence of the Atlantic. Many have crossed the North Sea and they are the most beautiful heralds of winter. Each of the birds outside my window weighs less than an ounce. I weigh the same as 3,500 of them and these little packages of life may have flown two thousand miles to be here, a quarter of it over the sea at night, while I have been at home adjusting the thermostat and listening to the news.

A swallow above Jim's Field

The brambling feels like a rarity maybe because they do not often winter in the same place twice and can deny us their presence two winters out of three. They are in fact a transcontinental species, breeding all the way from the Atlantic to Siberia and across to Alaska. In the open birch woods or juniper and willow shrublands of the far north, there are millions of uncounted pairs.

In winter, their crowds come south and west, the cocks before the hens, feeding in large flocks, usually looking for beech mast. Beech trees themselves do not always fruit reliably and so the bramblings and the beeches share this intermittency: where the beech trees produce quantities of mast, numbers of bramblings gather to consume it. Where the beeches are barren, the bramblings are absent. How the birds do this on the scale of an entire winter continent is not known but the phenomenon is unequalled.

Ian Newton, the modern English expert on the biogeography of birds, has described one brambling flock in the winter of 1951–2 near Hunibach in Switzerland, perhaps drawn in by an exceptional crop of beech mast that year:

> From mid-afternoon each day, the Bramblings that had gathered there began to fly towards their roost in some conifers, small parties converged to form small flocks, small flocks to form large ones, so that a few kilometres from the roost they formed continuous streams, which poured non-stop through a small valley for 45–60 minutes each evening. One stream was about 200 metres across and four metres high ... and was estimated to contain 36 million birds. But only about half the birds could be seen properly, so the total number was probably at least 70 millions ... This single concentration, the bulk of which roosted within one small valley, could easily have accounted for the entire breeding population between the Norwegian coast and the Urals.

About a month after the bramblings, at the end of October, the little Scandinavian redwings arrive. These small 'rakish' thrushes, as *The Birds of the Western Palearctic* describes them, 'with sharp wing-points and tail-corners', as if they were black-market spivs arriving in their Jags for the winter, like to hide in the hedges between Jim's Field and Great Flemings, one or two going down to the wood, flashing white in the cold of the October sunshine. They dive and dart into the blackthorn at the top of Long Field, *kewk-kewking* in alarm as they make their way along the covert run.

The redwings seem to behave as suddenly as any bird. If I disturb them late in a dark afternoon, the little flock of twelve or so makes a joint and jagged plunge into the hedge-thicket, swerving together as sharply as a cyclist before a pothole. I listen to them in flight and hear the stirring of their wings, the mechanism of feather in air, a fan-like repercussion, stiff and taut. It is the sound of someone doing the laundry in a wind, or shaking the sheets out when making a bed. Winter music from the north.

The third of these northerners arrives in the autumn probably at night and hides in the wood. Not until a day in late January did I first meet one: at the end of a long and dark afternoon I was beating down some blackthorn bushes at the top of Hollow Flemings, armed with leather gauntlets, and cutting the thorned stems with loppers, pushing them down to make a substantial ground layer that would, I hoped, be enticing nesting territory for nightingales. I knew from a famous poem by John Clare that 'matted thorn' was the best of all frames for a nightingale's nest, an asylum in a hostile world, 'a blackthorn clump by which the bird could sing unseen', and so I slashed and lopped as deep as I could.

As I cut my way through the brambles, playing the part of the trampling herds and trying to make a large growing protective *kraal* for the summer migrants, I came to a patch of bracken.

With no warning a big dark woodcock burst from the tangle at my feet. It can have been no more than two feet from me as it rose and I watched it as if in slow motion, the wings digging into and clawing at the air, like an oarsman with his first heavy strokes at the start of the race, its eye beside me looking enormous as it escaped, each of us just grasping the other's presence for an instant before it disappeared, the long pale bill held down and close to its chest as it struggled and banged away from its hiding place. All I was left with was the retinal image of what seemed like a hen's body, marked brown and dark like a ploughed patch of winter field, carving away through the ash wood, in italic cuts through the maze.

Eight times I disturbed the woodcock that winter in Hollow Flemings, and thought of them more often: lurking, secret, inward. These were the wood-spirits and as I lay awake at night I loved knowing they were here, creeping from their hiding places to find the worms in the wet winter pastures of Great Flemings above them.

A man I know slightly, not understanding the road I was on, sent me in the post a woodcock he had shot a few days before. It was delivered by courier in a plastic bag, damp, bruised as if bitten, perhaps by a retriever, and empty-eyed. Its perfect crypsis had gone – one or two feathers had been stirred and broken by the shot – disrupting the flicker of wood colours, the tapestry of pale and dark, black and dark, chestnut brown and dawn brown. You could see how perfect it must have been in life. Its wood existence had created this pattern for it, a visual thickness and subtlety. Each wing was made up of about eighty overlapping silk-lined feathers, sleeker and softer to the touch than any dog or cat.

Only the tips of the underside of the stubby tail were a dazzling white, intended either for cocks to signal to hens on the ground when flying over them, or for hens to signal to overflying cocks, that sex might be in the air. Biologists have found recently that these tail feathers are the whitest of any feather in any bird, including snowy owls, winter ptarmigans and Caspian terns, a spike of brilliance in the dark of a summer wood.

The brilliant tail feathers

Most disturbing in the dead creature on my kitchen table were the sunken hollows of its eyes, because woodcock eyes are one of its marvels. They are essentially wading birds, related to sandpipers, oystercatchers and stilts, which have wandered ashore from the estuaries where their cousins live and become the secret dwellers in the woods. Their bills like those of other waders have a sensitive and grasping tip that can feel its way to the earthworms underground and grab them once discovered.

But the wood and its surrounding fields are dangerous, full of predators, and while poking for worms the woodcock must remain alert to any threat from behind or above. That is why its eyes are set high and well back on its head. When its long bill is buried in the ground, it can see an entire domed world above it, a panoramic helmet of vision that stretches left and right, forward and back, to all horizons, with no blind spot. It lives in a hemisphere of vision, as if it had a sky observatory in its head. In very narrow fields in front and behind that vision becomes binocular. Most of the woodcock's vision is provided by each eye separately, since detecting a predator, even roughly, is more important than precisely fixing it in space. Like a pilot in a commercial jet who needs to know where the limits of the aircraft are but cannot see them, the woodcock's own bill is invisible to its constantly watching and wary eyes.

As winter ends, in March and early April, the woodcock start to put on layers of fat and think of leaving Hollow Flemings. Because they are big enough to carry modern trackers, there is no need to guess where they go. From the whole of western Europe, they head east and north for Russia, Scandinavia and Finland, flying on average 1,800 miles, but a small proportion go further. Some fly more than six thousand miles

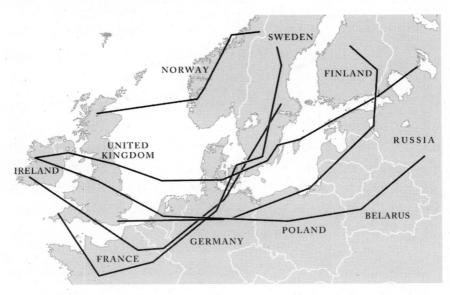

Spring migration routes by British and Irish woodcock: direct to Norway from Scotland, multiple sea-crossings to Russia, the long way round to Sweden and Finland

Photograph by Paul Williams of migrant woodcock on the Tartan Alpha oil platform, 12 April 2018: 80 miles from the nearest point of Scotland, 180 from the Norwegian coast

deep into central Siberia, sometimes covering 430 miles or more in a single night.

The numbers are vast: there are more than seventeen million woodcock in Europe, with about 1.4 million of them spending the winter in Britain and Ireland. Although some remain here to breed, most leave each spring for the longer days of the Arctic and sub-Arctic.

I wondered if any stayed here and from mid-April, I looked out evening after evening for the famous *roding* flights of the breeding birds, their leisurely cruises in the dusk, ten or twenty feet above the edges of the woods, appealing through a series of dark woody groan-croaks to any hen that might be lurking below.

It was a cold spring and the evenings colder. I signed up to be part of the national survey of woodcock for the British Trust for Ornithology and in my designated square a mile or two away in the valley of the River Dudwell, I listened shivering to the last songs of the song thrushes, the chaffinches, the wrens, robins, blackbirds and nuthatches, all falling away as the night settled in and the tawnies began their chorus. One evening I heard the unmistakable and haunting sound of a snipe drumming, flying high above me and then dropping towards the reedy fields of the valley: a quiver in the feathers of its tail, again and again giving a distant half-train-hoot, half-fluting. For the first time in my life I photographed a snipe above me as it stated its territory with its hollow feather-song and owned its air. But no woodcock. They had all left for the north.

The woodcock journeys are heroic. Those that cross to Norway cut straight over the North Sea, sometimes resting on the oil rigs they encounter on passage but many not surviving the journey: after storms, woodcock are often found by fishermen drowned and floating. Others take the land course across Europe, usually resting for four or five days en route.

One woodcock, tracked by the wader specialist Andrew Hoodless, left the west of Ireland and flew to Lake Onega in northern Russia, not by following the European landmass but by unequivocally aiming for its destination. It crossed the Irish Sea (93 miles), the North Sea (380 miles), the Kattegat (island-hopping), the Baltic (280 miles), the Gulf of Finland (250 miles) and Lake Ladoga (80 miles), before finally

coming to the lakeside summer birch wood in which it may well have been born.

It was outdone by one Italian woodcock from just north of Venice that flew east one spring across Austria, Slovakia, Ukraine, Belarus and Russia, passing just north of Kazakhstan and ending up in the forest near Ust-Ilimsk in Irkutsk Oblast north of northern Mongolia. The following autumn, it returned on an almost identical track to within a hundred yards of where it had spent the previous winter, having completed a round-trip of some eight thousand miles.

The turning year makes for migration. In a constant world, without seasons, there would be no need for it. As it is, birds migrate south and west at the beginning of winter to avoid death; and migrate north and east at the beginning of spring to engender life. It is, at root, as simple as that, a metronomic swaying with the geometries of the earth and its orbit. In the dark of the northern winter, plants stop growing and many invertebrates die or hide. If the birds stayed there they would starve to death before they died of cold.

But why bother to go north in spring? Could the birds not stay here all summer? The answer to that is subtler and larger: without migrants, the opportunity provided by the long northern summer, with its extended hours of sunlight, would not otherwise be exploited. Given the expansive drive that is the essence of any living system, that is a biological impossibility, particularly in animals that have mobility at their core. If an opportunity exists, birds will use it.

The urge to migrate is pervasive. It is part of the restlessness that seems inseparable from bird existence and is no arcane specialism of a few elaborately adapted species. About half of all the bird species in the world undertake seasonal migrations of some kind, a total of about fifty billion individuals, if the young ones are included, all of them airborne in spring and autumn, as if they formed another beating layer

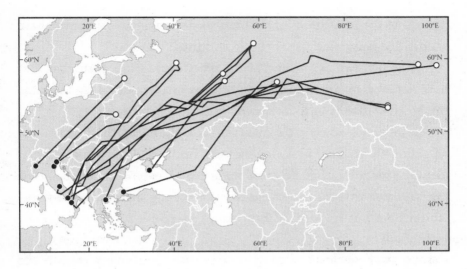

*The autumn migrations of southern European woodcock from their
Russian breeding grounds to their winter quarters. Departure points
in white, arrivals in black*

in the atmosphere, a living coat for the planet. Most fly at night and
high, often at four thousand feet, sometimes up to thirty thousand,
where the birds can catch the jet stream and travel to their destinations
at over a hundred miles per hour.

Even the tiny goldcrests (year-round residents in the wood and
garden here) are migratory further north, making their annual transcontinental travels to England from Finland and Poland. Large
numbers gather on ships in the North Sea but 'vulnerability to extreme
weather conditions may lead to large-scale disorientation or loss'. For
all that, there are goldcrests that spend the summer in Murmansk and
the winter in Crete or Tunis. These birds weigh a fifth of an ounce,
with a wingspan of just under five inches. Is there anything in those
facts that does not inspire a sense of awe?

Exposure to the hazards and rigours of long voyages is a form of
choice and the urge to migrate is variable, not hard-wired into a bird's
life. It comes and goes within populations according to need or incli-

nation. Many populations of the birds surrounding me in the birdhouse are divided between those that stay and those that go.

Tawny owls are at one end of the spectrum, so sedentary that they have not even managed to cross the narrow western or northern seas to the Scottish islands or to anywhere in Ireland.

Several of the others – the marsh tit, coal tit, nuthatch, magpie – are all genuinely resident here, inching out from wood to wood, generation by generation, but no more than that. Most of the others – blue tits, skylarks, wrens, robins, blackbirds and song thrushes – spend the winter here but in parts of Europe migrate south and west for the warmth.

Even swallows are not reliable migrants. They may seem like the most relentless travellers, but for at least a century some have refused the migrating instinct and been seen wintering in Britain. Most do make for South Africa but some don't bother and winter in southern Spain or Morocco.

And birds can change their habits. Siskins, the little yellow and black finches, live in Hollow Flemings all year but I think they have been joined by new arrivals recently. It has been shown that when migratory siskins are housed with their non-migratory cousins they soon learn to be non-migratory themselves, showing no restless anxiety to leave in spring or autumn.

Should one be surprised that adaptability and elasticity are embedded in the life habits of these birds? The tiny African warbler, the beautiful greenish, lemon-yellow chiffchaff, which used to announce the beginning of spring in England by saying its name ('loud enough to fetch an echo out of the wood from a bird the size of my thumb', as Tim Dee relentlessly quotes Gilbert White celebrating him in his journal), can now spend all winter here. The blackcaps that leave in the autumn for southern Spain and Africa, only returning to signal the beginning of the English spring, now overlap with blackcaps that come to England from central Europe for the winter, even while the English birds are leaving for the south. I cannot know, when I hear the high brilliance of an April blackcap, if it is an African bird, a Czech bird or a bird that has decided to make England its year-round home. There is one I know, a beautiful brown-capped blackcap hen, that lurks in the oak trees by the birdhouse, and she, I am assuming, is now Sussex through and through.

Birds are vessels for our hopes and longings. We want to see beauty and possibility in them, to identify with their quickness, their brightness, their liberty. The migrating impulse gives them a glamour that we, in our rooted, repetitive habits, spending thirty years or more walking the same paths, our boots getting *slubbed up* as they say round here with the same lumps of intractable Sussex clay, can never have.

An early hint that birds did indeed migrate came in May 1822 when a white stork was shot on its nest near Mecklenburg in north-east Germany. It had clearly been somewhere else over the winter as a large spear from central Africa was embedded in its neck.

In some ways, every migrant bird that you see in an English wood is a version of that stork: all have undergone travails to be present in front of you. You do not meet the untold numbers that have not made the journey. For Europe alone, perhaps five billion land-birds cross and recross the Sahara each year. That number is largely a guess and measuring mortality is difficult. Some attempts have been made and on average, during the autumn migration when adults and young return to warmer winter quarters, about a third of all the juveniles die en route, and perhaps 5 per cent of the adults. The weather and the unpredictability of storms, added to drought and the failure of seed harvests in those parts of Africa to which they travel, mean that several billion migrating European songbirds die each year. Many more die than do not, so that only 30 per cent of small songbirds survive their first migrations to their wintering grounds and back again. The level of mortality from the rigours of migration is not very different from

The Mecklenburg stork

the proportion of birds that die from the rigours of the northern winter.

The steady assault on numbers, particularly of the young, continues unseen and largely unnoticed but occasionally a cataclysm makes the underlying truth apparent. Storms have from time to time killed millions of swallows and house martins, particularly when early and unexpectedly wintry conditions have hit the migratory movements in autumn. It happened in central Europe in 1974, when at one blow, lasting a day or two, the Swiss population of house martins was cut by 30 per cent and of Danish swallows by 50 per cent. Scandinavian swifts, held too long in the north by storms into which they were reluctant to embark, died in untold numbers when the summer invertebrates, on which they relied to build up fat reserves for the journey, were no longer around for the taking. The swifts died of starvation in their summer haunts.

Occasionally a catastrophe strikes. On the night of 13 March 1904, what was called 'the great bird shower' fell around the villages of Worthington and Slayton in south-western Minnesota. With a light breeze from the south and temperatures above freezing, and soft wet snow falling from overcast skies, the birds began to appear from eleven in the evening in a shower that kept coming until the following dawn. Over an area of 1,500 square miles, from 1.5 million to 2 million Lapland buntings, or Lapland longspurs, a small black and brown migratory songbird, fell out of the sky.

They had been on their way to their breeding grounds in northern Canada but now lay scattered on fields and frozen lakes five or six feet apart. Some were still alive, in the bushes around the lakes, showing signs of the injuries they had sustained when falling to earth, many of them buried in the snow with only their heads protruding. In many, the skulls had been fractured and indented, leading to cerebral haemorrhages. In others the bones had been crushed. 'A Mr Drobeck' was reported as saying

that on the morning following the storm he noticed lumps or balls of snow on the roof of his barn and that when they thawed in the morning sun, they were found to contain live birds.

Although the birds were fat, their stomachs were empty. Those that were picked up alive fed greedily when offered seeds and so it seems likely that as a result of the weakness of extreme hunger, combined with the wet snow soaking their flight feathers, the buntings fell to their deaths from high on their migratory flight north.

No birds hibernate. Movement is of their essence. Those that commit to long migrations find their bodies sculpted by the journeys, with longer and more pointed wings for fast flying, and a larger proportion of the brain taken up by the hippocampus that controls and preserves spatial memory.

The routes they take are not rationally derived outcomes but step-by-step extensions of the first forays made as the Ice Age came to an end.

The red-backed shrikes that spend the summer in northern Spain and southern France – dramatic, black-masked predators that like to impale their victims on thorn trees where the meat can be eaten at will – migrate to sub-Saharan Africa for the winter but not by flying south across the Strait of Gibraltar. Shrikes have been tracked on their autumn migration flying east from around León in north-west Spain to northern Italy, on to Greece and only then turning south for the coast of Libya before heading down towards Zambia, Malawi and onwards. The flights are twice as long as they need to be, obeying the conservative mentality of survival.

They are only responding to genetic instruction. The first post-Ice Age shrikes came into Europe at the eastern end of the Mediterranean and since then have spread west through Europe. The genetic path back to Africa follows that origin story. What guaranteed their survival in the past remains the route to follow now. The spring-time migration goes even further east, over Saudi Arabia and Iraq before turning west towards Europe over Kurdish Turkey. It may be that the spring path is the ur-route out of Africa – the winds are more sympathetic there – and the autumn route is something of a short-

*Red-backed shrikes breeding near León in north-west Spain do not
head directly for their stopovers (white and grey dots) and wintering
refuges (black dots) in south-east Africa but take the routes in
autumn (black lines) and spring (grey lines) which it is thought
their ancestors pioneered in the years after the Ice Age*

cut across the Sahara that has developed in the last few thousand
years.

Migration is both heritable and malleable. Old methods stay in use
if they deliver; new methods and locations can be adopted when they

work. Birds inherit from their parents a sense of direction but that does not always remain fixed. Swainson's thrush, a fluty woodland bird that summers in western Canada, is split into two subspecies that travel south to their winter grounds along different routes: one keeps to the Pacific coast, the other tracks far to the east over the southern United States and the Gulf of Mexico.

Kira Delmore and Darren Irwin from the University of British Columbia mated groups of two Swainson's thrushes from the different subspecies, and put trackers on the offspring. Those hybrids were found to follow migration paths halfway between their two parents', often over difficult and hostile mountainous terrain, an incontrovertible sign that the choice of flyway was not made by following other birds but was genetically encoded. Somehow, in ways that are not understood, genes tell birds where to go. The bramblings, redwings and woodcock that winter in Hollow Flemings had Hollow Flemings already fixed in their minds when they were born somewhere in the distant north or the Russian forest.

As they mature and make the return journey, they get to know more about the route, recognising landmarks, learning to adjust when blown off course, becoming more accurate and economical in the flights they make. In effect, while they are born with a compass, they must learn to acquire a map. Like most animals, they have an internal clock to recognise the time of day and with that knowledge use the sun to orientate themselves. The same is true at night, when most songbirds migrate: they learn to recognise not only the celestial pole, the point around which the night sky turns, but individual constellations and their relationships. Just how birds can perceive the slow turning of the night sky remains unknown. Many of them, as they near their destination, can also smell their way to the precise wood or valley where they have sheltered or bred before.

More astonishing, and perhaps in the end more revelatory, is the birds' extraordinary capacity to sense the earth's magnetic field.

Goldfinch

Siskin

Greenfinch

Marsh tit

Nuthatch

Redpoll

Ring ouzel

Female siskin

Migrants that have to cross oceans or deserts need to accumulate fat to fuel the journey, sometimes doubling their weight with the load. When Swedish thrush nightingales, aiming for their winter quarters in tropical Africa, arrive each autumn at the Egyptian coast, they pause to build up the reserves that will enable them to make the thousand-mile Sahara crossing. The Stockholm biologist Thord Fransson and others caught and held some Swedish thrush nightingales outside Stockholm just before they left on their first migration. At the appropriate moment the birds were exposed to a magnetic field that mimicked the conditions in northern Egypt, while a control group was allowed to remain in unchanged Swedish conditions. In a matter of days and in response to this magnetic change and no other, the birds that felt they were in magnetic Egypt put on the fat they needed for the demands of the journey. The others, still in conceptual Stockholm, stayed much as they were.

We need to recalibrate the idea we have of the songbirds' minds. They live within the grid of a magnetic world, and it is probably a consciousness of the earth's magnetic field that lies at the root of their inherited direction-finding ability. The ornithologist Henrik Mouritsen, from the University of Oldenburg near Bremen in north-west Germany, kept some garden warblers in an aviary and watched them in the days before they were due to head south on their autumn migration. They displayed all the usual migratory restlessness of birds on the brink of departure, hopping from stance to stance and wing-flicking as their systems responded to the changing light levels at the beginning of winter.

Mouritsen exposed some of these warblers to conditions in which the usual magnetic field was neutralised. The birds that received no magnetic information were literally disorientated, turning their heads from side to side, sometimes through 90 or even 180 degrees, more than 140 times an hour, as if to sort out where they were. Those warblers in a normal magnetic field scanned their surroundings only a

third as often, 52 times an hour, and unlike those in the zero-mag-
netism field soon orientated themselves to the south, the direction
their migration would take them.

Mouritsen concluded that these birds, and perhaps all migratory
birds, used head movements 'to detect the reference compass direction
of the earth's magnetic field'.

The inbuilt detector, which allows birds to tell what is north and
what is south, is somewhere in the birds' heads, but where exactly?
Mouritsen and Peter Hore, professor of chemistry at Oxford, have
begun to make some mind-boggling discoveries about the way the
birds grasp that all-important information. The chemistry is complicated but essentially Hore and Mouritsen have found that the birds are
sensing the earth's magnetism in their eyes. Highly responsive molecules in the retina can detect variations in the earth's magnetic field and
communicate the signal through the optic nerve to a specialised part of
the fore-brain labelled Cluster N.

Cluster N is part of the visual system and in a way that is not
entirely understood, birds can apparently 'see' the earth's magnetic
field, as if the world itself were equipped with a magnetic version of
the latitudinal grid we draw on maps. Nerve impulses encoding the
field direction are sent along the optic nerve to the brain but only
when there is a small amount of light entering the eyes. Light acti-
vates Cluster N. If blindfolds are put over the birds' eyes, that part
of the brain does not respond to the magnetic field. In that way the
birds' perception of the field is *like* seeing but not the same as
seeing.

In migrating meadow pipits, the special receptors in the eyes and
Cluster N are highly active at night but not during the day. Daylight
probably drowns out the subtle magnetic signals and here, for the first
time, is an explanation of why birds might have evolved to migrate at
night. They need a small amount of light but not too much for the
magnetic compass to work. What they need, in fact, is starlight. The

receiving material, a protein called cryptochrome, becomes particularly sensitive to the magnetic field when it absorbs blue light of the kind most stars emit. Red light of the kind that washes over the world during the day disrupts them.

Mouritsen has also shown that levels of this blue-receiving cryptochrome are higher in migratory birds during the spring and autumn than during the winter and summer, when birds do not migrate. Radar tracking has shown that birds are more disorientated when the sky is overcast than when it is clear and that migrating birds do not like to fly within clouds, choosing to go either above or below them, using landmarks when that is possible or the stars themselves. Fog or long, thick overcast skies can be responsible for the kind of catastrophic crash that killed the millions of buntings in Minnesota in 1904.

This astonishing fact seems to be true: night-migrating birds can grasp the shape of the earth's magnetic field by using starlight to activate a chemical-visual compass in their eyes and brains. The sensitivity is dazzling. The magnetic field of the earth is ten to a hundred times weaker than a fridge magnet. Henrik Mouritsen found that when the magnetic compasses of robins were tested in wooden huts on his campus at Oldenburg, they were unable to orientate themselves. Very faint radio-frequency noise – Mouritsen used the term 'electrosmog' – generated by computers and other equipment in the nearby labs was interfering with the birds' magnetic compasses. When he and his team lined the huts with aluminium sheets to block the frequencies, the robins orientated themselves without trouble.

It is as if the birds are flying in a kind of ultra-informed virtual reality, by which magnetic information is transmitted to their brains and bodies through their eyes, and to which brain and body respond in acutely effective ways. Just as the tawny owls, in which the nerves from the ears bifurcate into the visual part of the brain, allowing them, in some senses, to *see* the sound of a mouse or a vole rustling in the leaves at their feet, the songbirds, it appears, can also see the magnetic geometries of the earth, a curving net of information through which they can navigate towards the lit summer north and the shelter of a warmer south. This is the miniature immensity of the birds: a microscopic consciousness that can encompass the earth.

Through the spring, I was impatient for the Africans to arrive. Everything in their evolution had equipped them for this journey. In past years I have heard turtle doves purring in our woods. Until a few years ago, nightingales sang in Hollow Flemings. I had never before thought to listen out for warblers singing here but they surely had. The year-round chiffchaffs and blackcaps were here but they could no longer count as spring arrivals. I waited for the others through April but nothing came. The wood was sprinkled with green light. The sedentary birds were breeding in the nest boxes, even in those I had repaired after the woodpeckers had done their worst. But a whole dimension of what this place should have been, and certainly had been since the end of the Ice Age, was missing.

I was witnessing the catastrophe that has unfolded over the last few decades thousands of miles away in the Sahel, that band of semi-desert Africa south of the Sahara that stretches from Senegal to Sudan. It is where the woodland birds of Europe have long gone to spend the winter.

Deep droughts in 1972–3 and again in 1984–5 killed millions of the acacia trees in which the birds roost. In the dry times, birds gathered at the few remaining pools, becoming an easy target for trappers. The drought meant a low supply of seeds and the seed-eating birds died of starvation. In this century, the summer rains have returned but for many birds the disaster that began with the droughts has continued. The list of those that have declined in the last five decades makes a melancholy roll-call: sedge warblers, turtle doves, lesser whitethroats, garden warblers, nightingales, cuckoos, house martins, willow warblers, wood warblers and spotted flycatchers – the most beautiful chorus of an English summer – have all crashed.

The Dutch ornithologist Leo Zwarts, who has been travelling the Sahel and recording its Eurasian migrants for many years, lays the blame for this continued decline on an ever-growing human population. The summer rains might have returned and the desertification of the 1980s and 1990s might have gone into reverse but a hundred million people now need to live and survive in the territory once used by the birds for their winters. Many people also live in cities and where the rural population used to collect branches for cooking and heating, modern urban people prefer charcoal. Charcoal can only be made from good lumps of roundwood and so where trees used to be trimmed they are now felled, in particular those species of acacia that woodland birds prefer. The human population, their sheep, goats and cattle are all growing at about 3 per cent a year. The wild country is being converted to farmland. Cashew plantations, devoid of birds, take the place of tree-pasture savannah. Massive bird hunts are conducted for food, using the cheap nylon nets originally developed for fisheries.

On top of that, the migrants must thread their way through the fields of hunters' guns, nets and traps, most of which are in the eastern Mediterranean and kill tens of millions of individual birds of hundreds of species every year. The numbers are by definition hazy but it is thought that between eleven million and thirty-six million songbirds are killed annually in the Mediterranean. More than two million birds die in Cyprus, Lebanon and Syria, not as a cumulative number but in each of those countries. Every year about 1.8 million blackcaps, 2.9 million chaffinches, 4.7 million house sparrows, 1.25 million song thrushes, 750,000 skylarks, 630,000 robins, half a million goldfinches and 360,000 chiffchaffs are caught or shot and eaten or kept in cages. In Italy, seven million birds are killed on their annual migrations, more than ten million in Egypt. Hundreds of thousands of those that make Malta their mid-sea stopover are killed as they land.

This illegal destruction of wild birds is not for subsistence. Birds are taken either as delicious titbits, supplied to restaurants or to be sold in local markets, or for the fun of killing them. It would be wrong to think of it as a charming artisanal practice. The trapping of blackcaps and robins for ambelopoulia in Cyprus – a dish consisting of grilled, fried, pickled or boiled songbirds – is now carried out on an industrial scale. Acacia plantations are cultivated solely with trapping in mind, lined either with mist nets or birdlime sticks, covered in a gluey substance made with the fruit of the Syrian plum tree applied to pomegranate branches in which birds' feet, wings and beaks get stuck.

On the Mediterranean coast of Egypt and eastern Libya, it is no better. About seven hundred kilometres of the Egyptian coast is lined with up to three rows of fine-meshed nets, forming a continuous barrier across the migrants' flight path. As the birds arrive at the shore exhausted from having crossed (in autumn) the Mediterranean or (in spring) the Sahara, and looking for somewhere to rest, they fly low straight into the nets.

As a result of these multiple and linked factors, the number of woodland birds that spend the winter in the Sahel and the summer in Europe has dropped by 80 to 90 per cent since 1970, some 12 to 15 per cent of the entire European bird population, a billion fewer individuals now than when I was a boy.

Autumn mist nets set on the Egyptian coast to catch migrants flying south from Europe for the winter

This human predation on the songbirds may seem marginal (perhaps twenty million songbirds taken each year) when set against the billion-plus that die annually from the natural effects of storm or drought. But it is more significant than one might guess. In the early twenty-first century, the shooting of turtle doves in western Europe had reached unsustainable levels. About a million birds a year were being shot and the population had dropped to around 1.5 million – until a moratorium was agreed by shooters in France, Spain and Portugal in 2021. For three years, no turtle doves were killed (at least legally) and in that brief pause their numbers increased by an additional 400,000 breeding pairs, the clearest possible evidence that direct human intervention – or the lack of it – has its effect.

Day after day I came down to the wood to hear them but all I heard was their absence. My attempts to make Hollow Flemings more nightingale-friendly had come to nothing. There was none there. The place seemed suitable for all the songbirds that should be arriving but, in all probability, they no longer existed.

Then, one day in the middle of May, a dazzling surprise awaited me. I walked down through the wood and felt that summer had arrived. The bluebells had collapsed, as if they had come and gone without fulfilling themselves. The oak flowers had browned but the hawthorn was full. The blue tit and great tit chicks were growing in their nest boxes. A blackcap and a blackbird were loud in Long Field Shaw. The robins were singing hard and bright.

At the top of Hollow Flemings, a few yards from the path, in a young, leafed-up oak tree, a bird I had never known: a garden warbler had arrived, furnishing the rough grounds with its song, ripple-burbling away in its high-stance inventiveness, an African perching for a moment in Sussex, an anthem for the Bird School. It had an occasional harshness in the voice, like a rough southern wine. He flew off when I was twelve feet from him to a blackthorn thirty feet away. But he didn't stop. Liquid sunshine in his song, sounding as if he was speaking French, a gift from abroad – or perhaps from the past.

At ten to nine in the evening, the song thrush by the birdhouse did its best to fill in for the nightingale that was not there. The others maintained their summer song: cadenzas and arpeggios from the black-cap, singing as if pirouetting on pinpoint toes; the garden warbler squeezing and folding the yeasty substance of its song; the woodpecker banging away like a carpenter at a hornbeam, but the four of them making a quartet for the summer wood.

The garden warbler in one of the blackthorns jumped to the top of the little oaks and then danced over to the upper branches of a hazel and then almost to the peak of an ash and then up further, creeping on until it was at the topmost sprig of the tree, where its open mouth was a black hole of song in its face.

Within a day or two, he was joined by another visitor, a willow warbler, one of the great migrants of the world, capable each spring and autumn of eight-thousand-mile journeys from Tanzania or Mozambique to the distant reaches of Siberia. This one had arrived from somewhere in west Africa south of the Sahara, voicing a gentle and lyrical melody that built to a high point and then fell away to a slow and perfected end. It sang in the birch trees, where the song hung elegantly and patiently, a sequence of many bubbled earrings for the trees. When the two warblers sang alongside each other, you could hear their difference: the willow warbler crooning but the garden warbler performing heights and depths of song above his neighbour's melody. I wished there were more of them, but there was some truth in their scarcity. These birds are now the elegists for a previous world, singing their anthems for the lost.

12.

Man

RECKONING

It is high, hot summer and the surge of the early year is spent. The wood is thick and quiet and a heaviness hangs over it like a brocade. The timbers of the birdhouse have shrunk in the sun so that the window-catches no longer catch. Outside, ragwort, bindweed, the first blackberries, the stillness of a year having come to its middle or end.

The horseflies move so slowly in the heat that I can take them between finger and thumb, feel their fragile, encrusted thinness, and let them out through the open windows where they zip away as if woken from a dream. I might have swatted them previously, but the birdhouse has had its effect. I look at them slowly crawling along the window frames and think of Uncle Toby in *Tristram Shandy*, a man with such a 'peaceful, placid nature, – no jarring element in it' that he scarcely had 'a heart to retaliate upon a fly'.

Go – says he, one day at dinner, to an over-grown one which had buzz'd about his nose, and tormented him cruelly all dinner-time, – and which, after infinite attempts, he had caught at last, as it flew by him; – I'll not hurt thee, says my uncle *Toby*, rising from his chair, and going a-cross the room, with the fly in his hand, – I'll not hurt a hair of thy head: – Go, says he, lifting up the sash, and opening his hand as he spoke, to let it escape; – go poor devil, get thee gone, why should I hurt thee? – This world surely is wide enough to hold both thee and me.

Tristram Shandy, his nephew telling the tale, never forgot 'the lesson of universal good-will then taught and imprinted' on his ten-year-old mind.

Hornets are in one of the nest boxes. They are making the waved cake-layers of their nest, a wood meringue, its fabric chewed and spat into a joint nursery. But it is too hot for them and one of them stands in the round wooden entrance to the bird box and burrs its wings like a fan wafting the cooler air in towards the nest, clicking on and off as if it were the thermostat in the corner. The sundae nest curves and grows, enclosing the cell body until it is the size of a small boxing glove, and I listen to the extraordinary instinctive understanding that instructs an appointed hornet to cool the surroundings in which its relatives are trying to breed.

There are minutes when the whole house vibrates with the hornet's hum. An occasional gust interrupts it, like a modest and welcome visitor blowing through from the window to the south, past me for a moment, touching the sweat on my neck and back, then out to the north and gone. The oaks remain unstirred. The acorns have lengthened and browned at the nipple. We are all left in the absolute quiet of a midsummer wood. Its life is folded in on itself. The culmination of all its vitality is a lack of it. The birdhouse sits inert in a stadium out of season, with no match in prospect and little maintenance being done. Territory for a moment means nothing, partnership nothing, parenthood nothing, childhood nothing. It is midsummer and the year is over. The nests in the bird boxes are dusty remnants. Nothing sings.

I sit in there and think of the different ways this birdhouse has given me of being with birds. There is, first of all, what the twentieth-century evolutionist Julian Huxley called the reward of 'new insights into the lives of familiar birds, new glimpses of their beauties and capabilities'.

The moment that came to Huxley's mind was one April morning in Surrey. He was standing on an old stone bridge over the River Wey.

> I saw an unaccustomed number of little birds in the bushes. Exploration revealed that these were warblers of many different kinds, and that the banks and bushes for a couple of hundred yards were crowded with them, feeding or talking softly to each other between whiles. They were a band of migrants, working their way up the guiding highway provided by the river, their subdued manner telling of the fatigues of their previous journey. They brought home the realities of migration more forcibly than could have a band of swallows in flight; the contrast between their quiet, tired little company in the English landscape and the thought of the thousands of miles they had come was overwhelming.

The fragility and humanity of those sentences, their open conversation between observation and implication, their soft-edged anthropomorphism and the sense of a shared destiny between bird and man came from no sentimentalist. Julian Huxley was a serious scientist, convinced of the essential purposelessness of evolution, one of the founders of the British Trust for Ornithology and later of the World Wildlife Fund, a man for whom an emotional response to nature was part of an analytical understanding of it.

To Laurence Sterne's Uncle Toby and Julian Huxley's benign, courteous absorbency of the bird world, add a third figure for this roster of senior staff in the Bird School: the Reverend Gilbert White, not the public and famous author of *The Natural History and Antiquities of Selborne*, in which he performed a series of curated letters (never actually sent) to an audience of gentlemanly friends, but an earlier phase,

Julian Huxley in 1922

less polished, more immediate, revealed in the 77,000 entries that make up the journals he kept between 1751 and 1783.

One after another, the pattern of White's years in his Hampshire parish are transmitted to his record as a necklace of bright instances. On a cold January day in 1768:

> It freezes under people's beds. Meat freezes so hard it can't be spitted. Several of the thrush-kind are frozen to death.

As the thaw comes on:

> Moles work. Cocks crow. Crows crie. Birds pull moss from the trees. Titmice [the old name for the birds we know as tits] pull straws from the eaves.

His world is full of news from the hedges and woods, straightforwardly seen or heard and plainly reported.

> The Rook assembles on the nest-trees
> The missel-thrush sings
> The Colemouse & the long-tailed titmouse chirp.
> The Hen-rook sits, the cock feeds her. Gold-finch whistles
> The titlark [a pipit] first sings. It is a delicate songster; flying from tree to tree, & spreading out it's wings it chants in it's descent. It also sings on trees, & on the ground walking in pasture fields.

There is no gradation. Each phenomenon arrives unfiltered and uninflected on the page, not as science, nor as a research programme destined for science but as the trace left by a listening and annotating mind. White himself seems scarcely to be involved but is somehow irrepressibly present.

> Columbines, & Monkshood blow.
> Lapwings on the down.
> Began to tack the vine-shoots.
> Men bring-up peat from the forest. The sycamores, & maples in bloom scent the air with a honeyed smell. Lily of the valley blows.

Above all, in the pages of the journal, the beings around him are alive:

> Nuthatch makes it[s] jarring, clattering noise in the woods
> Nuthatch chatters. It chatters as it flies.
> The grasshopper-lark chirps concealed at the bottoms of Hedges
> … it haunts the tops of tall trees, making a shivering noise.

The gizzard of a red-backed shrike is full of the legs and parts of
   beetles.
The capsule of The twayblade bursts at a touch, & scatters the
   dust-like seeds on all sides.
The white owl has young. It brings a mouse to its nest about
   every five minutes, beginning at sunset.

White's plunging perceptions of the natural world are birdlike in their
immediacy: a jab, a pounce, a sharp turn, a long look, the head held
sideways for a moment like a listening thrush, a worm retrieved.

Bucks grunt. Hedge-hogs cease to dig the walks. Wood-cocks in
   the high wood.
Vast swagging rock-like clouds appear'd at a distance.
A Martin seen: it was very brisk and lively.
Green woodpecker begins to laugh.
Cock-turkey struts, & makes love.
Golden-crowned wren [the goldcrest] sings. His voice is as
   minute as his body.
Goose sits, while the gander with vast assiduity keeps guard, &
   takes the fiercest sow by the ear & leads her away crying.

White conquers no mountains and fords no torrents. The word 'I'
scarcely appears in the journal, but when he does arrive on the page, it
is with the warmth and empathetic amusement that seem to be usual
among people who love birds.
   One April:

Green wood-pecker laughs at all the world.

And in May:

Black-cap sings sweetly, but rather inwardly: it is a songster of
    the first-rate. It's notes are deep & sweet.
Sheared my mongrel dog Rover, & made use of his white hair in
    plaster for ceilings. His coat weighed four ounces. The N:E:
    wind makes Rover shrink.

In June:

    The house-martins, which build in old nests begin to hatch, as
        may be seen by their throwing out the egg-shells.

In July:

    Swifts dash & frolick about, & seem to be teaching their young
        the use of their wings

He is not without anxieties and often wakes at night, but even then the
attention does not flag.

    Bees begin gathering at three o'clock in the morning: swallows
        are stirring at half hour after two
    The woodlark sings in the air at three in the morning.
    Stone-curlews pass over the village that hour.

For decade after decade he remains present in his world.

    Sweet harvest weather. Sweet moon-light.
    Golden-crowned wrens [goldcrests], & [tree]creepers bring-out
        their broods.
    The vipers are big with young.
    Bees eat the raspberries.
    The air is full of flying ants & the hirundines live luxuriously.

Gilbert White's Selborne might be seen as a theatre for nostalgia, the pastoral picture of a charming, unmarried, slender, eighteenth-century clergyman (he was light-limbed, five feet three inches tall, ever active) at home in a yet-to-be-damaged nature, but the value of his journal is more current than that: the beauty of attentiveness, as much bodily as intellectual. White hears, sees, smells, tastes and touches his world. He is interested in understanding the life around him, in untangling the mysteries of migrating birds, in distinguishing one warbler from another and the chiffchaff from them all, not as problems or biological categories but as the conundrums of feathered lives that persist and pullulate alongside him.

As he describes a chiffchaff in April 1793, you know that he is hearing it as he writes:

> The small willow-wren, or chif-chaf, is heard in the short Lythe
> [a plantation near his house]. This is the earliest summer bird, &
> is heard usually about the 20th of March. Tho' one of the
> smallest of our birds, yet it's two notes are very loud, & piercing,
> so as to occasion an echo in hanging woods. It loves to frequent
> tall beeches.

White loved the chiffchaff as much as the chiffchaff loved the beeches and his journals are an enormous, sustained act of love. They are almost shapeless, both in daily detail and in their bulk, but that is their virtue. As the critic and writer Rhian Williams has said, 'by committing to a *project* rather than a *structure*', White avoided abstract definition and instead created 'a breathing space … a medium in which we are immersed, rather than a category to be analysed'.

A simple, curious openness is the key, combined with an attention to the real, a rich ability to allow free rein to the lives of others and an indifference, as Virginia Woolf said of him, to public opinion, so that without embarrassment he could 'bawl through a speaking trumpet at his bees' and indulge his fondness for his lonely pet bachelor tortoise Timothy whom he used to watch in the first days of June each year carefully making his way along the garden paths at Selborne, teetering on tip-toe, sadly and hopelessly – or so Woolf thought – in search of love.

One last member of staff, perhaps the most unlikely: St Francis of Assisi. Sarah and I went to find the place one day late in the summer where the young saint, barefoot, in a rough habit held at his waist with only a rope, preached his famous sermon to the birds. It was out in the agricultural flatlands to the south of Assisi, at Pian d'Arca on the road between Cannara and Bevagna. Someone put a shrine up on the spot in the 1930s, where it stands now on the edge of the fields opposite a petrol station, shaded by a big oak and two ilexes. Sweeps of gold-finches were crying and squeaking in the trees and from time to time a long-tailed tit joined them as the cars gathered speed again and again away down the road to Bevagna.

Francis, then in his twenties or early thirties, had lived a luxury youth, the son of a rich cloth merchant, who had fought as a knight in the wars between Italian cities, before turning one day, as the medieval practice had long been for those who were gripped by a vision of the metaphysical, to a life of caves and huts, telling his friends that the only girl he would marry would be Lady Poverty. But like many hermits his charisma was undeniable and he soon gathered around him a band of followers. The authority of godliness came naturally to him and in the tradition of many such medieval holy men, if he heard birds calling as he was about to start on a sermon, he would order them to be silent as he preached, and to remain silent until he had finished. He was doing no more than voicing the traditional authority and dominion of west-ern Christianity over the natural world.

But the sermon of the birds marks something new. That morning, he had preached in a small town 'with such fervour that the inhabitants wished to follow him out of devotion; but St Francis would not allow them, saying: "Be not in such haste, and leave not your homes. I will tell you what you must do to save your souls."'

He left them 'much consoled' and walked out into the country, 'letting himself be guided by the Spirit of God, without considering the road he took':

> And as he went on his way, with great fervour, St Francis lifted up his eyes, and saw on some trees by the wayside a great multitude of birds; and being much surprised, he said to his companions, 'Wait for me here by the way, whilst I go and preach to my little sisters the birds'; and entering into the field, he began to preach to the birds which were on the ground, and suddenly all those also on the trees came round him, and all listened while St Francis preached to them, and did not fly away until he had given them his blessing. And Brother Masseo related afterwards to Brother James of Massa how St Francis went among them and even touched them with his garments, and how none of them moved.

The tone is suddenly different. The saint is not instructing the birds to submit but finding reciprocity in them and experiencing them as a willing audience around him.

> Now the substance of the sermon was this: 'My little sisters the birds, you owe much to God, your Creator, and you ought to sing his praise at all times and in all places, because he has given you liberty to fly about into all places; and though you neither spin nor sew, he has given you a twofold and a threefold clothing for yourselves and for your offspring. Two of all your species he sent into the Ark with Noah that you might not be lost to the world; besides which, he feeds you, though you neither sow nor reap. He has given you fountains and rivers to

quench your thirst, mountains and valleys in which to take
refuge, and trees in which to build your nests; so that your
Creator loves you much, having thus favoured you with such
bounties.'

No one had spoken to birds in this way before, or treated them as a
congregation worthy of what he had to say. As the environmental
historian Roger Sorrell has written, 'It is a sign of the birds' prestige
and position' – as St Francis sees it, and by implication in the mind of
God – 'that they are taken care of without working. They have their
own niche, "a home in the purity of the air."'
For the first time a vision of apostolic harmony was allowed to
spread across the species barrier. The birds, according to the thir-
teenth-century account, took Francis for what he was and responded
in an equally epoch-making way.

All the birds began to open their beaks, to stretch their necks, to
spread their wings and reverently to bow their heads to the
ground, endeavouring by their motions and by their songs to
manifest their joy to St Francis. And the saint rejoiced with
them. He wondered to see such a multitude of birds, and was
charmed with their beautiful variety, with their attention and
familiarity, for all which he devoutly gave thanks to the Creator.

Sarah and I walked out from the little shrine beside the road, where
Francis had left his companions, down the pale dusty track through the
heavy ploughlands towards the fields where he had preached. Beehives,
cattle sheds, the tall silhouettes of some poplars, the blue-grey heat on
the hills to the east, vineyards on the slopes and olives among the
villages to the south.
Rich orange-yellow butterflies, Gatekeepers, were flirting through
the scabious and chicory in the ditches. A flight of swallows came over

Giotto's depiction of the Sermon to the Birds by the
east door in the Upper Basilica in Assisi

us, skirling in the blue, their wings tick-pause-ticking in flight, like a telex machine, the wire with the news coming through.

The next morning, as early as we could, before anyone was about except the priests and monks up for the sunrise service of Prime, we crept into the Upper Basilica in Assisi to find Giotto's famous depiction of this moment. The frescoed panel is high on the wall by the east door, the early sunlight streaming in through the opening beside it. A calm wash of grey and blue is settled over the picture. Giotto has painted an expanse of air. This is not a moment of crisis. The saint is out in the flat farmland, a couple of broccoli-like trees beside him. He is portrayed as a man of strength and substance. His left hand is open and welcoming, the right instructing or urging the birds to be with him. They are gathered on the ground and a few come down from the tree to join them. Francis's brother, perhaps Masseo, is with him, his sandal and toes just breaking through the edge of the picture. The surprise, even alarm, on the brother's face throws into relief the step Francis has made into settledness and ease. For the saint, it is an undramatised encounter, almost a private event that overbrims with gentleness and confidence. In the vast, empty medieval church, lit by those marble reflections of the morning light, Giotto's picture felt like a pool of grace.

The birds are in outline, semi-present, attentive, some with their heads raised to meet Francis, the blue wash over the top of them half-concealing their bodies after they were first drawn. He bends towards them as they look to his words. Even the trees on each side seem to incline towards the saint.

But the colours have faded. These monochrome and scarcely identifiable creatures are surely not what Francis met or Giotto intended. In their fadingness they are half-spiritualised, when the story's essence is the birds' physical and real presence, brilliantly feathered, with an unreduced standing in the world.

There is another version of this painting, also by Giotto, once in Pisa, stolen by Napoleon's troops and now in the Louvre. It was painted a few years after the Assisi frescoes and in a more durable medium: tempera and gold on a wood panel. Here you can still see the birds in the radiant reality Giotto intended. They stand in their Ark-ready pairs: identifiable goldfinches, chaffinches, greenfinches, blackbirds, magpies, rails, geese, red-legged choughs, swallows, pigeons, a cockerel, a mallard and what may be a woodlark coming down from the tree, some of their beaks open and all their bodies attendant, listening to the saint as he tells them of their blessedness. It is a painting of a miracle. Nothing is naturalistic. St Francis stands over the birds like another Noah, inviting them into the Ark he wants to share with them.

The culture frame for these four figures – St Francis, Gilbert White, Julian Huxley, Uncle Toby – at least within the western tradition, could scarcely be more different. Medieval mystic Christianity, eighteenth-

century proto-science, a part-Darwinian, part-Mendelian understanding of genetic inheritance, the Enlightenment cult of sensibility: these
are distinct branches of our culture, but whether it is godliness, curiosity, amusement or a sense of wonder that forms the frame for these
people's attitude to birds (or flies), the root instinct is the same: to
recognise, when seen in a perspective longer and larger than our own
clamorous demands, their equivalence to us, that we share a world.

To love and be close to the birds is neither new nor old. The
ninth-century BC prophet Elijah, near-contemporary of Homer, was
fed by ravens. As the medieval historian Robert Bartlett has described,
one of the first accounts of a Christian saint being sustained by wild
creatures describes a raven bringing food to St Paul the Hermit.
'Usually it brought half a loaf every day, but, on the occasion when St
Antony visited Paul, it knew to bring a whole loaf.' To St Baldomarus,
an early medieval saint in Lyon, the birds used to come for breakfast,
lunch and dinner at pre-arranged mealtimes. St Matilda, wife of Henry
I of Germany, told her staff to scatter breadcrumbs under the trees, so
that the birds 'might find alms there, in the name of the Creator'.
Bishop Ansfried of Utrecht who died in 1010 went one better and 'had
sheaves [of wheat] placed in the trees to feed the little birds in winter'.

Francis followed in their wake. 'If I speak to the emperor in the
future,' he once said, in a remark that throws some light on his nuanced
relationship to power and worldly authority,

> I will beg that a general law be passed, that everyone who is able
> should scatter grain and seed on the streets, so that on such a
> solemn feast-day there should be plenty for the birds, especially
> our sister larks.

Ernest Renan, the pioneering nineteenth-century historian and the
first to advocate seeing the past on its own terms, wrote a paean to
Francis that should be put up over the door of every birdhouse and

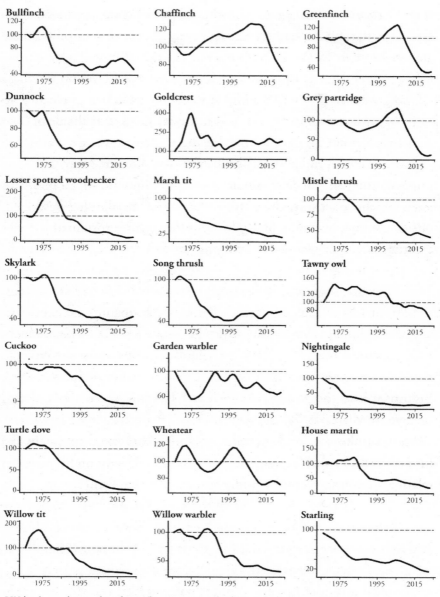

UK bird population abundance (long-term trend 1960s–). Index base = 100.

British Trust for Ornithology graphs of the collapse of English birds

hide. 'The great sign by which one recognises souls preserved from typical narrowness – namely the love and understanding of animals,' Renan wrote in 1884,

> was greater in [Francis] than in any other human being. He recognised only one form of life; he saw degrees in the scale of beings but not sharp divisions. He did not acknowledge, any more than did India, the classification that puts the human person on one side and, on the other, the thousand forms of life of which we see only the outside, where the inattentive eye sees only uniformity and which perhaps hides different infinities. Francis himself heard only one voice in nature.

I can't imagine more inspiring words than those but we live in a different world and a changed nature. The expectations of wholeness that drove these ancient figures can no longer apply and for one reason: the expansion and impact of human civilisation. The nature encountered in this book does not resemble the one known to St Francis, Gilbert White or even the young Julian Huxley but has in part been deeply changed and in part is residual, what is left over after what we have done to it. The large and overarching story of English birds in the last century is mournful.

These graphs, generated by the British Trust for Ornithology, show the fate since the 1960s of many of the birds I might have expected to find in the woods and their surrounding fields. They tell of catastrophic and in many cases relentless decline, some with an initial fillip followed by a crash, some steeper, others shallower, some maintaining themselves until a sudden collapse, others plunging for oblivion from the start. Collectively, the graphs portray the ending of a multiple form of life, driven by an indifference to everything Huxley, Uncle Toby, Gilbert White and St Francis treasured. It is the indifference that led me finally to build a birdhouse and to write this book – the landscape of a general carelessness and ignorance, made knowable, ironically, only through the years of close attention and record-keeping by those who knew something was wrong.

The roll-call of these birds' names reads like a list of regiments decimated in battle:

Bullfinch – 50 per cent lost
Chaffinch – 25 per cent lost
Greenfinch – 70 per cent lost
Dunnock – 40 per cent lost
Goldcrest – 50 per cent lost since 1975
Partridge – 90 per cent lost
Lesser Spotted Woodpecker – 90 per cent lost
Marsh Tit – 80 per cent lost
Mistle Thrush – 70 per cent lost
Skylark – 60 per cent lost
Song Thrush – 40 per cent lost
Tawny Owl – 50 per cent lost since 1970
Cuckoo – 80 per cent lost
Garden Warbler – 40 per cent lost
Nightingale – 50 per cent lost
Turtle Dove – 90 per cent lost
Wheatear – 40 per cent lost since 1995
Whitethroat – 75 per cent lost
Willow Tit – 90 per cent lost
Willow Warbler – 75 per cent lost
Wood Warbler – 75 per cent lost
House Sparrow – 75 per cent lost
House Martin – 80 per cent lost
Swallow – 50 per cent lost

I can imagine them carved into the stones of the village memorial next to the church in Burwash, laid out beside the mossed-up names of the village men killed in the wars.

Nevertheless, there are complexities to the picture. The populations of a few birds have remained more or less steady in the last sixty years, some with gentle upward trends, others coming and going:

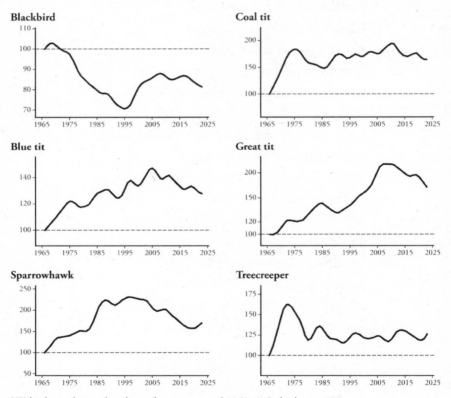

UK bird population abundance (long-term trend 1960s–). Index base = 100.

Birds whose numbers have remained almost steady

And some have grown more or less sharply in numbers:

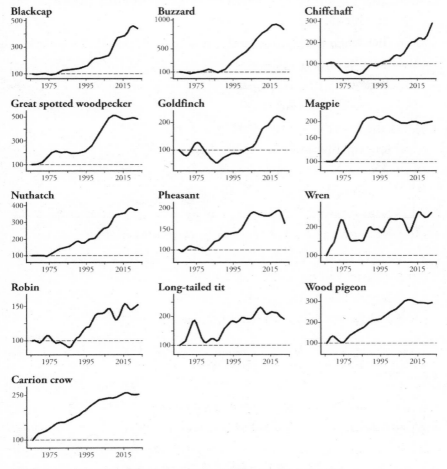

UK bird population abundance (long-term trend 1960s–). Index base = 100.

Birds whose numbers have risen

What dictates the different destinies? What is behind the general catastrophe? The woods should be teeming with life. I think of the medieval greenwood that surrounded John and Richard Ringmer when they first came to the Swetyngcroft here in the years after Agincourt. These little creased valleys would have been filled with deer and bird-

song then. 'In summer when the shaws are bright', one of the ballads
contemporary with their arrival in the fifteenth century begins:

> In somer when the shawes be sheyn
> And leves be large and long
> Hit is full mery in feyre foreste
> To here the foulys song
> To se the deer draw to the dale
> And leve the hilles hee
> And shadow hem in the leves grene
> Undur the grene wood tre.

As the deer seek the cool of that shady green midsummer wood,

> Itt is merry, walking in the fayre forrest,
> To hear the small birds singe.
> The woodweele sang, and wold not cease,
> Amongst the leaves a lyne.

The 'leaves a lyne' describes a midsummer tree with a full head of foliage
and the 'woodweele' may be a golden oriole, hidden up in there, cease-
lessly singing as a presence that has long haunted the English imagination.
The oriole was probably common enough in the warm years of the thir-
teenth century, singing each summer its exotic, echoing song. But it was
probably only ever at the northern limit of its range in southern England.
By the time a hundred years later when that rhyme was being sung and
this farm was first occupied, the weather had worsened. Its presence
might already have been shrinking away, perhaps even then coming to
represent a remembered state of perfection. It was not Proust who was
the first to think that *Les vrais paradis sont les paradis qu'on a perdus*.

I long to find the oriole here again. I heard it once in southern
Champagne, in a wood east of Troyes. Its name means 'the golden

golden' and on that sunlit morning it had sounded hypnotic, almost tropical, echoing through phrases that seemed to grow and extend even as it sang them, as if a flute had been fitted with the slide of a trombone. It was the song, as Olivier Messiaen (for whom this was a favourite bird) wrote, of

> a royal prince, very colourful, full of laughter. The song reflects the sun of Africa as well as the supernatural influence of another world. Whistling, gliding – always gliding – the timbre is strange: golden, laden with harmonics (all the sounds are complex), brilliant, triumphant, luminous and shimmering.

I could not see the oriole through the packed trunks of the beech trees that morning but I listened to it in the green-leaved sunlight as if caught in a spell.

But it is not here. Apart from a few wanderers that come to England and Ireland each year, it can now be heard only further south in Europe. In 2021, it was finally removed from the list of English breeding natives. There is just one small paradoxical hope amid all the damage being done by the changing climate: with the rising temperatures, hot summers are moving north at about two miles a year, a slow tide of warmth from which many English breeding birds are already benefiting. It may be that *Oriolus oriolus oriolus*, the golden golden golden, will one day be coming up with it.

Although some birds have colonised Britain recently from the south – the firecrest, the collared dove and Cetti's warbler among them – the long story is of birds that are either deeply diminished or no longer here. Throughout the nineteenth century, under the pressure of what the twentieth-century chronicler of Sussex birds John Walpole-Bond called 'pheasant-worship', the attack on birds turned relentless. Sussex peregrines and kestrels were both driven to the coastal cliffs through 'constant persecution by gunners of every description'. 'Forky-tailed kites' had been the commonest predators in the late eighteenth century, taking many young ducks and chickens, but a hundred years later were almost entirely gone. Choughs and buzzards had both been locally exterminated by 1830. Tawny owls were much reduced ('victims of insensate persecution') and barn owls regularly shot as they were 'much sought for making fire screens'. The ravens had taken refuge in the sea cliffs but even there they were shot out by 1895. So pervasive was their poisoning that by the 1930s Walpole-Bond thought that 'inland in Sussex the Raven as a nester now stands no chance whatsoever'.

By the end of the nineteenth century the crow in Sussex 'from its persecution by the gamekeeper … bids fair to become altogether extinct'. Large numbers of magpies were caught in steel traps baited with hens' eggs and by the 1880s 'from constant persecution has now betaken itself chiefly to the thorn trees in the deep valleys of the Downs'. Until the First World War, magpies were 'comparatively scarce', killed on estate after estate.

Only when Kitchener's recruiting drive drew thousands of young men away from gamekeeping to the western front did the magpies make the beginnings of a recovery from which they are still benefiting.

Cuckoos became rare as keepers shot them, mistaking them for hawks. The wheatears that had been hunted in their thousands were by the 1880s no longer worth the trouble. Goldfinches, prized as cage birds, were taken near Worthing for the London market, an astonishing 13,848 dozen in 1860, still more at Brighton. By 1890, 'not a hundred may now be seen'. At least until 1900, skylarks and greenfinches were still in their tens of thousands. In January 1897, a thousand dozen skylarks were netted above Brighton, along with '8 or 10 dozen linnets, ditto greenfinches, and 2 or 3 dozen lesser redpolls'.

A steady traffic in Sky-Larks and Song-Thrushes was carried on between Brighton and Paris throughout every winter … From twelve to twenty hampers, all choked with victims – each basket averaging about 14 lbs of them – were sent across the Channel daily.

Tens of thousands of birds were taken for the millinery trade to decorate women's hats. It is a picture of mass destruction but also of mass presence. You can read of a scene recorded in the spring of 1872 only as if it came from another world: the beach at Brighton that April was so covered in nightingales newly arrived from Africa that they found shelter under the wheels of the bathing machines along 'the whole length of the shore'.

Birds have lived under our shadow for thousands of generations. In the nineteenth and early twentieth century, one bird after another was driven into local or national extinction: ospreys, harriers, eagles, bitterns, bustards and grebes were all devastated. The late twentieth century was, for different reasons, just as destructive. We may hold our heads in our hands at the cruelties of the past, but they have been equalled by what has been done to bird populations in my lifetime.

First, intensive agriculture. In the spring of 1999, Christopher Mason from the University of Essex wanted to find out how blackbirds, song thrushes and mistle thrushes were doing in a part of Essex near the port of Harwich. Most of his study area was intensively and chemically farmed for arable crops, with a heavy use of fertilisers and pesticides; the majority of hedges had been removed and those that survived were in thin and poor shape. Towns, villages and industrial areas also formed part of the survey district, as did woodland. Mason walked all the paths, lanes and field boundaries in his 6,500-acre patch over two and a half months, from the middle of March to the end of May, listening and watching in the early mornings and early evenings. If a bird was singing or carrying nest material or food for nestlings or mates, he marked it on his large-scale maps, finding nearly a thousand territories for his three birds, most of them blackbirds, eighty-five of them song thrushes and only a few mistle thrushes.

The shocking aspect of his survey was not the number of birds but where they were. While farmland made up two-thirds of the study area, only 36 out of 826 blackbird territories were found there, and even those were on small patches of grass and set-aside in the arable desert. As for song thrushes, Dr Mason could not find a single one in the 4,300 acres of Essex farmland he surveyed. Even the mistle thrushes preferred the towns and brownfield sites to the modern denuded and poisoned agricultural acres.

'Farmland in the study area,' he concluded, 'although occupying the greatest proportion of land, is no longer a suitable habitat for these three thrush species.' In contrast, the lawns and shrubberies of the towns and villages were a refuge, providing ideal feeding conditions and nesting sites. That was where these singing birds felt at home. The blackbirds and thrushes, alongside starlings, dunnocks and house sparrows, all in savage decline on the brutalised farms, were feeding and breeding happily enough in the gardens of Harwich and its surrounding villages. They liked nothing better than one new development of executive housing, 'with open-plan front lawns and shrubberies', which had more than seven times the number of blackbirds that Mason could find in the gardens of Victorian terraced houses. The blackbird density in those executive gardens reached 386 per square kilometre; in the arable fields beyond them, the equivalent figure was one blackbird territory per square kilometre, one blackbird in every 250 acres. And not a single song thrush.

It will benefit the birds (and the nature on which they depend) to build low-density housing estates, or even industrial estates with plenty of green space, on intensively farmed land. Jamie Tratalos, now at University College, Dublin, has measured birds' preferences over a wide range of sites in Britain. In places with no houses at all, you will be likely to find about eight species of bird and 250 individuals in every square kilometre. But where houses are built and gardens made, that number goes up, peaking in conditions of about six hundred households per square kilometre, equating to a leafy suburbia, in which you will find on average twenty-one species of bird and about 1,100 individuals in each square kilometre. Above that human density, the number of bird species (and so the biodiversity) goes down, even if the numbers of individuals continue to rise. Unfortunately, present planning guidelines, which are keen to minimise the amount of land taken for new development, suggest very dense housing patterns of between three thousand and five thousand households in every square kilometre, far too high for the kind of distribution of building and garden that will encourage birdlife. The outcome is that government rules favour sterilised fields over enriched gardens. The requirement for builders now is to make a 10 per cent 'biodiversity net gain' on any project. But if the pre-existing conditions are next to zero, what good is 10 per cent of zero?

The conclusion that Tratalos and his fellow authors come to is unequivocal:

> In the United Kingdom at least, our results suggest that building
> new developments at intermediate housing densities over a
> larger area of land will result in higher overall avian abundance
> than building housing at the very high densities suggested by
> current guidelines.

In the last twenty years of the twentieth century ten million breeding individuals of ten species of farmland birds disappeared from the British countryside. It is a figure that makes those few thousands of wheatears and skylarks shipped to Parisian restaurants look paltry. This was not the poisoning of nature with DDT and other organochlorine insecticides that had fuelled the green revolution and which had summoned *Silent Spring* from Rachel Carson in 1963. It was the next generation of intensification in farming that did the damage, removing hedges, increasing the use of more targeted pesticides, draining most of the remaining wetlands, massively fertilising the soil, re-seeding and 'improving' pastures, making silage rather than hay, sowing the new year's crops in autumn rather than in spring so that the winter supply of fallen seeds in the old stubbles disappeared, all of which drove deep body blows into the traditional ecologies of farmland and its surrounding woods. This was the second Silent Spring, the dismantling of life webs on which the birds relied.

It has happened in North America, where 29 per cent of breeding birds have disappeared since 1970, a net loss of 2.9 billion individuals. In Europe, over roughly the same time there has been a drop of nearly a fifth in the overall numbers, a loss of about six hundred million birds from a total of about 3.2 billion in 1980.

Even though all biomes and lifestyles are implicated – in America even introduced, non-native birds have been in decline – much of this collapse has taken place in farmland where modern techniques have been focused on food production and nature exclusion. Seed eaters such as grey partridges, bullfinches and turtle doves (in summer) and yellowhammers (in winter) found little to sustain them after the weed-killers had been through. Thrushes, starlings and wheatears dependent on invertebrate-rich grasslands found nothing in an earth that had been stripped of otherwise unproductive life. Modern farming was designed to maximise the human take and minimise anything from which other non-human inhabitants could benefit. As the Cambridge biologists C.S. Dolton and M. de L. Brooke have put it:

> Modern arable agriculture captures energy at the lowest possible trophic level, in crops such as wheat, and uses pesticides and efficient harvesting methods to prevent the passage of energy to higher trophic levels, for instance to insects and thence to birds.

In the late winter of 2023, I bought a bag of seed from a large agricul-tural supplier, having asked for grains that I could scatter in the clearings of the wood during the so-called 'hungry gap', the months at the end of winter when the previous year's seeds are exhausted and the spring has yet to produce any more. The bag came with a label printed on it:

CHEMICAL HAZARD WARNING
THIS SEED MAY HAVE BEEN TREATED WITH A CHEMICAL
SEED TREATMENT

1. Treated seed can be toxic, harmful or an irritant. Do not inhale dust. It must not be used as food or feed.
2. When handling seed, wear butyl rubber or PVC gloves and an approved respirator. Avoid handling treated seed with bare hands.
3. Wash hands and exposed skin before meals, after work and after dealing with seed spillages.
4. In the case of seed spillage, clean up as much as possible into the related seed sack and reuse clean seed. Bury the remainder completely. Treated seed can be hazardous to children, game, wildlife and other animals.
5. Empty treated seed sacks are hazardous … Treated bags must never be used for any other purpose.
6. In case of contamination flush the affected area or body with plenty of water. If you feel unwell seek medical advice and inform your doctor of the seed treatment used. Take the seed bag label with you.

It so happened that my seed had not been given the toxic treatment and could be used to feed wild birds, but the seed merchants use only one kind of bag for all kinds of seeds. This was their usual product.

Modern agriculturalists do not usually admit that poisons are essential to the nature of their trade but you only have to read that warning to recognise the terrifying nature of what has been and is being done.

In the woods, more subtle dynamics are at work. Less than an eighth of England is covered in woods but even so, 40 per cent of all bird species use them to feed or breed. They are a reservoir for birdlife, yet in the modern era different birds have fared differently. Those that depend exclusively on woods – the lesser spotted woodpecker, lesser redpoll, spotted flycatcher and willow tit, above all – have crashed in numbers by at least 50 per cent since 1970, some by far more. Most of the birds that use both woods and fields have maintained their populations, but even among those so-called generalists, some such as the tawny owls, bullfinches, dunnocks and song thrushes have suffered, while others – the blackcaps, nuthatches and the great spotted woodpecker, all thriving in mature woods with large trees – have boomed.

It is not clear what explains these differences. Bullfinches have lost many wide old hedges with their understoreys full of invertebrates and weed seeds. The bullfinches here like to sit on low branches in a hedge and jump down to eat the grass and sorrel seeds in the field beside them. The wood and willow warblers and other African migrants may have suffered in their wintering grounds, or on the journey there and back. Cuckoos taking a western route south seem to be dying on the way to Africa in a drought-afflicted Spain. Those that go via Italy are doing better. Other woodland birds may be finding it hard due to a lack of coppicing in old woods, meaning there is less rough and brambly cover for them in the new tall-tree openness, making for a habitat rife with foxes, and where the lack of cover is exacerbated by too many deer browsing out the understorey. Nightingales, willow tits, the warblers and dunnocks that like to hide in dense low leafy places may all be suffering from more open woods. It is the modern combination: over-managed fields and under-managed or abandoned woods have delivered a double blow.

The biologists find it difficult to be certain of the effects of climate change. It is so overarching and all-pervasive a factor. Certainly it has dried out summer soils, which makes life difficult for birds trying to penetrate them. Warmer winters have made life easier for small birds staying in England, but the effects are ambivalent. Blackcaps and chiff-chaffs are now either spending the winter here, travelling only to the south of Spain and Morocco or arriving from Africa eighteen days earlier each spring.

Meanwhile, the natural responsiveness in birds to annual shifts in the weather seems to enable them to cope with longer-term changes in climate. Great tits, marsh tits and blue tits can all control the date at which their chicks hatch by deciding when to begin incubating the eggs they have already laid. If the spring feels cold, and the emergence of the prey caterpillars will be held up, the birds can wait before starting to incubate their eggs and so synchronise hatching dates with peak food supplies. If the spring is warm (as it now generally is) the tits will begin to lay earlier than before but will still wait to start incubation until a large clutch is laid, all of which will hatch when the caterpillars emerge.

In very broad terms, farmland birds have declined more than wood-land birds. The migrants that fly to and from the African tropics have declined more than the birds that spend the winter in England. Birds that eat insects (which have also suffered a catastrophic decline) have done worse than those that eat seeds. And birds that nest in trees or bushes have done better than those that nest on the ground, largely because of the ever-growing number of cats, foxes and crows.

The overall picture remains dire and the number of species described as threatened on the BTO's Red List has doubled from thirty-six in 1996 to seventy in 2021.

At the same time, some birds have thrived. There are now ten times as many buzzards as there were in the 1960s, rebounding from decades of shooting and poisoning. It is now the commonest English raptor. Ravens are booming, as are magpies and crows (with all the implications that carries for their impact on songbirds). The commonest bird in England now is the pheasant, which, once modern farming had destroyed the grey partridge, entered its boom years in the 1970s and 1980s when shooters realised they needed something to shoot. Excluding seabirds, the biomass of all birds in Great Britain fell from over 13,600 tons in 1968 to 9,600 tons in 1988, a drop of nearly a third. At the same time, the weight of all the pheasants in England – an odd image comes to mind of a large serge-suited diner tucking into his pheasant dinner – grew by 2,500 tons.

Nowadays, every year somewhere between thirty-nine million and fifty-seven million pheasants are released into the woods of the United Kingdom, with 7/8ths of them in England, plus eight to thirteen million red-legged partridges (to replace the grey partridge that agriculture has destroyed). Half arrive in the country from Europe as eggs or chicks and no one counts them precisely but about 40 per cent of the released birds, more than twenty-eight million each year, are shot, using between 2,500 and 6,700 tonnes of lead pellets, which are poisonous and kill up to a hundred thousand waterfowl annually. The other pheasants and partridges are run over or otherwise die to feed the crows and foxes. Half of the entire mass of wild English birds by weight consists of these industrially raised creatures.

There is something else in the life of wild birds for which two-thirds of us are responsible: the food we give them and the nest boxes we provide. In this country every year we put out 150,000 tons of bird food, £250 million-worth, enough to feed the entire population of birds that would think of coming to bird feeders three times over. There is now one bird feeder in England for every nine birds. We have at least 4.7 million nest boxes in private gardens, very nearly one for every pair of blue and great tits. We keep nine million cats which kill twenty-seven million of the birds that live in our gardens because of the food we have put out for them.

I have been as guilty as anyone of feeding and overfeeding a certain sort of bird and of providing nest boxes for them. In the trees outside the birdhouse I have strung up wires and pulleys to allow me at times to have five different feeders there, some filled with nyger seeds for the goldfinches, others sunflower hearts for the great, blue and marsh tits, for siskins and almost any bird that comes, some with fatballs in which indeterminate insects are embedded, for robins, nuthatches, woodpeckers and chaffinches, a table below for the dunnocks and blackbirds.

One hot summer afternoon, after the feeders were fully charged, I sat in the birdhouse for ninety minutes and counted the birds that came to them. Without colour-rings, I couldn't distinguish individuals but could register, one by one, the visits of the different species.

The little census I took revealed only what I knew but when I put the figures into a bar chart, they showed something more. Most of the birds outside the window were effectively invisible. Of the 476 visits in the ninety minutes, 312 were by blue tits, a further 64 by great tits and 52 by goldfinches. All the others (coal tit, robin, marsh tit, chaffinch and nuthatch) represented a mere 10 per cent of the total. It is a pattern that mirrors quite closely the dominance hierarchy among the birds. The shy nuthatches, chaffinches and marsh tits scarcely visit at all, or at

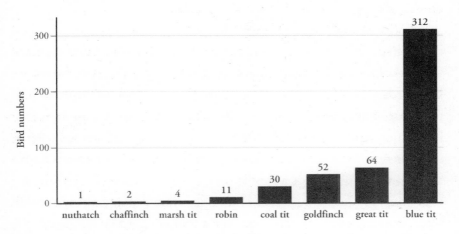

Birds visiting the birdhouse feeders over ninety minutes, August 2023

A marsh tit tries to get in to the feeder as young grey-headed
goldfinches and a siskin dominate it

least only when the dominant gangs of goldfinches and siskins are absent. Great spotted woodpeckers, which happened not to have come on this afternoon, are in fact a near constant.

All of these birds are strong and dominant in the wood. They are not threatened. Great spotted woodpeckers have tripled in numbers since we all started feeding them and have become hungry predators of the songbirds around them. Goldfinches, often arriving in intimidating mobs, are rampant with success. Blue tits and great tits are breeding more successfully than ever in provisioned woods and gardens. From midsummer on, the trees are full of scratchy tit fledglings peeping for their parents. And this is a problem.

A study by Jack Shutt and others has shown that half of all wild birds, wherever they were caught on a long transect across Scotland, had eaten from feeders, mostly peanuts. Blue tits were flying nearly a mile to get to them. And the effect was pervasive. Of twenty insect-eat-ing woodland birds the study looked at, those that were using feeders were steeply increasing in numbers; those not using feeders were in decline; birds that could hold their own against blue tits were increas-ing, those dominated by them were in decline; those that were competing for nest sites against blue tits were declining; if not, they were increasing. The evidence is accumulating that wild birds are living in an ever more man-shaped world.

I have seen or heard fifty-six different species of birds at the bird-house but feeding them like this favoritises and prioritises a very few while disadvantaging the others. Nightingales, willow tits, willow warblers, lesser spotted woodpeckers: all are precious and beautiful birds, but none of them comes to the feeders and all are in decline. The marsh tit, which is still quite strong in Sussex but failing in most of the country, is the only one of the declining birds that visits the feeders. But when it does so, it has to battle through crowds of more aggressive birds.

Can this be a coincidence? The science has not been done but as Jack Shutt and Alexander Lees at Manchester Metropolitan University have suggested, it looks as if feeding birds and providing (some) of them with nest boxes is wrenching this wood, or the whole country, into a different man-engendered shape. We are not attending to nature; we are re-sculpting it – again.

Goldfinch–siskin face-off at a feeder

Chaffinch and greenfinch: decimated by dirty feeders

It is well established that birds that have been artificially fed become more productive, with more and healthier chicks, are less likely to starve in hard times and have better immune systems. Those, like the blue tits, which have suffered in the past from harsh winters are now to some extent insulated against them. Nest boxes increase the size of populations – there is less competition for suitable breeding spaces – and help with raising chicks. And the whole process, inevitably, makes the people who are providing the food and shelter both more aware of bird lives and happier because of it.

But the philanthropy – or philaviary – carries dangers. The transmission of disease from dirty feeders has been catastrophic for greenfinches and chaffinches. From 2005 onwards, a parasite called *Trichomonas gallinae*, transferred from bird to bird at dirty feeders, swept through these finch populations, killing at least five million birds over ten years, first greenfinches of which two-thirds disappeared and then the chaffinches. The affliction, trichomonosis, is an ironic fate to be handed out at feeders: the parasite creates open wounds in the birds' throats, making it difficult for them to swallow. They soon regurgitate what they try to eat, starve and die.

Despite the drama of that, it is the more systematic threat that is most troubling. By feeding the birds, was I simplifying and homogenising a bird population that had already suffered more than it should? And if I was, which way should I turn?

13.

Perch Hill

RECULTURING

I am in a Cambridgeshire wood on a light and breezy October morning with Dr Richard Broughton. He is one of the world's leading experts on woodland birds, a busy senior scientist at the UK Centre for Ecology & Hydrology in Oxfordshire. I have been emailing him for weeks and he has been tireless in doling out help and tips. Now I have come to find him at his research station in Cambridgeshire, wanting to ask what any of us might do to redeem the birds. The answer, as I come to hear it anyway, is clear enough: be more like Richard Broughton.

I say 'research station' but it is in fact a steel shed (Broughton calls it 'the bunker') sadly marooned in the middle of a field next to some tall, ancient woodland. This is Monks Wood, a National Nature Reserve and for decades a famous place in English biology. From 1961 onwards it was where government-funded, world-changing research was done into the effects of DDT, the persistence in animals and soils of other poisons and heavy metals, on what happened to farmland if it was abandoned, on the history of hedges and the way of looking after them, the slow effects of climate change, the pattern of woodland flowers over time and many other pioneering, long-term experiments in the natural world.

Next to no one comes here now, but Monks Wood is one of the most important places in the world for the history of conservation biology. Much of what we know about our effects on nature began here. Its glory years were brought to an end in the late twentieth century by re-organisation and deep cuts. The place was closed in 2009 and the buildings sold off. Richard Broughton now makes his tea and writes up his records in the steel box while the neat 1960s complex of tower and laboratories is used to train young Cambridgeshire policemen. Little groups of them were standing around outside having a cigarette as I drove in to find the biologist in his steel shed.

Broughton has been here for a quarter of a century, recording the lives and behaviours of two beautiful and endangered woodland birds: the marsh and willow tits, one of which survives here and one of which does not. His container is wallpapered inside with aerial images and Lidar surveys of the woods beside us, plus enormous photographs of his chosen birds.

He has the usual manners of the ornithologist: quiet, definitive, straightforward, thinking before answering, not hurried, attentive and careful, used to being on his own, every sentence spoken in his light and burry, easy Hull accent. 'As a boy I lived on a council estate,' he says,

> the last house, right on the edge. Go one way and you could play with the stolen motorbikes, the other and it was rough, wet grasslands. We used to spend hours and hours with my brothers and friends, all day, catching sticklebacks, finding newts. There were willow tits there then. When I was a boy and teaching myself birds, I would record all the willow tits. Years and years of it. Then I wasn't seeing them very much and then they were gone.
>
> I remember the last one. It was on a New Year's Day I think. It sat in the top of a bush calling *ni ni ni ni* and then it flew off and I have never seen a willow tit there since.

That memory. It is unique to me. My nieces and nephews,
who live in that same street, they can't go and hear a willow tit.
There are plenty of blue tits. But is that enough?

His boyhood immersion, and a long year off school seriously ill when
he was ten, led him onwards. He loved painting but was fascinated
with the microbiology of viruses and was unsure whether to do science
or art. In the end, 'science seemed a better bet' and that took him to
geography and ecology at university, a master's degree at Edinburgh, a
PhD in woodland birds and since 1999 a career as a research scientist.
You could imagine him in a novel: a man's life dedicated to forms of
life that were disappearing as he watched.

We set off for a walk through what has long been his territory.

It is a place full of marvels. On the edge of the ancient ashes and
oaks of Monks Wood, a ten-acre field, first farmed by the Romans, was
let go in 1961, ploughed up after a final crop of barley. Kenneth
Mellanby, then director of Monks Wood, left a small typed note in the
files. 'It might be interesting to watch what happens to this area if man
does not interfere. Will it become a wood again, how long will it take,
which species will be in it?' Since then, nothing has been done to it in
six decades and it has become one of the ur-rewilding sites of Europe.

Broughton took me into the tall, airy woodland. When he first knew
it, twenty-five years ago, nearly forty years after the experiment had
begun, it was impenetrable. Standing outside, you could hear it was
full of willow warblers, blackcaps, dunnocks and other birds of the
shrubland, as well as all the usual robins, blackbirds and song thrushes
– not that different from the rough grounds as they are at the moment
in Hollow Flemings.

But the ashes and oaks, originally protected by that thicket, have
grown and now this barley field is turning into what Broughton calls
'high forest'. Only after fifty years did the marsh tits, which need the
cracks and hollows that develop in substantial trees for their nests, start

to breed here. They had long been living in the ancient wood next door but hadn't come into the old barley field until the conditions were right.

That is the repeated lesson from this graduate school: particular birds need particular places. 'The evolving wood goes through a warblery phase,' Broughton says,

> rough, dense at first, but that comes to an end as it grows higher. You get the willow warblers in the dense shrubby stuff, the nightingales, willow tits, and turtle doves if you are lucky, then chiffchaffs as it matures, then the willow warblers move out into the ride edges and other scrubby places, and only then do the marsh tits move in. They like complexity, a really three-dimensional structure – ground layer, dead wood on the ground, a good understorey and this massive architecture above us.

We picked our way easily through the fallen limbs and standing trunks of what had been the barley field. Its ten acres are the territory of a single pair of marsh tits, two birds weighing a third of an ounce each, possessing and controlling this high, wide, multi-layered woodland. 'They find everything they need here,' Richard said. Fledglings, if they can find a vacant territory, pair up within two weeks of leaving the nest and remain faithful to their partners for the rest of their lives.

> When they are settled, they are settled for life. Sometimes one will go to another territory for the winter, but it will be back in the spring. The adults sometimes allow a juvenile to settle as a spare. But if at the end of the winter both adults are alive, the juvenile gets kicked out and the pair resumes their territory alone.

Although, as with all small birds, there is a high mortality in the first winter, and only 8–10 per cent reach the next spring, if they can survive that, marsh tits can live for five to ten years, almost entirely loyal to each other. 'There is quite a bit of infidelity going on,' Richard says. 'About half of the nests contain an egg fertilised by another male. And a little polygyny, one male with two wives, two separate territories and two separate nests. That is what happens when the population starts breaking down and there are not enough males. The male looks after both females until the first eggs hatch and then he abandons the second one. The two females hate each other. They know they are in competition. But it is just possible for the single female to raise a brood on her own.'

Richard and I are in the wood together and for the moment no marsh tit is apparent, but somehow they are all present around us. 'You almost have to lift your imagination off the ground to feel how they are perceiving it,' he says. 'It is a cathedral-like structure, isn't it?'

We walk into the older parts of Monks Wood, where Richard has set up one of his small, home-made cage-traps. There is a short bird feeder full of seed inside, and a trapdoor he can operate with a long string from thirty or forty yards away. We stand and whisper together at the end of the string, waiting for a marsh tit to come.

'They definitely have an inner world,' Richard says. 'A phenomenal spatial memory. They store food everywhere, in the tops of broken grass stems, in nettle stems, a single seed in each hiding place, or a berry crammed into a crevice, or on the tops of horizontal boughs, the seeds pushed into the moss. And they remember things, sometimes for only a few hours, sometimes for weeks.'

There is nothing sentimental in this description but it is profoundly fond.

They will call to each other. They will sing at each other, with complex call systems that have a syntax, in which different chunks mean different things.

Such as?

It has not quite been unravelled yet. It's not as specific as dolphins, where certain noises are like names, but ... The marsh tit call is *pichou di di di*. The number of *di di di* notes is what matters. The more of the *di di di*, the more they mean it.

The function of the calls, and their posturing visual warning systems, in which they flick a wing or show off a dark bib like a badge, is to preserve their territories, to prevent too high a density of marsh tits for any of them to survive. It is all-important for each pair to own its part of the wood.

Interlopers are not attacked but they read the signals, respond submissively and back off.

A Monks Wood marsh tit nibbles Richard Broughton's finger

We crouch in the near silence of the autumn wood as Richard continues quietly describing his world.

It is difficult to know what they are feeling but you can definitely see signs of emotion in them. They definitely have individual characters. Even the ways they use the trap. Some are really assertive, coming straight in, putting a foot up [he imitates a runner stretching a leg against a wall] and every time puts his head under the leg to get the seed. Some just lean forward. Some are tolerant of you.

Some of them really hate you. Some scold you for following them, really pissed off, assertive, swaggering. A *bibibibibi*. None of them likes you near a nest. Some can be really relaxed and user friendly. Others are more elusive and tricky.

He had been with a bird whose partner had been killed by a sparrow-hawk that same morning, an hour or so earlier.

It was going everywhere calling for it, a soft call, *pichou pichou*, going everywhere around its territory, obviously looking for it and feeling the loss. It wasn't just getting on with its day. Where is she? What has happened? Where has she gone? It is hard not to see emotions in that, their feeling of loss.

The birds might have spent five years together, they know each other. A dynamic will have developed between them, with a strong socially monogamous bond. Really reliant on each other. If one of them dies, the other's life chances go right down. Because then they have no partner looking out for each other.

A great tit lands on the edge of the trap, hops in, takes a seed and is away. 'That's good,' Richard says. 'It shows the marsh tit that everything is fine.' A second or two later, a marsh tit is into the trap, Richard pulls his long light fisherman's string, the trapdoor flips and the tit is caught. We scurry up, Richard retrieves the bird and holds it between fingers and thumb.

After all the talk we have had this morning, nothing is more wonderful than how tiny it is, its head smaller than Richard's thumb, its bright eye not much larger than a pin head. He has caught and ringed it before and on its minuscule, fragile-looking left leg are the blue and yellow rings he attached in September. The tit bites at his fingers, he puts it in a cotton bag and gives me the bag for a moment as he takes the scales from his rucksack. The bag trembles slightly at the end of its string.

I know there is a marsh tit in there but as far as I can tell I'm holding a quivering nothing. When Richard weighs the bird, it turns out to be 10.9 grams, 0.384 ounces. 'This is what I will be doing for the next week, catching and measuring all the marsh tits in the wood, perhaps thirty-five, forty of them.' The entire marsh tit population of the four hundred acres of Monks Wood, with their overarching psychological presence, will add up to less than a pound in weight.

There are no willow tits to be caught. They have gone within Richard's time of knowing them.

It is very difficult watching a population I have known for more than twenty generations disappear. I used to walk through here and I still remember finding nests here, nests there, a territory here, a territory there, and now I come through in the spring and it is empty. It does get to you. You try not to let it. But there is a bit of despair, because it is very difficult to find the answers. The willow tits have gone and the marsh tits year by year are doing badly. We know for sure what isn't causing the declines but we don't know exactly what is.

It is not deer grazing: deer are no threat to marsh tits, which nest in cavities on average ten feet above the ground. It's not habitat change: the area of old broad-leaved woodland in Britain doubled between 1964 and 2000, so there is more mature, unmanaged woodland that the marsh tits like. It's not nest predation by woodpeckers, which is low. And it is not a problem with the survival of adults because they are continuing to live and breed from year to year as well as any other population elsewhere.

It is something happening to the juveniles between fledging in June and when we come to catch them in the autumn. By then, most of them have gone.

Disappeared. This year there are about ten adult pairs in the wood and so we should have something like sixty, seventy, eighty juveniles. There are probably about twenty or twenty-five. We know it is something happening to them then.

Richard's best guess – at least as one factor: the decline in insect food may be another – is that blue tits and great tits are outcompeting the young marsh tits.

When you try to think what has changed, we know those species have increased. The young marsh tits are newly independent. They're inexperienced.

They're trying to forage and they are lowest on the ladder under all the blue tits and the great tits.

If you think of the hundreds of blue tits and great tits competing for the same food in the wood, then all of those young birds are after the same caterpillars and the same insect eggs. The marsh tits are going to lose out. Something is squeezing them in that window. Competition. That's the best idea I have got. But testing it? That is really, really, really difficult.

The modern world is coming to pinch on the natural ecology of the birds. Marsh tits and willow tits are both adapted for tough, northern conditions. Having such large territories ensures they can hoard enough food to keep them going in the winter. Milder winters release blue and great tits from the stress of the conditions that marsh and willow tits are adapted to survive. Previously, these birds' populations would have been kept more in balance by the cold and difficulties of winter knocking back the numbers of blue and great tits.

Not now, partly because of climate change and partly because every day, within a few hundred yards of almost anywhere, they can fly to gardens and their bird feeders, fill up and come back into the wood. A marsh tit will come to a feeder in its own territory but will rarely fly out to a garden to find one, and only then if it is alongside its own territory in the wood. The result, as Richard says, is that 'every year is now a good year for blue tits and great tits. Marsh tits and willow tits still have to survive through good years and bad.'

Blue tits and great tits, the beneficiaries of garden feeders, have been booming. The natural density of these tits in primeval forest conditions in Poland, where Richard's partner, the Polish bird ecologist Dr Marta Maziarz works, is about two to three times more than that of the marsh tits. In modern Britain, the ratio in many places, of both blue and great tits combined, is more like twenty or thirty to one. The failure rate of great tit nests in their natural state in Poland is about 60 per cent. In England, the nests of fat, contented, garden-fed great tits fail only 10 per cent of the time.

The conclusion to all this? The young Monks Wood marsh tits are starving to death because they are being outcompeted by the great and blue tits to which we have given a decisive advantage by feeding them. Quite unawares, and carelessly, we have killed off the willow tits and are in the process of doing the same to the marsh tits.

A marsh tit: 70 per cent decline in fifty years

Bird feeding is a massive experiment and we don't really know the outcome. It changes the competitive landscape. It tips the balance in favour of the species that can be at home with us and against those that can't.

It seems that we are cultivating pets. So should we ban the feeding of garden birds?

No. I don't have bird feeders myself but it is very difficult to tell an old lady with a lonely life who loves seeing the birds in her garden, it is very difficult to tell her that she is doing something wrong.

But that is not true of most people. Most people can walk out to see wildlife. They don't need to attract artificially large numbers into their garden.

On top of that, he asks, is it really right to import sunflower seeds from Ukraine or nyger seeds from India when the effect on the birds here is so distorting? Not to speak of food security in those countries, the ecological impact of growing those bird foods or the carbon costs of transporting them.

'If it was a natural food supply,' Richard said at one corner in the wood,

> like these knapweeds here, they would give the birds lots of food for a few days or a few weeks and then run out. The bird moves on and switches to other seasonal foods. With a bird feeder, it is a constant source. The sparrowhawk just sits there. It only has to be lucky once.
>
> And if a marsh tit is taken out by a predator, there is probably not going to be another one to take its place. That cannot be a good deal.

We had a final cup of tea in Richard's metal shed.

> Feeding the birds in such widespread and massive quantities is starting to feel increasingly wrong. You used to be able to watch and listen to willow tits in this wood. Now we don't hear them. The soundscape is impoverished. When I started here, there was one pair left and they were actually coming to the garden bird table which I had in the bungalow then. It was before I realised how much bird feeding was distorting the bird communities! Anyway, we caught and ringed them and we saw them one more time and then we never saw them again. It is symptomatic of a simplification of ecosystems, simplified by generalists, by human intervention, by unintended consequences. Even the chaffinches are in steep decline. A virus and a mite means they get growths on their feet, which eventually fall off. There's salmonella,

trichomonosis, a cocktail of diseases, a constant exchange of pathogens. It can't be the right way to go.

And so what should we do?

I think we have to make the environment right for the birds.

At first, I wondered if I should embrace passive rewilding, as the Nature Conservancy had done in 1961 with the barley field at Monks Wood: let the whole of Perch Hill go, remove the sheep and cattle, let the form of the historic landscape sink slowly under the impenetrable tangle of thorn and bracken that would erupt there, and allow the birds to come as a new Perch Hill Wood gradually emerged over the next sixty years.

I had heard of one fascinating example of this totalising, no-intervention approach in the depths of Bedfordshire, one of the most chemicalised counties in England, and so I drove there early one May morning, leaving home at two, arriving just before sunrise at five.

It was a long, empty, three-hour drive. Even in the dark, the English Midlands were glowing in the white of May time, the lanes piped with the white of cow parsley under the flowering hawthorns. In the headlights, the country looked as perfect as a sofa or a cake, as much regal as bridal. The place I was going is blessed with a wonderful name: Strawberry Hill Farm. It had been part of the enormous estates of the Dukes of Bedford, who in the 1860s and 1870s had built a handsome house, some cottages and a capacious yard of High Victorian red brick.

Until about 1960, Strawberry Hill was a 365-acre mixed farm on the heavy boulder clay of the North Bedfordshire Wolds. There were sheep and cattle, pigs and poultry and a little bit of arable. All the six cottages were occupied by farm labourers and their families. One was a shepherd.

When Hugh White, an ambitious farmer from south Bedfordshire then in his thirties, took it over with his uncles in the 1950s, he was intent on joining the modern world. Within ten years, he had transformed the place.

Everything was turned to arable except for ten acres of grass around the house. He put 95 per cent of it into winter wheat, one year after another, with no break crops to clean the ground or improve the soil.

The farm lies across a shallow valley with marshland in the middle and on the heights to either side goodish agriculture ground. The crops rolled in, a mixture of bread wheat and feed wheat, two tons an acre or more, year after year. White made money and reached a position where he didn't have to sell his corn straight after harvest, but would keep it until the next June or July, when prices were high.

Hugh died in 2014 aged ninety but his son Graham, a sports journalist and publisher, now lives in a cottage at Strawberry Hill. I asked him what it had been like.

All this was field after field after field before. But we took the hedges out where we could. We were never quite able to have the fields as huge as we wanted. He wanted as few fields as possible in order to do the ploughing. He wanted a good run. He didn't want to be turning around the whole time. Or take the combine. It was a fiddle with the Klaas Dominators we had. And with a five-metre bar. And when you get into these corners all you are doing is whizzing round the steering wheel trying to get the thing round.

But we managed. Bourne Wood [one of the fields] forty-nine acres, that was a nice run. Arno's that was forty-two acres. Little Field, that was far from little, thirty-five acres. He took all those hedges out. He transformed the farm from what it had been before.

They were only doing what every arable farmer in the country was doing at the time, and with lower pesticide and fertiliser use than most. Production and efficiency were the goals.

By the 1980s, a note of disenchantment had begun to creep in. Like many farmers, Hugh White was his own man, intent on following his own path, and with government increasingly involved in farming, he became politicised. He disliked the way the rules of the European Union were always interfering with his task of producing crops. He often went on the Jimmy Young show on Radio 2, standing up for the farmers' cause. The BBC took him out to France to meet the French and put his point. In particular, he thought the British government was lying when they said there was a surplus of wheat in the EU. It was nothing but a way of keeping the price down. Things got worse when he was told to stop burning the stubbles after harvest. And 'to cap it all,' as Graham says, 'he was being told to take a certain amount of land out of production. Into set-aside.'

> They wanted us to take the headlands out on each field. Two yards or three yards of the headland right the way round. Dad said – it was almost two fingers up to Thatcher – he said, 'I am going to take all of it out' and that was it.

The government wanted a reduction in the farmed area to reduce the surpluses that farmers were producing all over the EU but Hugh White was not going to be told what to do. He decided, on the instant in the late summer of 1987, that the whole farm was going to be taken out of production. The Whites would continue to receive set-aside payments on their 365 acres but he wasn't going to half-farm the place. The last harvest at Strawberry Hill was in 1988. Graham drove the combine and when the final acres of wheat were cut, they took the machines to the barn and left them there, unused until sold as antiquated relics in 2022.

Everything was kept, the tractors, trailers, ploughs, harrows, seed drills and the combine, all gathering dust for decades.

Hugh White never did anything again with his land. He continued to receive various forms of government subsidy for habitat creation until 2014. In all the time he had, he raised barn owls, which he loved, but he never farmed again. The ditches were maintained, as was required, but the pattern of fields that Graham remembers today as he walks around them with me – Man Meads Grass, Man Meads Arable, Mill Hill Grass, Mill Hill Arable, Bourne Wood ('there must have been a wood there in the distant past'), Little Field ('not little!'), Strawberry Hill Paddocks, Wassalls, New Ground, Twin Trees, Charley, Arno's – was subsumed under the tide of a resurgent nature. Nothing grazed it beyond the hares and rabbits and the wild deer. No plough entered the ground. Any boundary between fields disappeared. The rest of Bedfordshire, even those fields all around it, continued on its sterilised way but Strawberry Hill became something astonishing.

Now, on this lit spring morning, it is an almost unbelievable silvery lushland, glimmering in the early light. Everything is wet with dew, a green-and-white overgrown wood, like an abandoned English common, scattered with thorns, or even an English Africa, a soft, damp green-white-and-silver shrubland ballooning into open grassy rides. The whole place is laden with white dead nettles and stitchwort, tall willows and teasels growing in the rough patches. Later in the year there will be knapweed, vetches, meadowsweet and wild carrot all flowering in the more open glades. But the old arable fields are now a wood full of young hawthorn trees in flower, all growing from seeds dropped by berry-eating thrushes that arrive en masse in autumn and winter. This is a wonder wood created by blackbirds, fieldfares, redwings and song thrushes. Walking through it feels like pushing your way into the rooms of a flower-filled palace.

It is difficult to believe that this is a chemical farm let go, or that such a place could be so intense with birdlife: thirty nightingale territories, plenty of cuckoos, one or two turtle doves and hundreds of warblers – whitethroats and lesser whitethroats, blackcaps, garden warblers, willow warblers, chiffchaffs and the high *zzzzz* of grasshopper warblers all alive among the flowering trees. It is a gift from nothing, scarcely comprehensible as a self-generated place.

Who would have thought that Bedfordshire had such resilience in it? Where did all these birds come from? The answer: a combination of the fledged chicks from any early pioneers who wandered in, and their descendants, and their descendants; and those migrants flying over that heard the birdsong loud beneath them as they passed and dropped in to join it. It is the purest demonstration that nature will thrive if allowed to. Nothing else is needed. People often talk about a shifting baseline – we do not know what we have not missed – but if you go to Strawberry Hill early on a May morning you will find that baseline rocketed into a vivid and vibrant present.

Strawberry Hill today

Graham White says that when his father died in 2015, he had to decide what to do.

> I got a quote from someone to ask how much it would cost to
> flatten all of this. We could have done it, return it to agriculture.
> Or a lot of it anyway. The drains are still running. But Natural
> England was not happy. Eventually they put a red line area
> which could not be touched, roughly half the farm. And what
> we could touch also had restrictions on it.

His hand was forced – half the farm was sold to the local wildlife trust in 2023 and by late 2024 the trust had raised the money to buy the rest.

Strawberry Hill is in what Richard Broughton calls 'the warblery phase'. It might last a while. The sources of any tall woodland tree seeds are quite distant – the nearest wood is more than half a mile away – and the birds that bring in the seeds, the jays in particular, not that common. These acres may remain as song-filled shrubland for decades to come, perhaps even for the next century, with taller groves or scattered trees only gradually increasing within it.

Oaks and field maples are already appearing among the hawthorns. The high forest architecture will eventually be there, at least in part, and the warblers and nightingales will move on. But the ecology, under its own impetus, will always be on the churn: thorns will topple and blow over in storms, new shrubs will take their place, the deer and rabbits will keep grassy patches open. The trust has already brought in some Highland cattle to graze the open glades. Perhaps in the style of the famous wildland project at Knepp in Sussex, they can introduce free-roaming gangs of ponies, cattle, red deer, beavers and pigs to keep things moving. That will need a long and expensive fence but what a prize to be gained.

*   *   *

A song thrush on her nest

Woodcock

Wood pigeon

Willow warbler

Giotto's depiction of
St Francis's sermon
to the birds

Giotto's birds stand in their Ark-ready pairs: goldfinches, chaffinches,
greenfinches, blackbirds, magpies, rails, geese, red-legged choughs,
swallows, pigeons, a cockerel and a mallard

Starlings on crab apples

Goldfinch on a teasel

Great tit on a sunflower

A fruity, seedy autumn
garden at Perch Hill

I took a long time wondering what to do at home. I was sure, from Richard Broughton, that we could do better than putting out bird feeders. With the idea of rewilding I was less certain. Hollow Flemings was, after all, a tiny experiment in passive rewilding and I have long been intrigued by it. The core idea is that we should allow land to return under its own dynamics to a 'self-willed' condition, one in which, as the biologists Nathalie Pettorelli and James Bullock have said, nature is seen not as an adversary or opportunity but as 'a formidable ally'.

Almost twenty years ago, with Isabella Tree and Charlie Burrell, who had already embarked on their inspirational rewilding project at Knepp, I visited the extraordinary experiment conducted on an abandoned polder at Oostvaardersplassen near Amsterdam, conceived by the controversial apostle of rewilding in Europe, the Dutch ecologist Frans Vera. Vera's idea was to see what would happen to a stretch of land if it was managed by nothing but roaming herds of deer, ponies, cattle and water buffalo, with the addition of some bison, elk, wild boar and beavers. That, he had proposed, was the dominant condition of Europe at the end of the last Ice Age: not the old picture of a continuous closed forest, but a shifting mosaic of woodland and glades, kept open by the herds of browsers and grazers, including bison, closing over again when forest trees, guarded when young by thorny scrub, got away for a century or two from those controlling mouths. The landscape would open again only as those trees aged and died – or when storms and hurricanes flattened whole forests, or fire, flood, disease and shifting climates transformed local ecologies. I asked Vera when he thought he might get some results from his experiment. 'Five thousand years?' he said. 'If then.'

It is the beautiful concept of a self-regulating system, oscillating through different conditions in which all the sequences of bird, flower, shrub and tree have their moment, a continent-wide vision of the intermediate disturbance hypothesis at work, both in time and space, a dynamic mosaic of life itself dancing and billowing across the centuries and through the widths of Europe. As anyone knows who has been to Knepp, to see and hear it radiating in the dazzling upsurge of its 'warblery phase', the sweeping vitality of a self-willed place under browser-and-grazer control is undeniable.

For a while I took to calling Hollow Flemings 'Little Knepp' but I did not want to rewild Perch Hill. I did not want to live surrounded by impenetrable thorny scrub for twenty years. Or lose what seemed like the most valuable thing about the place, its late medieval landscape, the interlacing of natural and cultural, the centuries-long pattern of pasture, wood, meadow, garden, house and rough grounds. Perch Hill is in its essence the memory of everything that has been done to it. It embeds the care of its inherited form.

Now, when I look out of the window at home, across the dip and rise of the farm, one word comes to mind: repair. Remake the place. Don't abandon it but mend it. Undo the damage that has been inflicted on it, along with most of lowland England, in the late twentieth century, when the litany unfolded of removal and reduction, an ignoring of the past, an imposing of the chemical and clarified, a denial of its multiplicity.

The only duty to a place like this must be to re-invigorate it, make it good, do what the world in general is coming to recognise – that undoing is as important as doing, that un-change can be as healthy as change, that the half-forgotten past can hold many answers, and that an accommodating place that allows the co-presence of other species alongside our own, in an ever-evolving and shifting relationship, is somewhere whose arc will tend to the good.

I don't often repair things but I know I should, and so when I found an old and beautiful bowl that was broken years ago and put away in pieces in a cupboard, I decided to mend it. Sarah had bought it from someone who imports pottery from Iran. It had all the allure of that country: a purity of form, wide and full, almost but not quite a hemi-sphere, about ten inches across. When complete, it could hold five or six oranges or pomegranates, all in the deep turquoise glaze of Isfahan, a colour used for tiles in the pools of Persian gardens to suggest the brightness of the sea or of the water in a clear river.

The bowl was in about eight pieces. And so: the table cleared and the pieces laid out. A good strong glue. Sleeves rolled up, hands washed. And slowly, perhaps over an hour, I fitted the pieces back together, finding in the slight bulges and ripples of the broken edges their coun-terparts on the other side, a protrusion here, a depression there, so that the mended edges met each other with a natural precision. It made me curiously happy. I was in no hurry to finish. The broken form started to become whole.

When everything was at last complete, it wasn't. A tiny piece was missing, just at the point where the body of the bowl reached the verti-cal. Other glued joints came up to its corners and met there, leaving a triangular hole. I looked in the cupboard where the other pieces had

been stored but could find nothing. This wonderful bowl could never hold a brimful of stew again. Fruit could sit in it but nothing liquid. And so I set it on the windowsill with its flaw turned away and left it for a while, seeming perfect.

I started to wonder more about that bowl and its missing triangle, and how it might reflect the remaking of a place. The gap in the bowl changes the thing. It is both the same and not the same bowl. It now carries some of its history with it, so that there is a self-recording chronicle in it which the smooth, cleanable surfaces would have resisted previously. Now it has more: on top of its everyday and usual qualities, there is its history of use, of breakage and mending, of being ours, of being dropped, forgotten and looked after.

The twentieth-century philosopher Henri Bergson thought a good existence was one that was taken up with the perpetual becoming of life: 'To exist is to change, to change is to mature, to mature is to go on creating oneself endlessly.' That idea has echoed through all cultures and all human history. Zen Buddhists, the builders of the Gothic cathedrals in Europe, the first Greek philosophers on the shores of the Aegean, modern physicists and the Romantic poets have all understood the centrality of becoming.

Nothing is essentially itself. Everything is always on the road from one state to another. Identity – of bowl or person or creature or building or place – is only the form through which the flow of the material world is currently passing.

This flood-in-time is the river in which we float. Mending, the habit of repair, is a conscious act within it, a swimming more than a floating, extending past into present, not to deny the passage of time but to make it explicit, to show that we are living within it, bringing our own existence into line with Bergson's perpetual becoming.

Those who tended the landscape, above all the premodern farmed landscape, always understood mending to be central to their lives. The ancient practice of agriculture, of shaping the growing world to our needs, is founded on six interrelated recognitions: many things will grow; others will break and decay; there is some good in that perishing; once mended, things will grow again; mending is a form of belonging; and a mended place carries the mark of its own (often repeated) breaking.

Modern destructive agriculture abandoned that vision and substituted for it a one-term doctrine of dominance. Care for places became essentially unitary and divorced from time: clear the ground by excluding competitors, clean it up and extract what value you can. The cyclicality of mend-and-grow was abandoned in favour of spray-and-run.

Why should we return to what the Swedish anthropologist Helena Norberg-Hodge once called our 'ancient futures'? Not only because our interests are biologically tied up with those of the plants and animals that we have been destroying, but because loss of memory is loss of meaning. Mending is one of the lamps of memory, lighting the way from past to future.

To remake a place is not to abandon it or to rewild it but in some ways the opposite: to reculture it, to allow the ancient connections between human use and animal and plant life to re-establish themselves in a way that persisted here for at least half a millennium before the locust years of the late twentieth century.

Richard Broughton was full of advice. We should increase the number of hedges,

especially if the hedges link up old hedges or woods. Increasing the number of nodes in a hedge network has benefits beyond the simple fact of being a hedge. The corners where hedges meet can create suntraps or sheltered spots away from the wind.
T-junctions contain more hedge than the same area in the middle of a linear stretch.

Hawthorn and blackthorn are always good, but multi-species hedges have multiple benefits. I might plant plenty of quick growing things to get the hedge thick quickly – sallow, elder, silver birch, poplar, aspen – and then let the hedge plants fill in after them. Hedgerow trees are also a good idea – oak being the classic – as birds such as the marsh tit can tree-hop along them when dispersing from their native woods.

> Wider hedges tend to be better, but there is the practical problem of maintaining them, to stop them becoming tree-lines over time. You have to think of periodic destruction of some of the width from time to time. A diversity of hedge heights has the greatest benefit for the birds.

The answer was to put gates into the fences that protected the hedges from the grazing cattle so that after a decade or so, they could be let in there and begin trashing the young trees.

Even better was Richard Broughton's ideas for green lanes.

A thick, rough, multiple, flowering wayward hedge

Two parallel hedges a vehicle-width apart, which can be
managed by an annual mow to keep it open, and also allow
access to the hedges for trimming. Green lanes tend to give a lot
of bang for their buck, as birds have double the habitat along
the same length.

I should allow the woods to develop scrubby edges.

Sunny, thorny and blossom-rich edges of hawthorn, bramble,
blackthorn and sallow are fantastic buffers for woodland,
helping to maintain their internal microclimate, and they're very
bird- and insect-rich.

And some of the fields should be turned into wood pasture:

Or a traditional orchard, which could have a similar outcome
but have the added value of blossom/nectar and fruit. It could
also help secure traditional local varieties. Perhaps even a mix of
both, e.g. oaks and apples/pears?

If we increased the number of fields by dividing them up with new
hedges, a whole crowd of benefits would come in. The hedges themselves would become a carbon sink. They would build even more
connectivity for birds and mammals across the farm. We could begin
to practise the traditional methods of moving the stock every few days,
allowing the sward long recovery periods. And we would restore the
close-grained pattern of the historic landscape of small fields, thick
hedges, a handmade place.

Finally, there was nothing like a pond to enhance the natural life in
a place.

* * *

Perch Hill as it is

Perch Hill as it might be

Rewilding may have a glamour to it but it was this mending that felt most beautiful. In the county archives I found the old maps that showed the shape of the farm in the past and transferred their outlines on to modern aerial photographs. With that information and the Broughton principles in mind, I made a double image to guide me: the farm as it is now, and another of what it might become again: every hedge allowed to balloon and roughen; little woods on steep slopes; no field bigger than three or four acres; trees growing in the middle of pastures; green lanes crossing the farm; ponds in the wet patches. This would be a place that could enable well-being for a wide range of nature and humanity.

There was one further element. Over the last thirty years Sarah has made a large and wonderful garden around the farmhouse. It became increasingly clear that this cultivated piece of ground could be a place in which, again according to the Broughton model, we could grow plants that would feed and nurture the birds, ephemeral sources that would come and go with the seasons.

We could plant the right kind of trees along the boundary. Many tits love aspens in March when the catkins are out. The birds pull the catkins apart to find the grubs. Blackbirds and thrushes love hawthorns and crab apples. We could add in berry-rich trees and shrubs such as guelder rose and holly. Ivy, honeysuckle and wild roses make dense cover for nests and have long-lasting fruits and all their attendant insects. We have now planted them all, plus some crab apples and a hazel, in the patch of open ground around the birdhouse. When wild garlic and other alliums are left to seed, they are a magnet for greenfinches. Seed heads left on lavender or teasels will bring in the goldfinches.

All this is a way of re-thickening the natural world, to allow human-made places to be good for nature, not by abstaining from involvement but by enlarging and deepening it. I asked Anita Oakes, a baker and gardener who lives down the road, who works with Sarah and is an inveterate birdwatcher, what she had noticed in her garden.

The garden at Perch Hill

Willow warblers eat forget-me-not seeds.

Bullfinches go through old bramble branches with any dried fruit or seeds on them.

Starlings tear off pieces of the apple mint and put it in their nests once they start feeding the young. The blue tits do that too.

Blue, great and coal tits use bits of clematis seed heads in their nests. Also artichoke seed heads – the fluffy bits.

Goldfinches eat the biennial evening primrose seeds. They open the seed heads from the top. Also cosmos and teasel seed heads.

Sparrows collect the fluff from a goat willow and take it to their nest.

Redcurrants and rowan berries ripen at the right time for the young blackbirds.

Blue tits bring their fledglings to the birch trees and go through
   them taking off the greenfly.
The berries on cotoneasters last well into the new year and often
   get fieldfares and redwings on them.
We leave old iris leaves for the female blackbirds who take bits
   for the base of their nest. It must feel strong to them.

Richard Broughton said that we should sow strips of seedy plants
which the farmland insects and birds would feast on. Wheat, barley,
triticale, kale, radish, millet, quinoa, oats, linseed, buckwheat, mustard,
chicory, fennel, phacelia, black medick and common vetch would all
be good.

Nothing would be too much. Diversify, enrich, multiply, protect.
Find insect-friendly plants and birds would devour them.

What could be more promising than all of this, a more-than-lifelong
project, stretching far beyond our own existence, to re-acquire the
culture of co-habitation we once had, to make a mended and
self-mending fragment of the world? Nothing seems more obvious. All
of it led by the birds and all leading to the birds.

There was one rather large remaining issue: cost. A new hedge with
enough plants to make it thick enough to be bird-friendly, with tree
guards and fences to prevent deer getting in and chewing everything to
the ground, will cost something in the region of £25 a metre. Fenced
on both sides, with gates to allow entry into it to manage it in the
future, might cost as much again. A green lane, with new hedges on
both sides, would be the ultimate in landscape luxury.

I have recently asked for and had approved a government grant
that will cover much but not all of those hedging and fencing costs
for at least part of my scheme. Without the grant, any proposal
would be impossibly expensive. The idea of restoring all of the
ninety acres of Perch Hill to their ancient woolly condition, with
green lanes, small new woods and shaws and wood-pasture trees out

in the fields, would at current prices cost many tens of thousands of pounds.

The annual income at Perch Hill from beef and lamb sales has never been more than a few thousand pounds. Until recently the farming operation has been sustained by what was called the Single Farm Payment, a legacy of Britain's membership of the EU by which all farmers were paid an annual sum according to the acreage they farmed. It too was a few thousand pounds a year. When combined with the beef sales, and after the costs of repairing fences, keeping the tractor running and making the hay, the annual hire of the bull, the shearing of the sheep and the vets' bills, the grant meant that in most years the income just about balanced the expenditure.

Richard Lambden plants the first strip of new wood to thicken up
Perch Hill: 3,500 field maples, hazels, birches, hawthorns, goat
willows and dog roses to make a bird-thicket for the ages

Without a grant, no small farmer could afford to keep going, let alone invest in environmental improvements of this kind. The average income of a lowland English grazing farm is about £17,000 a year. Most places like this, where there is no income from other sources, are scratching along on the thinnest of margins. It is not surprising that most small farmers, of the kind that made this precious landscape, the vision of yeoman England, have now been forced to give up. According to Savill's, the upscale land agents, 54 per cent of land sold in England in 2023 was bought by non-farmers, most of it as a hedge against inflation.

For a while, in the early twenty-first century, it seemed as if a widespread belief in the restoration of nature might result in effective government policy. The EU's much-derided Common Agricultural Policy developed a whole series of environmental schemes by which farmers would be paid for looking after their land in a way that went beyond food production at any price. When Britain voted to leave the EU in 2016, there was little mention of these green European policies in the widespread attack on 'the dead hand of European bureaucracy' and when in 2018 Michael Gove came to proclaim the brave new world as the government's environment secretary, he talked about 'a green Brexit'. The government was going to 'strengthen environmental protection measures and to create new mechanisms to incentivise environmental improvement'.

The Single Farm Payment was to be renamed the Basic Farm Payment and gradually reduced to nothing by 2027. Its place was to be taken by a dazzling cornucopia of Environmental Land Management schemes, involving a Landscape Recovery scheme, a Farming in Protected Landscapes scheme, a Sustainable Farming Initiative or Incentive, as well as the leftovers from the EU of a Countryside Stewardship scheme and an Environmental Stewardship scheme.

It was complicated and muddled. Years passed in which no detail was added to these heroic conceptions. Government stuttered and stumbled in a string of botched attempts to get these things off the ground. There are 82,000 farms in England and by early 2023 a total of 224 payments had been made to farmers under the Sustainable Farming Incentive. Even in 2024, fewer than 12 per cent of all English farms had been signed up. Most of those were the big farms and estates that had the expert management that could navigate the bureaucracy these schemes involved.

Meanwhile, the Basic Farm Payment, on which farms had relied for years to balance their books, was cut year by year. A general stress on government budgets in 2024 brought an accelerated end to that scheme, bringing its funding to near zero by 2025. The new environmental grants were also cut, so that a government agricultural budget of £3.5 billion in 2015 had shrunk by £1 billion ten years later, over a period in which farmers were already weighed down by rising costs for feed, fuel and fertiliser, by extreme weather and by the demand to shift to lower-carbon and more sustainable farming. Largely as a result of the confusion and muddle, and the daunting design of most of these schemes, the government's farming budget as a whole was underspent by hundreds of millions of pounds.

There is no doubt the Common Agricultural Policy was unfair. The top 10 per cent of large landowners usually received 50 per cent of the money, the bottom 20 per cent no more than 2 per cent of it. Small-scale farmers, of the kind that made the landscape at Perch Hill, were gradually driven out of business. The number of farms with cattle in Britain shrank from just over 100,000 in 2005 to 75,000 today. Apart from any environmental benefits, a green Brexit might have been their saving. Government money could have remade their world.

But that vision has been lost. The Farming in Protected Landscapes scheme, which had in mind something very like the reculturing this book has described, has been allowed to wither. Other green schemes will be cut. Farms will go bust. Big money will buy them up, perhaps for rewilding or carbon offset projects, and an entire tranche of our culture, in which human and natural history were for centuries richly folded together, will have been lost. A good future will have been lost. A farmed landscape alive with the creatures of the natural world, and with the memories of the families that farmed it, will have been lost. And the world will have been coarsened and diminished.

The nightingale that I had been hearing in the rough grounds by the birdhouse was no longer there. I thought its loss must be yet another symptom of the general decline, perhaps because of conditions in Africa, or on the migration route. But I was wrong. It had moved a third of a mile away. I hadn't realised that Hollow Flemings, after only twenty years, was already growing up beyond its 'warblery phase'.

An email arrived from Anita Oakes. 'Have you heard the nightingale down by the Dudwell, in that brackeny gorsey rough patch just above the meadows by the river?'

I went down that evening and lay in the long grasses above the rough bank, the broom in flower, the thicket impenetrable with blackthorn and bramble. Children were playing in the shallows of the river just below me unseen. Young oak seedlings were pushing up through the grass of the pasture. There was cuckoo spit on the stems beside me.

A blackbird, a robin and a chiffchaff were trio-ing away with each other in the thorny shrubland, the blackbird taking the leading part. All the birds sounded exhausted, none of them at full whack. The chiffchaff seemed on the verge of sleep. I had thought the blackbird was sounding nightingalish, having borrowed a phrase or two from the exotic stranger, but then I realised. The nightingale itself was singing. The totemic moment of the summer. *Didididididi chugchug.* Long pauses. *Ch ch ch chrrrr.* And then occasional morse signals from his distant mind. *Schwitt schnitt schwitt.*

'I have listened till I felt/A feeling not in words,' John Clare wrote of the presence and indescribability of birdsong and the insufficiency of language when faced with it. But having confessed his inadequacy, he

embarked on one of the most adventurous pieces of bird-voice transcription ever attempted. '"Chew-chew chew-chew" & higher still,' he
had the nightingale sing,

> 'Cheer-cheer cheer-cheer' more loud & shrill
> 'Cheer-up cheer-up cheer-up' – & dropt
> Low 'Tweet tweet jug jug jug' & stopt
> One moment just to drink the sound
> Her music made & then a round
> Of stranger witching notes was heard
> As if it was a stranger bird
> 'Wew-wew wew-wew chur-chur chur-chur'
> 'Woo-it woo-it' – could this be her
> 'Tee-rew tee-rew tee-rew tee-rew
> 'Chew-rit chew-rit' – & ever new
> 'Will-will will-will grig-grig grig-grig'

'The alphabet [has] no letters that can syllable the sounds,' he wrote of
these descriptions, but no one has come nearer to catching a nightingale in full song. With these proclaimed and half-gurgled mutterings
to hand, I listened to the nightingale singing and heard the precision
of Clare's account. He catches the uncertainty and oddness, the lack of
connectedness between one phrase or set of phrases and the next, the
sudden silences as if the nightingale would say nothing again, the
jerked resumption and wrenching transitions, the apparently uncontrolled and rapid repetitions, the lack of any form or frame we might
understand, putting the listener not in a position of power in relation
to the bird – Clare is never the man to own a bird through knowing it
– but accepting the impotence of incomprehension.

Set that alongside Keats's 'Ode to the Nightingale'. Nothing could
be more different. We might long, with Keats, on a warm night in early
summer for the bird to sound like the tenderness of the night itself, a

The ride through Hollow Flemings

poured-out, melancholy, transient richness that cascades across the darkness in undiluted ecstasy. But it is obvious Keats was no naturalist. So deep was his absorption in himself as the bird was singing in the warmth of May 1819 that its identity disappeared. There is some suggestion he might have been listening not to a nightingale but to a song thrush. The beautiful continuities, the slip-sliding of thought and feeling between him and bird, night and place, unmatched as it is as an account of the absorbent mind and soul, is not nightingale-ish at all. The seductive Ode reads more, in fact, as if the nightingale had understood Keats and written an ode to him. It is, in its tantalising way, a model of how not to be.

So here now in the dusk of the Dudwell valley, the children gone home from the river, it is Clare's nightingale I am with: 'a stranger bird', not a pet, nor a version of me or of anyone I know, but its own thing, still just here, still wild, its own apostle for its own anxious future.

Birds in the Garden

AN AVIARY WITHOUT THE CAGE

By Sarah Raven

It first dawned on me how important birds are as a gardener while I was sitting writing at a table in the garden over the long Jubilee weekend in 2022. Bored with what I was doing, I spent most of the day looking around, being in and watching the garden. It was early June and our band of lupins was at its most splendid, but we had a bad case of lupin aphid, along with a heavy infestation of greenfly, coating and devouring an increasing number of stems.

The evening before, I'd jetted the flower spires with a hose – that's a good way to get rid of the pests – but it only works before numbers get hold and I was pretty sure I'd left it too late. That would be that for another year with my beloved lupins.

The following morning I noticed a clutch of just-fledged blue tits, still pretty rough and ready with their new punk-rocker plumage, going to and fro from their nest in the hawthorn hedge on the southern side of the garden. There was a continual circuit of young birds moving between the hedge and lupin row. Once there, they were hopping around at ground level for a moment and one by one, proceeding up the flower spires.

Soon a pair of blackbirds came to join them and then three robins, down at ground level. After an hour I went to see what was going on.

The day before, the spires had been moving with bugs before my eyes, along the whole line of at least thirty plants, but now there was not a single aphid.

This was my Eureka moment – look after our garden birds and they'll help keep our pests in balance and under control.

With record wet years, many gardeners struggle to grow dahlias, particularly those that have been left in the ground and mulched for winter protection. All sorts of people reported that as soon as their dahlias sprouted in April and May, they were mown off by hideous numbers of slugs and snails. The mild winter had not killed off their eggs and the wet spring had enabled scary numbers to thrive. Instagram was full of it. How were our dahlias coping with the plague of molluscs?

Fine, in fact rather triumphant! Garden birds are the answer. Along with toads and frogs (they eat adult slugs and a fair number of snails, making it worth having a pond or damp area if you can), as well as plenty of garden beetles (which you'll get if you go organic – they devour mollusc eggs), the bigger garden birds, the thrushes and blackbirds, help keep our slug and snail population under control.

Smaller birds are crucial in spring and early summer as shoots and leaves unfurl and with them the invertebrates (or pests) arrive. Whereas finches, tits and dunnocks eat seeds in summer and autumn, in spring the adults are on the lookout for protein-rich caterpillars, aphids and the smaller slugs to feed their young. They need the concentrated protein to get their babies from the hatching to fledging stage in three weeks or so and that's what garden pests provide.

The more birds, the less molluscs and the Perch Hill garden is the living, flowery, abundant proof of that.

So garden birds it's got to be – but which is the best way to encourage them to visit, or better still come to live and breed in your garden?

I've always gardened for production, cut-and-come-again flowers and edible plants – and for twenty years I've gardened for pollinators, but now I plant consciously to feed the birds and am always on the lookout for ornamental, non-invasive plants that attract a good range of birds to feed on their fruits, hips and seeds.

The problem with feeders is twofold. First, as Adam has described, the cross-contamination from one bird to another of fatal diseases; second is the advantage given to those birds that visit the feeders over those that don't. Rarities suffer and it looks as if feeders literally reduce biodiversity. They diminish the breadth of bird life.

Current advice seems to be that sporadic feeder use is okay (feast and famine is more natural) with proper regular washing of your feeders. And move the feeders around. Both are important *and* growing ever-more plants to feed the birds naturally is the way we should all be going.

We have an ever-evolving calendar of birds we notice feasting on certain plants, with the key time now being the early months of the year before the garden greens up again. We concentrate on when the temperatures get cold and carry on till April when the garden and countryside fill with invertebrate food.

OCTOBER AND NOVEMBER BIRD FOOD

Trees, shrubs and climbers

One of the best fruits for autumn is a crab apple, even more than an apple and pear. If you watch our garden birds, this is where they're visiting more than anywhere else with us. Malus hupehensis and 'Dartmouth' are two of our and their favourites. The mini cherry fruits of hupehensis get stripped first and then the birds move on to 'Dartmouth'.

Blackbirds also love yellow pyracantha berries in October, then the holly and ivy berries start to be eaten by pigeons, blackbirds and thrushes in November.

At ground level – for smaller birds

There is a huge range of plants with autumn seed available, and the verbena, sunflower and amaranth family (love-lies-bleeding) are being visited most. They are stellar (along with the grasses and grains – see next month). Teasels could be included here but are too invasive and any late-flowering thistles. We've got a pair of marsh tits that visit here each afternoon. They go for the sunflower hearts and strip them one by one, hiding them in the top of our chestnut posts or in cracks in the walls of our so-called Chelsea garden shed. We now put pinecones in the holes and when we go back to check, they've put the sunflower seeds in there.

DECEMBER AND JANUARY BIRD FOOD

Trees, shrubs and climbers

Holly, famously, has berries in midwinter and ivy has berries which some birds eat. And the Malus 'Dartmouth' and 'Red Sentinel' in our garden still have fruit – and birds – until Christmas, whereas M. hupehensis is stripped bare by then.

The winter-flowering clematis C. cirrhosa varieties also have good seed production at this moment. C. 'Paul Farges' (aka 'Summer Snow') and tangutica are also good for now, still covered in seed.

Hawthorn berries are loved by blackbirds, as well as great and blue tits and sparrows. Rose hips are also favoured – the ramblers that have small hips, such as R. 'Veilchenblau', attract house sparrows. They nibble off the flesh and leave the hairy seeds.

And with us at this time of year we have robins and blackbirds eating the black berries of our myrtle.

At ground level

The shoo-fly plant, Nicandra physalodes, holds its mini apple-filled seedheads longer than almost anything in our garden, loved by blue tits in particular which excavate the seed with their beaks from the apex of the pod, straight into the apple, rather than accessing from below. The Chinese lantern-like seed pods may have been browned by frost by now, but the plants and seedheads still hold plenty of forage.

It's also the moment for late-season grasses and grains such as Chasmanthium and Panicum 'Frosted Explosion'. Looking like spun sugar, 'Frosted Explosion' is the only grain I know that forms axillary buds: one head grows, ripens and dries and is blown away, but then along comes another, and on and on it goes till Christmas.

FEBRUARY AND MARCH BIRD FOOD

Trees, shrubs and climbers

There aren't that many plants which hold their berries, hips and haws as late as the new year, so they are a precious commodity. The non-native Cotoneaster and Pyracantha are famous for holding their berries longer than even holly. I wonder if that means they're not delicious – but they are at least still there for keeping birds alive in this hungry gap. The redwings, mistle thrushes, fieldfares and waxwings go for them if cold weather pushes them south and west. A birdie friend of mine reported a good cotoneaster/bird story one February. She arrived at work at 7 a.m. and parked her car under a cotoneaster tree that was heavy with berries, noticing that about forty waxwings were roosting there. When she got in her car to go home that evening the tree was bare!

By the middle of February sloes come too, but only the bigger black-birds go for these. And again, the winter-flowering clematis. We have also found that rather than cutting back old blackberry stems that might have old dry berries on, leave them over winter and the bull-finches like them.

At ground level

Flower-filled gardens will have plenty of seed that has dropped and not yet been eaten in the hungry gap, which is why annual, biennial and perennial plants that shed plenty of seed are good to grow in the main summer season. Verbena bonariensis and all the cosmos, cerinthe and salvias are ideal for this, plus the stinking iris, Iris foetidissima, the fat orange seedheads of which are ripening now, and I've seen blackbirds eating these.

The way to cultivate a big bird population is to mimic as much as possible what nature would have given them in a pre-manipulated world – that is, lots of cover, old, thick climbers over everything, a succession of fruity and seedy plants, the place filled with food and shelter.

Notes

1. Bird School: Learning

4 *his excoriating 2018 account* Mark Cocker, *Our Place* (Jonathan Cape, 2018)

5 *Heraclitus wrote* André Laks and Glenn W. Most (eds and trans.), *Early Greek Philosophy*, Vol. III: *Early Ionian Thinkers, Pt 2* (Loeb Classical Library, Harvard University Press, 2016), 124–7, from Themistius, *Oration*

5 *The eye-spots on butterfly wings* A.D. Blest, 'The function of eyespot patterns in the Lepidoptera', *Behaviour*, 11, 2/3 (1957): 209–56

5 *a pair of eyes is more frightening* Robert R. Hampton, 'Sensitivity to information specifying the line of gaze of humans in sparrows (*Passer domesticus*), *Behaviour*, 130, 1/2 (August 1994): 41–51; M. Scaife, 'The response to eye-like shapes by birds II. The importance of staring, pairedness and shape', *Animal Behaviour*, 24, 1 (February 1976): 200–6; Julia Carter et al., 'Subtle cues of predation risk: Starlings respond to a predator's direction of eye-gaze', *Proceedings of the Royal Society B*, 275 (2008): 1709–15

2. Birdhouse: Absorbing

10 *'hum with the frequencies of the unconscious'* Kapka Kassabova, *Border* (Granta, 2017), xv, xviii

14 *'In place of aurochs-grazed pastures'* Benedict Macdonald, *Rebirding* (Pelagic, 2019), 31, who quotes M.G. Paoletti, *Invertebrate Biodiversity as Bioindicators of Sustainable Landscapes* (Elsevier, 1999)

14 *intermediate disturbance hypothesis* David M. Wilkinson, 'The disturbing history of intermediate disturbance', *Oikos*, 84, 1 (January 1999): 145–7; Joseph H. Connell, 'Diversity in tropical rain forests and coral reefs', *Science* New Series, 199, 4335 (March 1978): 1302–10; Douglas Sheil and David F.R.P. Burslem, 'Defining and defending Connell's intermediate disturbance hypothesis: A response to Fox', *Trends in Ecology & Evolution*, 28, 10 (October 2013)

16 *now in East Sussex Record Office* ESRO listing as: 'Rounden, Coomb, Blackbrook Wood, Flat Weard, Little Weard, Willingford, Worge and Peach Hill in Brightling and Burwash' Finding/Object Number: ACC 2452/1

19 *Swetyngcroft* ESRO ref: 1419 Grant SAS-RF/9/1/1

20 *they have the same etymology* J.H. Prynne, 'Huts', *Textual Practice*, 22, 4 (2008): 613–33

22 *'a wave that ripples out'* T. Morton, *Humankind: Solidarity with Nonhuman People* (Verso, 2017), 15

22 *'the top access mode'* Ibid., 11

22 *'brushing against'* Ibid.

22 *'a loose, thick, wavy line'* Ibid., 14

22 *'necessarily ragged'* Ibid., 36

3. Wrens: Surviving

27 *'the cheerful one'* Edward Armstrong, *The Wren* (Collins, 1955), 53

29 *'it perks, bobs, teeters'* Ibid., 24

30 *'I am small, like the Wren'* Emily Dickinson to T.W. Higginson (268), July 1862, in *The Letters of Emily Dickinson*, ed. Thomas H. Johnson (Belknap Press of Harvard University Press, 1958), 2: 409–10

30 *'excels my Piano'* Letter 261, 25 April 1862

30 *'an unspectacular joy'* Quoted from Seamus Heaney's lecture 'John Clare's Prog', in Jonathan Bate, Introduction to *John Clare: Selected Poems* (Faber, 2003), xxviii

31 *'many a time hath sought'* 'The Wren', first published in the annual *Friendship's Offering* (1829), 334. In John Clare, *Selected Poems* (Faber, 2003), 152

31 *'the efforts of the lady'* Armstrong, *The Wren*, 56

32 *sixty-one were once found* D.W. Snow, C.M. Perrins et al., *The Birds of the Western Palearctic*, Concise edition, Vol. 2 Passerines (OUP, 1998), 1123

32 *population fell by 79 per cent* Kenneth Williamson, 'Habitat preferences of the Wren on English farmland', *Bird Study*, 16, 1 (1969): 53–9

32 *The oldest recorded* https://www.bto.org/understanding-birds/birdfacts/wren

33 *began as an American species* Carl H. Oliveros et al., 'Earth history and the passerine superradiation', *Proceedings of the National Academy of Sciences of the United States of America*, 116, 16 (April 2019): 7916–25

33 *'the wee brown button'* Armstrong, *The Wren*, 7, 23

34 *solemnly killed and buried* Karl P. Wentersdorf, 'The folkloristic significance of the wren', *Journal of American Folklore*, 90, 356 (April–June 1977): 192–8; Bryan J. Jones, 'Wren Boys', *Folklore*, 19, 2 (June 1908): 234–5

35 *'The wren goes to't'* William Shakespeare, *King Lear*, Act 4, scene 6

36 *males start to build* Matthew R. Evans and Arthur R. Goldsmith, 'Male wrens with large testes breed early', *Animal Behaviour*, 60, 1 (July 2000): 101–5

37 *hold less ground* Armstrong, *The Wren*, 34

37 *a mate worth having* Amotz Zahavi, Avishag Zahavi, *The Handicap Principle: A Missing Piece of Darwin's Puzzle* (OUP, 1997)

38 *five, six or seven eggs* Matthew R. Evans and Joe L. Burn, 'An experimental analysis of mate choice in the wren: A monomorphic, polygynous passerine', *Behavioral Ecology*, 7, 1 (Spring 1996): 101–8

39 *population pump restores* Barry J. Kentish, *Home range and territory of woodland wrens (Troglodytes Troglodytes Troglodytes linn.) in spring and summer* (1976), Durham theses, Durham University: http://etheses.dur.ac.uk/9208/

40 *every single one of the eggs* M.L. Berg, *Sexual selection and reproductive strategies in songbirds: Territoriality, mate attraction, parentage and parental care* (2007), [Thesis fully internal (DIV), University of Groningen]. [s.n.]

40 *neighbour hatred* Ibid.

40 *'dear enemy effect'* Ronald J. Brooks and J. Bruce Falls, 'Individual recognition by song in white-throated sparrows, I. Discrimination of songs of neighbors and strangers', *Canadian Journal of Zoology*, 53, 7 (1975): 879–88; J. Fisher, 'Evolution and bird sociality', in J. Huxley, A.C. Hardy and E.B. Ford (eds), *Evolution as a Process* (London, 1954), 71–83; Ethan J. Temeles, 'The role of neighbours in territorial systems: when are they "dear enemies"?', *Animal Behaviour*, 47, 2 (1994): 339–50

41 *Wren song* Armstrong, *The Wren*, 57

41 *form of highly expensive exclusion* H. Courvoisier, S. Camacho-Schlenker, T. Aubin, 'When neighbours are not "dear enemies": A study in the winter wren', *Animal Behaviour*, 90 (April 2014): 229–35

4. Songbirds: Proclaiming

45 *'the stirring hour'* Robert Louis Stevenson, 'A Night Among the Pines', *Travels with a Donkey in the Cévennes* (1879)

50 *'human-in-the-loop'* See Van Horn's website: https://gvh.codes/

50 *using AI to integrate new observations* merlin.allaboutbirds.org/sound-id

51 *Bell spectrographs could distinguish* Peter R. Marler, *Nature's Music: The Science of Birdsong* (Academic Press, 2004), 1

51 *first used in the 1950s* Luis F. Baptista and Sandra L.L. Gaunt, 'Advances in studies of avian sound communication', *The Condor*, 96, 3 (August 1994): 817–30

51 *app was released to the world* Interview in *Fast Company*: https://www.fastcompany.com/90694460/how-a-cornell-scientist-created-shazam-for-birds

52 *'the common cry of the Magpie'* C.B.M., 'The song of birds', review of C.A. Witchell, *Cries and Call-Notes of Wild Birds. With Musical Illustrations, Irish Naturalist*, 8, 8 (August 1899): 183–4

54 *calling for its American cousin* Native American languages heard the same bird. In Cherokee the black-capped chickadee is *tsigili'i*, in Yupik *cikepiipiiq*, in Oneida, an Iroquoian language spoken in upstate New York, *tsiktsile·lé*, all of which, more accurately, have one more syllable than chickadee. The bird when alarmed adds extra *-dees* to the end of its call, and most often sings *chickadee-dee*

54 *'We listen to be elsewhere'* Walter Benjamin quoted by Amit Chaudhuri in *Finding the Raga: An Improvisation on Indian Music* (Faber, 2022), 90

57 *Francis Allen* Francis H. Allen, 'More notes on the morning awakening', *The Auk*, 30, 2 (April 1913): 229–35

57 *George Marples* G. Marples, *British Birds*, 33: 4–11, in Armstrong, *The Wren*, 70–1

57 *Diego Llusia* 'Mean time of the first song for a temperate avian community in Île-de-France', data by Diego Llusia, Thierry Aubin and Jérôme Sueur (France) in T. Aubin, N. Mathevon (eds), *Coding Strategies in Vertebrate Acoustic Communication*, Animal Signals and

Communication 7 (Springer, 2020), Chapter 3: Diego Gil and Diego Llusia, 'The Bird Dawn Chorus Revisited'

58 *'dressed quickly'* Armstrong, *The Wren*, 70

58 *'a rather orderly fashion'* Robert J. Thomas et al., 'Eye size in birds and the timing of song at dawn', *Proceedings of the Royal Society B*, 269 (2002): 831–7

58 *'By the time birds'* Ibid.

59 *completely fill the skull* K. Tansley and J.R. Erichsen, 'Vision', 623–9, in B. Campbell and E. Lack (eds), *A Dictionary of Birds* (Poyser, 1985)

60 *Bart Kempenaers at the Max Planck Institute* Bart Kempenaers, 'Artificial night lighting affects dawn song, extra-pair siring success, and lay date in songbirds', *Current Biology*, 20 (October 2010): 1735–9

60 *Noise levels on the runway* M.J.T. Smith, *Aircraft Noise* (Cambridge, 1989); 'Levels of noise', https://audiology-web.s3.amazonaws.com/migrated/NoiseChart16x20.pdf_5399b28aaef0d9.27446344.pdf

60 *birds were shuffling their songs back* Diego Gil et al., 'Birds living near airports advance their dawn chorus and reduce overlap with aircraft noise', *Behavioral Ecology*, 26, 2 (2015): 435–43

62 *Whether that decision is genetically determined* Calandra Q. Stanley, Michael H. Walter, Madhvi X. Venkatraman, Gerald S. Wilkinson, 'Insect noise avoidance in the dawn chorus of Neotropical birds', *Animal Behaviour*, 112 (February 2016): 255–65

62 *the same mechanism that birds use* Stuart Alan Brooker, *The avian dawn chorus across Great Britain: using new technology to study breeding bird song* (2020), Durham theses, Durham University: http://etheses.dur.ac.uk/13709/; S.E. Goodwin, J. Podos, 'Shift of song frequencies in response to masking tones', *Animal Behaviour*, 85 (February 2013): 435–40

64 *sparrows which have had the gland cut out* S. Gaston and M. Menaker, 'Pineal function: The biological clock in the sparrow', *Science*, 160, 3832 (June 1968)

64 *when birds are exposed to constant bright light* J. McMillan, 'Pinealectomy abolishes the circadian rhythm of migratory restlessness', *Journal of Comparative Physiology*, 79 (1972)

65 *When the blackbird pours out his song* I.C. Cuthill, W.A. Macdonald, 'Experimental manipulation of the dawn and dusk chorus in the blackbird *Turdus merula*', *Behavioral Ecology and Sociobiology*, 26 (1990): 209–16

66 *outweighs the competition it has to face* Timothy J. Brown and Paul Handford, 'Why birds sing at dawn: The role of consistent song transmission', *Ibis*, 145, 1 (January 2003)

66 *marsh tits that pair for life* Richard Broughton, *The Marsh Tit and the Willow Tit* (Poyser, 2025)

66 *idea that it is even more directly about sex* Angelika Poesel et al., 'Early birds are sexy: Male age, dawn song and extrapair paternity in blue tits, *Cyanistes* (formerly *Parus*) *caeruleus*', *Animal Behaviour*, 72, 3 (September 2006): 531–8

5. Robins: Occupying

69 *More than 70 per cent of female birds* K.J. Odom et al., 'Female song is widespread and ancestral in songbirds', *Nature Communications*, 5, 3379 (2014): 1–6

69 *in papers on female birdsong* Casey D. Haines et al., 'The role of diversity in science: A case study of women advancing female birdsong research', *Animal Behaviour*, 168 (October 2020): 19–24

70 *They are not entirely quiet* Javier Sierro et al., 'Female blue tits sing frequently: A sex comparison of occurrence', *Behavioral Ecology*, 33, 5 (2022): 912–25

70 *They use song as the cock birds do* Virginia Morell, 'Why some female birds don't sing', *Science*, 12 January 2016

70 *Singing is expensive* R. Thomas et al., 'The trade-off between singing and mass gain in a daytime-singing bird, the European robin', *Behaviour*, 140, 3 (March 2003): 387–404

70 *No northern female bird has been heard* Evangeline M. Rose et al., 'Why do females sing? – pair communication and other song functions in eastern bluebirds', *Behavioral Ecology*, 30, 6 (2019): 1653–61; Sonia Kleindorfer, Christine Evans and Katharina Mahr, 'Female in-nest chatter song increases predation', *Biology Letters*, 1 January 2016

71 *'That's the wise thrush'* R. Browning, 'Home-Thoughts, from Abroad'

72 *'song is a war-cry'* David Lack, *The Life of the Robin* (4th edition, 1965), 45

73 *double the size of their English cousins* European density map: https://ebba2.info/maps/species/Erithacus-rubecula/ebba2/abundance/

74 *tall trees and bushes from which to sing* Snow and Perrins et al., *The Birds of the Western Palearctic*, Vol. 2 Passerines, 1142

76 *'Silence is either dead or married'* Lack, *The Life of the Robin*, 36

77 *'the redbreast's delectable resonancie'* Quoted in ibid., 13

77 *'As the observer approaches'* Ibid., 32

77 *'seep' calls* Joe A. Tobias and Nathalie Seddon, 'Female begging in European robins: Do neighbors eavesdrop for extrapair copulations?', *Behavioral Ecology*, 13, 5 (September 2022): 637–42

78 *A now-horrifying experiment* Robert E. Stewart and John W. Aldrich, 'Removal and repopulation of breeding birds in a spruce-fir forest community', *The Auk*, 68, 4 (October 1951): 471–82

80 *total of 528 adult birds had been killed* M. Max Hensley and James B. Cope, 'Further data on removal and repopulation of the breeding birds in a spruce-fir forest community', *The Auk*, 68, 4 (October 1951): 483–93

80 *The territories are not permanent fixtures* See I.G. Johnstone, *Space use by passerine birds: A study of territory economics in robins* Erithacus rubecula *and dippers* Cinclus cinclus (1994), PhD Thesis, Department of Biological and Molecular Sciences, University of Stirling

81 *Winter female robins are unique* Charlène Dudouit et al., 'Vocal performance during spontaneous song is equal in male and female European robins', *Animal Behaviour*, 193 (November 2022): 193–203

81 *independent territories are more likely* Michael Dunn et al., 'Trade-offs and seasonal variation in territorial defence and predator evasion in the European Robin *Erithacus rubecula*', *Ibis*, 146, 1 (December 2003): 77–84

81 *hen robins in winter behave like their tropical ancestors* H. Schwabl, 'Winter and breeding territorial behaviour and levels of reproductive hormones of migratory European robins', *Ornis Scandinavica*, 23, 3 (1992): 271–6

81 *Habiter en Oiseau* Vinciane Despret, *Living as a Bird* (Polity, 2022)

82 *'He knew every species'* Maylis de Kerangal, *The Heart* (Picador, 2017), 136–7

6. Tawny Owls: Haunting

90 *'vocifération douloureuse et lugubre'* Roderick Chadwick and Peter Hill, *Olivier Messiaen's* Catalogue d'oiseaux (CUP, 2017), 29

91 *'It was the stillness'* J.A. Baker, *The Hill of Summer* (1969), 87

92 *'part of the hearing nerve'* Jennifer Ackerman, *What an Owl Knows* (Oneworld, 2023), 30–1

92 *'an illuminated dot of light'* Ibid.

93 *'All of the night'* Edward Thomas, *Poems* (1917)

94 *hoot in the daytime* Jeff R. Martin and Heimo Mikkola, 'The changing face of Britain's Tawny Owls', *British Wildlife* (August 2014): 399

94 *their young only rarely travel far* With a few extreme exceptions see: R.A. Robinson, D.I. Leech and J.A. Clark, The Online Demography Report:

Bird ringing and nest recording in Britain & Ireland in 2022 (British Trust for Ornithology, 2023)

95   *came up from south-east Europe* Patricia H. Brito, 'The influence of Pleistocene glacial refugia on tawny owl genetic diversity and phylogeography in western Europe', *Molecular Ecology*, 14, 10 (2005): 3077–94

95   *easing north into the post-glacial grasslands* J.R. Martin, *The Tawny Owl* (Poyser, 2022), 26

95   *Gamekeepers … still set traps for them* 'Gamekeeper fined for illegally setting traps', Bird Guides, 1 August 2014, https://www.birdguides.com/news/gamekeeper-fined-for-illegally-setting-traps/; 'Gamekeeper charged with illegally killing wild birds', ShootingUK, 24 December 2013, https://www.shootinguk.co.uk/features/gamekeeper-charged-with-illegally-killing-wild-birds-20370/

96   *now have as many as there ever were* M. Stenning, *The Blue Tit* (Poyser, 2018), 32; Derek Yalden and Umberto Albarella, *The History of British Birds* (OUP, 2009)

96   *The air flows unbroken* H.D. Gruschka, I.U. Borchers and J.G. Coble, 'Aerodynamic noise produced by a gliding owl', *Nature*, 233 (1971): 409–11; R.A. Kroeger, H.D. Gruschka, T.C. Helvey, 'Low speed aerodynamics for ultra-quiet flight', US Air Force Flight Dynamics Laboratory (1971), TR 971–5

97   *'Eat this'* T.H. White, *The Once and Future King* (1958), Chapter 18

97   *two broods of young tawny owls* H.N. Southern, Richard Vaughan and R.C. Muir, 'The behaviour of young tawny owls after fledging', *Bird Study*, 1, 3 (1954): 101–10

99   *'But as we walked'* Eric Hosking, *An Eye for a Bird* (Hutchinson, 1970), 18–20

100 *'I was there within twenty-four hours'* Ibid., 21

101 *An owl's hearing* Ackerman, *What an Owl Knows*, 23; Bianca Krumm et al., 'Barn owls have ageless ears', *Proceedings of the Royal Society B: Biological Sciences*, 284, 1863 (2017): 20171584

101 *more than likely you are hearing an old man* Paolo Galeotti, 'Correlates of hoot rate and structure in male tawny owls *Strix aluco*: Implications for male rivalry and female mate choice', *Journal of Avian Biology*, 29, 1 (March 1998): 25–32

101 *most owl chicks will starve and die* G.J.M. Hirons, 'The effects of territorial behaviour on the stability and dispersion of Tawny owl (*Strix aluco*) populations', *Journal of Zoology*, 1, 1 (August 1985): 21–48

102 *a tawny owl territory* Graham R. Martin, 'Sensory capacities and the nocturnal habit of owls (*Strigiformes*)', *Ibis*, 128, 2 (April 2008): 266–77

102 *'the driver is quite often operating'* Brian L. Hills, 'Vision, visibility, and perception in driving', *Perception*, 9, 2 (April 1980)

7. Ravens: Thinking

105 *after 1895 they had all gone* John Walpole-Bond, *A History of Sussex Birds*, 3 vols (1938), Vol. I, 1

107 *'a plunderer then'* William Wordsworth, *The Prelude*, I (1805), 336–50

108 *That image of the boy* See the fragments from the *Prelude* notebooks collected in *The Prelude 1798–1799*, ed. Stephen Parrish (Cornell UP, 1977), 107, 113

109 *'My anxious visitation'* The Prelude 1798–1799*, ed. Stephen Parrish, 72–3

110 *'among the hills I sate'* The Prelude*, II (1805), 361–4

110 *as happened to a young and frightened friend of Bill Wordsworth* T.W. Thompson, *Wordsworth's Hawkshead*, ed. Robert Woof (OUP, 1970), 211–23

111 *'sounds unfrequent as in desarts'* The Prelude*, VII (1805), 637–8

111 *a pre-mammalian voice more ancient* J. Yoshida, Y. Kobayashi and M.A. Norell, 'An ankylosaur larynx provides insights for bird-like vocalization in non-avian dinosaurs', *Communications Biology*, 6, 152 (2023)

113 *'in northern Europe a vulture substitute'* Derek Ratcliffe, *The Raven* (Poyser, 1997), 75

113 *rarely kill a living thing as large as a lamb* See Ratcliffe, *The Raven*, 82–5, for a long and careful discussion of this question. Raven attacks on lambs have been witnessed but are rare

113 *white quartz* George Bolam, *Wild Life in Wales* (Frank Palmer, 1913), 223–4

114 *reveal the time-depth of our companionship with ravens* Chris Baumann et al., 'Evidence for hunter-gatherer impacts on raven diet and ecology in the Gravettian of Southern Moravia', *Nature Ecology & Evolution*, 7, 8 (June 2023): 1–13; Krzysztof Wertz, Jarosław Wilczyński et al., 'Bird remains from Dolni Vestonice I and Predmosti I (Pavlovian, the Czech Republic)', *Quaternary International*, 421 (2016): 190–200

114 *in the damp birchwood of the Mediterranean* See Anne Eastham, *Man and Bird in the Palaeolithic of Western Europe* (Archaeopress Archaeology, 2021)

114 *A commanding height is one of the fundamental aspects of a raven's world* Sascha Rösner et al., 'Raven Corvus corax ecology in a primeval temperate forest', *Ptaki krukowate Polski [Corvids of Poland]* (Bogucki Wyd. Nauk., 2005), 385–405; from ninety-eight raven nests found during 1985 and 1994, 91.8 per cent were built on pines, 4.1 per cent on spruce, 2.1 per cent on triangulation towers and 1 per cent on birch (Pugacewicz, 1997). The highest nest was found on a pine at a height of forty metres

115 *Analysis of the human remains* Hervé Bocherens et al., 'Reconstruction of the Gravettian food-web at Předmostí I using multi-isotopic tracking', *Quaternary International*, 359–60 (2015): 211–28

116 *ravens fed mostly on the meat of large herbivores* Zbigniew M. Bochenski et al., 'Fowling during the Gravettian: The avifauna of Pavlov I, the Czech Republic', *Journal of Archaeological Science*, 36, 12 (2009): 2655–65; Piotr Wojtal, Jarosław Wilczyński et al., 'The scene of spectacular feasts: Animal remains from Pavlov I south-east, the Czech Republic', *Quaternary International*, 252 (2012): 122–41

118 *naturalists have tried to transcribe the raven's voice* Richard N. Conner, 'Vocalizations of Common Ravens in Virginia', *The Condor*, 87, 3 (August 1985): 379–88

118 *gurgle-plop-clink* Ratcliffe, *The Raven*, 266

118 *'chewing and chuckling to himself'* George Bolam quoted in ibid., 267

119 *Roah never made that call* K. Lorenz, *King Solomon's Ring*, trans. M.K. Wilson (1952), 90–1

121 *never any traces of butchery* Dale Serjeantson and James Morris, 'Ravens and crows in Iron Age and Roman Britain', *Oxford Journal of Archaeology* (January 2011)

121 *booty ended up buried in the garden* John Forster, *The Life of Charles Dickens Vol. I. 1812–1842* (1872), 232–40; Paul Kendall, *Charles Dickens: Places and Objects of Interest* (Frontline Books, 2022), 83

122 *Raven is a high-powered* Marjorie Mandelstam Balzer, 'Flights of the sacred: Symbolism and theory in Siberian shamanism', *American Anthropologist*, New Series, 98, 2 (June 1996): 305–18; Elizar M. Meletinsky, 'The epic of the raven among the Paleoasiatics: Relations between Northern Asia and Northwest America in folklore', *Diogenes*, 28, 110 (1980): 98–133

122 *Raven liberated them* J. Oosten and F. Laugrand, 'The bringer of light: The raven in Inuit tradition', *Polar Record*, 42 (2006): 187–204

122 *'The birds were angry'* James A. Teit, 'Tahltan Tales', *Journal of American Folklore*, 32, 124 (April–June 1919): 208–9

123 *'The loon was to be tattooed first'* K. Rasmussen, *The Netsilik Eskimos: Social life and spiritual culture* (Copenhagen, 1931), 399

124 *'adapts, innovates, and transforms'* Thomas F. Thornton and Patricia M. Thornton, 'The mutable, the mythical, and the managerial: Raven narratives and the Anthropocene', *Environment and Society*, 6 (2015): 66–86

125 *As the flood withdrew* John Reed Swanton, *A New Siouan Dialect* (Torch Press, 1909); Franz Boas, 'Tsimshian mythology', US Bureau of American Ethnology, 31 (1916)

125 *he impregnated her* Teit, 'Tahltan Tales', 206–7

126 *'The trees and roots'* Ibid., 209–10

127 *driving out intruding ravens* J. Haffer and H. Kirchner, '*Corvus corax*: Kolkrabe', *Handbuch der Vögel Mitteleuropas*, 13 (1993): 1947–2022; Sascha Rösner and Nuria Selva, 'Use of the bait-marking method to estimate the territory size of scavenging birds: A case study on ravens *Corvus corax*', *Wildlife Biology*, 11, 3 (2005): 183–91

128 *extent of the territory of a breeding pair* The mean size of raven territories during the 2001 breeding season was 13.1 km2, as estimated by the bait-marking method (Rösner and Selva, 'Use of the bait-marking method to estimate the territory size of scavenging birds'). That is a circle with a two-kilometre radius. See Ratcliffe, *The Raven*, 102, for hearing at two kilometres

130 *looking for giant bonanzas* William C. Webb, John M. Marzluff and Jeff Hepinstall-Cymerman, 'Differences in space use by Common Ravens in relation to sex, breeding status, and kinship – Diferencias en el uso del espacio por *Corvus corax* con relación al sexo, estatus de cría y parentesco', *The Condor*, 114, 3 (August 2012): 584–94

130 *the birds will gorge for many days* Matthias-Claudio Loretto, Richard Schuster and Thomas Bugnyar, 'GPS tracking of non-breeding ravens reveals the importance of anthropogenic food sources during their dispersal in the Eastern Alps', *Current Zoology*, 62, 4 (2016): 337–44

130 *as many as 1,500 birds* Richard E. Stone, Nigel Brown, 'Communal roosts as structured information centres in the raven, *Corvus corax*', *Journal of Animal Ecology*, 72, 6 (2003): 1003–14

131 *'large groups of soaring birds'* John M. Marzluff, Bernd Heinrich, Colleen S. Marzluff, 'Raven roosts are mobile information centres', *Animal Behaviour*, 51, 1 (1996): 89–103

131 *'giving a few noisy kaws'* Ibid.

131 *'super-abundant, permanently renewed'* William C. Webb, William I. Boarman and John T. Rotenberry, 'Common Raven juvenile survival in a human-augmented landscape', *The Condor*, 106, 3 (2004): 517–28

131 *they are outcompeted for food* Bernd Heinrich and J.M. Marzluff, 'Do common ravens yell because they want to attract others?', *Behavioral Ecology and Sociobiology*, 28 (1991): 13–21

132 *Heinrich watched the ravens* Bernd Heinrich, *Ravens in Winter* (Summit, 1989), 215

132 *They liked to yell as they arrived* Ibid., 213

132 *fighting turns fierce* Ibid., 214

132 *in the end sheer numbers count* Ibid., 217

132 *'14 ravens at 11 am'* Ibid., 89

134 *Each raven has memories* Markus Boeckle and Thomas Bugnyar, 'Long-term memory for affiliates in ravens', *Current Biology*, 22, 9 (2012): 801–6

134 *Bigger birds will dominate* G. Kaplan, 'Long-term attachments and complex cognition in birds and humans are linked to pre-reproductive prosociality and cooperation. Constructing a hypothesis', *Annals of Cognitive Science*, 4, 1 (2020):127–42; Thomas Bugnyar, 'Social cognition in ravens', *Comparative Cognition and Behavior Reviews*, 8 (2013): 1

135 *all of them are playing* M. Osvath and M. Sima, 'Sub-adult ravens synchronize their play: A case of emotional contagion?', *Animal Behavior and Cognition*, 1, 2 (2014): 197–205

135 *Many adults remain single* O.N. Fraser, T. Bugnyar, 'Do ravens show consolation? Responses to distressed others', *PLoS ONE*, 5, 5 (2010): e10605

135 *pilferer just as quickly pretends* Bugnyar, 'Social cognition in ravens', 1–12

136 *no bird that is more like us* Thomas Bugnyar and Kurt Kotrschal, 'Observational learning and the raiding of food caches in ravens, *Corvus corax*: Is it "tactical deception"?', *Animal Behaviour*, 64, 2 (2002): 185–95; Thomas Bugnyar and Bernd Heinrich, 'Ravens, *Corvus corax*, differentiate between knowledgeable and ignorant competitors', *Proceedings of the Royal Society B: Biological Sciences*, 272, 1573 (2005): 1641–6; Thomas Bugnyar and Bernd Heinrich, 'Pilfering ravens, *Corvus corax*, adjust their behaviour to social context and identity of competitors', *Animal Cognition*, 9 (2006): 369–76

8. Buzzards: Flying

143 *Studies of different tit populations* Svein Haftorn, 'Contexts and possible functions of alarm calling in the willow tit, *Parus montanus*; the principle of "better safe than sorry"', *Behaviour*, 137, 4 (April 2000): 437–9; Millicent S. Ficken and Steve R. Witkin, 'Responses of Black-capped Chickadee flocks to predators', *The Auk*, 94, 1 (1977): 156–7

146 *a bird's heart* Herbert J. Levine, MD, FACC, 'Rest heart rate and life expectancy', *Journal of the American College of Cardiology*, 30, 4 (October 1997): 1104–6

146 *Birds can distinguish the passage of time* Kevin Healy et al., 'Metabolic rate and body size are linked with perception of temporal information', *Animal Behaviour*, 86 (2013): 685–96

150 *dinosaur legacies* Kevin Padian and Luis M. Chiappe, 'The origin of birds and their flight', *Scientific American* (February 1998): 38–47; Per G.P. Ericson, 'Evolution of terrestrial birds in three continents: Biogeography and parallel radiations', *Journal of Biogeography*, 39, 5 (May 2012): 813–24

150 *The short feathers covering* Quanguo Li et al., 'Plumage color patterns of an extinct dinosaur', *Science*, 327, 5971 (2010): 1369

151 *leaving the fore-limbs free for flight* Stephen L. Brusatte, Jingmai K. O'Connor and Erich D. Jarvis, 'The origin and diversification of birds', *Current Biology*, 25, 19 (5 October 2015): R888–R898; illustration by Jason Brougham (http://jasonbrougham.com/); Mark N. Puttick, Gavin H. Thomas and Michael J. Benton, 'High rates of evolution preceded the origin of birds', *Evolution*, 68, 5 (May 2014): 1497–1510

152 *following a long and worldwide series of ice ages* Nicholas R. Longrich, Tim Tokaryk and Daniel J. Field, 'Mass extinction of birds at the Cretaceous–Paleogene (K–Pg) boundary', *Proceedings of the National Academy of Sciences*, 108, 37 (2011): 15253–7

152 *their beginnings emerged* M. Andreina Pacheco et al., 'Evolution of modern birds revealed by mitogenomics: Timing the radiation and origin of major orders', *Molecular Biology and Evolution*, 28, 6 (May 2011): 1927–42; J. Stiller, S. Feng, A.A. Chowdhury et al., 'Complexity of avian evolution revealed by family-level genomes', *Nature*, 629 (2024): 851–60

153 *died with the trees among which they lived* Alan Feduccia, 'Avian extinction at the end of the Cretaceous: Assessing the magnitude and subsequent explosive radiation', *Cretaceous Research*, 50 (2014): 1–15

153 *They arrived much as they are now* Carl H. Oliveros et al., 'Earth history and the passerine superradiation', *Proceedings of the National Academy of Sciences*, 116, 16 (April 2019): 7916–25

154 *originated in South America* Scott V. Edwards and Walter E. Boles, 'Out of Gondwana: The origin of passerine birds', *Trends in Ecology & Evolution*, 17, 8 (August 2002): 347

156 *little birds of the wood can get airborne with a jump* Kathleen D. Earls, 'Kinematics and mechanics of ground take-off in the starling *Sturnis vulgaris* and the quail *Coturnix coturnix*', *Journal of Experimental Biology*, 203, 4 (2000): 725–39; Bret W. Tobalske, 'Biomechanics of bird flight', *Journal of Experimental Biology*, 210, 18 (2007): 3135–46

156 *'otherworldly and feminine'* Chadwick and Hill, *Olivier Messiaen's Catalogue d'oiseaux*, 158

161 *ready for the next downbeat* Crawford H. Greenewalt, 'The flight of birds: The significant dimensions, their departure from the requirements for dimensional similarity, and the effect on flight aerodynamics of that departure', *Transactions of the American Philosophical Society*, 65, 4 (1975): 1–67; Tobalske, 'Biomechanics of bird flight', 3135–46; D. Lentink, A.F. Haselsteiner, R. Ingersoll, '*In vivo* recording of aerodynamic force with an aerodynamic force platform: From drones to birds', *Journal of the Royal Society Interface*, 12, 104 (2015): 1283

163 *small birds do not dawdle* Matthew W. Bundle, Kacia S. Hansen and Kenneth P. Dial, 'Does the metabolic rate–flight speed relationship vary among geometrically similar birds of different mass?', *Journal of Experimental Biology*, 210, 6 (2007): 1075–83

164 *'wandering about the fields'* John Clare, *John Clare by Himself*, eds Eric Robinson and David Powell (Carcanet, 1996), 37

165 *seem like anomalies* Bret W. Tobalske, 'Morphology, velocity, and intermittent flight in birds', *American Zoologist*, 41, 2 (April 2001): 177–87

165 *Pulsed flight increases* Donald L. Kramer and Robert L. McLaughlin, 'The behavioral ecology of intermittent locomotion', *American Zoologist*, 41, 2 (April 2001): 137–53

165 *'a product of our own poor sampling rate'* D.R. Warrick, M.W. Bundle and K.P. Dial, 'Bird maneuvering flight: Blurred bodies, clear heads', *Integrative and Comparative Biology*, 42, 1 (February 2002): 141–8

9. Tits: Breeding

171 *lack of light generates a hunger for it* A.J. Lewy, T.A. Wehr, F.K. Goodwin et al., 'Light suppresses melatonin secretion in humans', *Science*, 210, 4475 (12 December 1980): 1267–9; A. Carlsson, L. Svennerholm, B. Winblad, 'Seasonal and circadian monoamine variations in human brains examined post mortem', *Acta Psychiatrica Scandinavica*, 61, S280 (March 1980): 75–85

172 *late summer moult is the better trade-off* Z. Barta, A.I. Houston, J.M. McNamara et al., 'Annual routines of non-migratory birds: Optimal moult strategies', *Oikos*, 112, 3 (March 2006): 580–93

172 *create interference patterns* K. Delhey, C. Burger, W. Fiedler, A. Peters, 'Seasonal changes in colour: A comparison of structural, melanin- and carotenoid-based plumage colours', *PLoS ONE*, 5, 7 (2010): 11582

172 *implanted small soluble tablets of testosterone* Mark L. Roberts, Erica Ras and Anne Peters, 'Testosterone increases UV reflectance of sexually selected crown plumage in male blue tits', *Behavioral Ecology*, 20, 3 (2009): 535–41

174 *carotenoid antioxidants* P. Hõrak, I. Ots, H. Vellau et al., 'Carotenoid-based plumage coloration reflects hemoparasite infection and local survival in breeding great tits', *Oecologia*, 126, 2 (2001): 166–73; Pablo Salmón et al., 'Urbanisation impacts plumage colouration in a songbird across Europe: Evidence from a correlational, experimental and meta-analytical approach', *Journal of Animal Ecology*, 92, 10 (October 2023):1924–36; Gergely Hegyi et al., 'Melanin, carotenoid and structural plumage ornaments: Information content and role in great tits *Parus major*', *Journal of Avian Biology*, 38, 6 (November 2007): 698–708

176 *this devastation may have been no more than* Martyn Stenning, *The Blue Tit* (Poyser, 2018), 129; map opposite page 161

178 *'Kevin feels the warm eggs'* Seamus Heaney, 'St Kevin and the Blackbird'

178 *'Why is the cuckoo's melody preferred'* Clare, 'The Wren'

182 *used cigarette butts incorporated* Adèle Mennerat et al., 'Aromatic plants in nests of the blue tit *Cyanistes caeruleus* protect chicks from bacteria', *Oecologia*, 161, 4 (October 2009); Monserrat Suárez-Rodríguez, Isabel López-Rull and Constantino Macías Garcia, 'Incorporation of cigarette butts into nests reduces nest ectoparasite load in urban birds: New ingredients for an old recipe?', *Biology Letters*, 9, 1 (2013): 20120931

185 *he might keep some energy in reserve* M.-J. Holveck et al., 'Eggshell spottiness reflects maternally transferred antibodies in blue tits', *PLoS ONE*, 7, 11 (2012): e50389

191 *allows them to see a caterpillar in dark silhouette* Stenning, *The Blue Tit*, 179

192 *hen's careful examination of his crown* Arild Johnsen et al., 'Male sexual attractiveness and parental effort in blue tits: A test of the differential allocation hypothesis', *Animal Behaviour*, 70, 4 (2005): 877–88

198 *the elimination of major predators* Density map: https://ebba2.info/maps/species/Cyanistes-caeruleus/ebba2/abundance/

199 *'The wind scatters'* Homer, *Iliad*, 6.146–9

199 *'One family of sparrowhawks'* Stenning, *The Blue Tit*, 61; Timothy A. Geer, 'Effects of nesting sparrowhawks on nesting tits', *The Condor*, 80, 4 (Winter 1978): 419–22. Geer found that in Wytham Woods outside Oxford 20–25 per cent of the population of breeding tits was taken by sparrowhawks each spring

10. Blackbirds: Singing

202 *'The development of song in the blackbird'* J. Hall-Craggs, 'The development of song in the blackbird *Turdus merula*', *Ibis*, 104, 3 (1962): 277–300

208 *expend so much energy on the brilliant* Krzysztof Deoniziak and Tomasz S. Osiejuk, 'Disentangling relations among repertoire size, song rate, signal redundancy and ambient noise level in European songbird', *Ethology*, 122, 9 (2016): 734–44

208 *blackbird's way of keeping ahead of those rivals* For sexual selection playing a part in the evolution of song repertoires see Donald E. Kroodsma, 'Correlates of song organization among North American wrens', *American Naturalist*, 111, 981 (1977): 995–1008; John R. Krebs and Donald E. Kroodsma, 'Repertoires and geographical variation in bird song', *Advances in the Study of Behavior*, 11 (1980): 143–77. For repertoires as a means of dominating rival males see J. Krebs, R. Ashcroft and M. Webber, 'Song repertoires and territory defence in the great tit', *Nature*, 271 (1978): 539–42; Ken Yasukawa, 'Song repertoires in the red-winged blackbird (*Agelaius phoeniceus*): A test of the Beau Geste hypothesis', *Animal Behaviour*, 29, 1 (1981): 114–25; Alfred M. Dufty, 'Singing and the establishment and maintenance of dominance hierarchies in captive brown-headed cowbirds', *Behavioral Ecology and Sociobiology*, 19 (1986): 49–55

208 *'Inspiration for one Cambridge blackbird'* Joan Hall-Craggs, 'Inter-specific copying by blackbirds', *Journal of the Wildlife Sound Recording Society*, 4, 7 (Spring 1984)

208 *Some bullfinches have been taught* Jürgen Nicolai et al., 'Human melody singing by bullfinches (*Pyrrhula pyrrula*) gives hints about a cognitive note sequence processing', *Animal Cognition*, 17, 1 (2014): 143–55

208 *'atonal noisemaker'* Paul Hindemith, Wikipedia, quoting Arnold Reisman, *Turkey's Modernization: Refugees from Nazism and Atatürk's Vision* (New Academia Publishing, 2006), 88–90

211 *'I value my garden more for being full of blackbirds'* John Addison, *The Spectator* (1711), 477

212 *'The first of these motifs'* Sylvia Bowden, 'The theming magpie: The influence of birdsong on Beethoven motifs', *Musical Times*, 149, 1903 (2008): 17–35

213 *'As for me, heavens above'* Beethoven's letter to Count Franz von Brunsvik, 13 February 1814, Emily Anderson (ed.), *The Letters of Beethoven*, Vol. I (Norton, 1986), 445

213 *'every musical idea that occurred to him'* Abbé Gelinek quoted by Bowden, page 33, from Elliot Forbes (ed.), *Thayer's Life of Beethoven* (Princeton, 1964), 248

218 *'fitter for the Spit than a Cage'* Nicholas Cox, *The Gentleman's Recreation, Book III, How to take, preserve, and keep all sorts of Singing-birds that are commonly known in England. Giving also an account of their Nature, Breeding, Feeding, Diseases of the same, with their Remedies* (London, 1686)

218 *Thorpe found the Kaspar Hauser chaffinches* P.J.B. Slater and P.J. Sellar, 'Contrasts in the songs of two sympatric chaffinch species', *Behaviour*, 99 (1986): 46–64

218 *if a group of those sound-deprived young chaffinches* K. Riebel et al., 'Learning and cultural transmission in chaffinch song', *Advances in the Study of Behavior*, 47 (2015)

218 *'complex but highly abnormal songs'* W.H. Thorpe, 'The Learning of song patterns by birds, with especial reference to the song of the chaffinch *Fringilla coelebs*', *Ibis*, 100 (1958): 535–70

219 *those from New York and Maine were somehow able to spread west* Donald E. Kroodsma and Hiroshi Momose, 'Songs of the Japanese population of the winter wren (*Troglodytes troglodytes*)', *The Condor*, 93 (1991): 1424–4320

220 *his potential for aggression* Torben Dabelsteen, 'An analysis of the full song of the blackbird *Turdus merula* with respect to message coding and

adaptations for acoustic communication', *Ornis Scandinavica*, 15, 4 (December 1984): 227–39

223 *meaning-structures of which the human ear was unaware* Stephen T. Emlen, 'An experimental analysis of the parameters of bird song eliciting species recognition', *Behaviour*, 41, 1/2 (1972): 130–71

223 *sing in imitation of two different birds at the same time* Martine Hausberger and Laurence Henry, 'Song sharing reflects the social-organization in a captive group of European starlings (*Sturnus-Vulgaris*)', *Journal of Comparative Psychology*, 109 (September 1995): 222–41

223 *Birdsong tends to be fluty* S. Nowicki and P. Marler, 'How do birds sing? Learning and development of bird song', *BioScience*, 38, 4 (1988): 265–74

224 *millisecond details* C.P.H. Elemans, A.F. Mead, L.C. Rome, F. Goller, 'Superfast vocal muscles control song production in songbirds', *PLoS ONE*, 3, 7 (2008): e2581

225 *It became clear to Dooling* Robert J. Dooling et al., 'Auditory temporal resolution in birds: Discrimination of harmonic complexes', *Journal of the Acoustical Society of America*, 112, 2 (2002): 748–59

225 *To birds in general* Beth A. Vernaleo and Robert J. Dooling, 'Relative salience of envelope and fine structure cues in zebra finch song', *Journal of the Acoustical Society of America*, 129, 5 (2011): 3373–83

225 *'a rich trove of information'* A.R. Fishbein, N.H. Prior, J.A. Brown et al., 'Discrimination of natural acoustic variation in vocal signals', *Scientific Reports*, 11, 916 (2021)

225 *'What Cartesian nonsense'* J.M. Coetzee, *Diary of a Bad Year* (2008), 132

227 *Ravel has written this music* The English flautist and composer Fiona Taylor provides an exceptionally helpful beginner's guide to this relationship in her blog https://fionajtaylor.com/blog/

228 *'suggests the song of nothing human'* Holly Watkins, 'On not letting sounds be themselves', *New Centennial Review*, 18, 2 (Fall 2018)

229 *'a train of thought that he can never fully unravel'* Immanuel Kant, *Critique of Judgment*, trans. Werner S. Pluhar (1987), 167

11. Migrants: Arriving

233 *'From mid-afternoon each day'* Ian Newton, *Finches* (Collins New Naturalist Library, 1972), 29–30

234 *'matted thorn'* John Clare, 'The Nightingale's Nest' (1832, published 1835)

235 *Biologists have found recently* Jamie Dunning et al., 'How woodcocks produce the most brilliant white plumage patches among the birds', *Journal of the Royal Society Interface*, 20, 200 (2023): 20220920

238 *most leave each spring for the longer days* Andrew N. Hoodless and Christopher J. Heward, 'Migration timing, routes, and connectivity of Eurasian woodcock wintering in Britain and Ireland', *Proceedings of the American Woodcock Symposium*, 11: 136–45; Gergely Schally, Sándor Csányi and Péter Palatitz, 'Spring migration phenology of Eurasian Woodcocks tagged with GPS-Argos transmitters in Central Europe', *Ornis Fennica*, 99 (2022): 104–16

239 *tracked by the wader specialist Andrew Hoodless* Andrew Hoodless et al., 'Migration and movements of Woodcocks wintering in Britain and Ireland', *British Birds*, July 2020; Schally, Csányi and Palatitz, 'Spring migration phenology of Eurasian Woodcocks tagged with GPS-Argos transmitters in Central Europe', 104–16

240 *About half of all the bird species* Ian Newton, *Bird Migration* (Collins New Naturalist, 2010), 8

241 *birds can catch the jet stream* Ibid., 98–9; F. Liechti, E. Schaller, 'The use of low-level jets by migrating birds', *Naturwissenschaften*, 86 (1999), 549–51

241 *'vulnerability to extreme weather'* Snow and Perrins et al., *The Birds of the Western Palearctic*, 1343

242 *seen wintering in Britain* www.bto.org/birdtrack; in the nineteenth century Howard Saunders in his *Manual of British Birds* (1899) recorded overwintering swallows, particularly in the mild winter of 1895/6

242 *when migratory siskins are housed with* Ashley R. Robart et al., 'Social environment influences termination of nomadic migration', *Biology Letters*, 18, 3 (2022): 20220006

243 *spear … embedded in its neck* 'Der Rostocker Pfeilstorch' [The Rostock Pfeilstorch] (PDF). *Der Sprössling* (University of Rostock, 2003), 9–10

243 *For Europe alone, perhaps five billion land-birds* Newton, *Bird Migration*, 152

245 *The swifts died of starvation* Ibid., 509

246 *fell to their deaths from high* Thomas S. Roberts, 'A Lapland Longspur tragedy: Being an account of a great destruction of these birds during a storm in southwestern Minnesota and Northwestern Iowa in March, 1904', *The Auk*, 24, 4 (October 1907): 369–77; Thomas S. Roberts, 'Supplemental note to "A Lapland Longspur tragedy"', *The Auk*, 24, 4 (October 1907), 449–50

246 *It may be that the spring path* A.P. Tottrup, L. Pedersen, A. Onrubia et al., 'Migration of red-backed shrikes from the Iberian Peninsula: Optimal or sub-optimal detour?', *Journal of Avian Biology*, 48, 1 (2017): 149–54

248 *mated groups of two Swainson's thrushes* Kira E. Delmore, Darren E. Irwin, 'Hybrid songbirds employ intermediate routes in a migratory divide', *Ecology Letters*, 17, 10 (July 2014)

249 *Stockholm biologist Thord Fransson* Thord Fransson et al., 'Magnetic cues trigger extensive refuelling', *Nature*, 414, 1 November 2001

250 *'to detect the reference compass direction'* Henrik Mouritsen, 'Migratory birds use head scans to detect the direction of the earth's magnetic field', *Current Biology*, 14 (9 November 2004), 1946–9; Henrik Mouritsen, 'Long-distance navigation and magnetoreception in migratory animals', *Nature*, 558, 7 June 2018

250 *specialised part of the fore-brain labelled Cluster N* The first suggestion had been made in the 1970s: Klaus Schulten, Charles E. Swenberg and Albert Weller, 'A biomagnetic sensory mechanism based on magnetic field modulated coherent electron spin motion', *Zeitschrift für Physikalische Chemie*, 111, 1 (1978): 1–5

251 *Red light of the kind* W. Wiltschko, U. Munro, H. Ford et al., 'Red light disrupts magnetic orientation of migratory birds', *Nature*, 364 (1993): 525–7

251 *Fog or long, thick overcast skies* Henrik Mouritsen, 'Night-vision brain area in migratory songbirds', *PNAS*, 102, 23 (June 2005): 8339–44

251 *lined the huts with aluminium sheets* S. Engels, N.L. Schneider, N. Lefeldt et al., 'Anthropogenic electromagnetic noise disrupts magnetic compass orientation in a migratory bird', *Nature*, 509 (2014): 353–6

251 *see the magnetic geometries of the earth* Peter J. Hore and Henrik Mouritsen, 'The radical-pair mechanism of Magnetoreception', *Annual Review of Biophysics*, 45,1 (2016): 299–344; Peter J. Hore and Henrik Mouritsen, 'How migrating birds use quantum effects to navigate', *Scientific American*, April 2022

253 *Massive bird hunts* L. Zwarts, R.G. Bijlsma, J. van der Kamp, 'The fortunes of migratory birds from Eurasia: Being on a tightrope in the Sahel', *Ardea*, 111 (2023): 397–437

253 *between eleven million and thirty-six million songbirds are killed* A.-L. Brochet et al., 'Preliminary assessment 884 of the scope and scale of illegal killing and taking of birds in the Mediterranean', *Bird Conservation International*, 885, 26 (2016): 1–28

254 *Acacia plantations are cultivated solely with trapping in mind* T. Shialis and N. Stylianou, 'Campaigning against illegal bird trapping in Cyprus', 121–6, in Sustaining Partnerships: A conference on conservation and sustainability in UK Overseas Territories, Crown Dependencies and other small island communities, Gibraltar, 11–16 July 2015 (ed. M. Pienkowski and C. Wensink). UK Overseas Territories Conservation Forum, www.ukotcf.org

254 *fly low straight into the nets* https://www.unep-aewa.org/sites/default/files/publication/poa_bird_trapping_egypt_libya.pdf

254 *dropped by 80 to 90 per cent since 1970* Zwarts, Bijlsma and van der Kamp, 'The fortunes of migratory birds from Eurasia', 397–437

255 *increased by an additional 400,000 breeding pairs* Turtle dove adaptive harvest management mechanism, March 2024. Technical update (western flyway) 1 Carles Carboneras, TFRB 24-04-05 TD AHM update – W flyway.pdf at https://circabc.europa.eu/

256 *eight-thousand-mile journeys* Kristaps Sokolovskis et al., 'Ten grams and 13,000 km on the wing: Route choice in willow warblers *Phylloscopus trochilus yakutensis* migrating from Far East Russia to East Africa', *Movement Ecology*, 6 (2018): 1–10

12. Man: Reckoning

260 *'the lesson of universal good-will'* Laurence Sterne, *The Life and Opinions of Tristram Shandy, Gentleman: ...* [pt.2] (London, 1760), in the digital collection Eighteenth Century Collections Online. https://name.umdl.umich.edu/004792564.0001.002, 78–9

261 *'I saw an unaccustomed number'* J. Huxley, *Bird-Watching and Bird Behaviour* (Chatto, 1930), from his talks on the wireless, 28

262 *'It freezes under people's beds'* *The Journals of Gilbert White*, ed. Francesca Greenoak, General Ed. Richard Mabey, 3 vols (London, 1986), Vol. I, 225

262 *'Moles work'* Ibid.

263 *'The Rook assembles'* Ibid., 229

263 *'The missel-thrush sings'* Ibid.

263 *'The Colemouse'* Ibid., 230

263 *'Gold-finch whistles'* Ibid., 233

263 *'The titlark'* Ibid., 234

263 *'Columbines'* Ibid., Vol. III, 35

263 *'Nuthatch makes'* Ibid., Vol. I, 235

263 *'Nuthatch chatters'* Ibid., 268

263 *'The grasshopper-lark'* Ibid., 237

264 *'The gizzard'* Ibid., 239

264 *'The capsule'* Ibid., 247

264 *'The white owl'* Ibid., 249

264 *'Bucks grunt'* Ibid., 262

264 *'Vast swagging rock-like clouds'* Ibid., 264

264 *'A Martin seen'* Ibid.

264 *'Green woodpecker'* Ibid., 274

264 *'Cock-turkey struts'* Ibid., 275

264 *'Golden-crowned wren'* Ibid.

264 *'Goose sits'* Ibid., 277

264 *'Green wood-pecker laughs'* Ibid., 320

265 *'Black-cap sings sweetly'* Ibid., 323

265 *'Sheared my mongrel'* Ibid., Vol. III, 223

265 *'The house-martins'* Ibid., Vol. II, 359

265 *'Swifts dash & frolick'* Ibid., 180

265 *'Bees begin gathering'* Ibid.

265 *'Stone-curlews pass over'* Ibid., Vol. III, 222

265 *'Sweet harvest weather'* Ibid., Vol. II, 230

265 *'Golden-crowned wrens'* Ibid., 267

265 *'The vipers are big'* Ibid., 269

265 *'Bees eat the raspberries'* Ibid.

265 *'The air is full of flying ants'* Ibid., 426

266 *'The small willow-wren'* Ibid., Vol. III, 455

266 *'by committing to a project'* Rhian Williams, 'Gilbert White's eighteenth-century nature journals as "everyday" ecology', *Interdisciplinary Studies in Literature and Environment*, 24, 3 (Summer 2017): 432–56, 449, in part quoting from Michael Sheringham, *Everyday Life: Theories and Practices from Surrealism to the Present* (OUP, 2006), 390

266 *'bawl through a speaking trumpet'* V. Woolf, 'White's Selborne', *New Statesman and Nation*, 30 September 1939

268 *'And as he went on his way'* From Ugolino Brunforte (1260–1345), *Fioretti di San Francesco* (*The Little Flowers of Saint Francis*), 1864 translation revised by Dom Roger Hudleston 1930, chapter 16, online at https://www.ccel.org/ccel/ugolino/flowers.iii.xvi.html

269 *'It is a sign of the birds' prestige'* Roger D. Sorrell, *St Francis of Assisi and Nature* (OUP, 1988), 65

269 *'All the birds began to open'* Chapter 16, *The Little Flowers of Saint Francis of Assisi in the First English Translation, Revised and Emended by Dom Roger*

Hudleston with an Introduction by Arthur Livingston (Heritage Press New York,1930s)

272   *The ninth-century BC prophet Elijah* I Kings 17

272   *'Usually it brought half a loaf'* Jerome, *Vita beati Pauli monachi Thebaci*, 10, 166 (PL 23: 25), in Robert Bartlett, *Why Can the Dead Do Such Great Things? Saints and Worshippers from the Martyrs to the Reformation* (Princeton UP, 2015)

272   *'had sheaves' Vitae Baldomeri epitome*, 684; the saint is also known as Galmier; see BS 2, cols. 725–6. *Vita Mathildis reginae posterior*, 17, 179; Thietmar of Merseburg, *Chronicon* 1, 21; 4, 36, 24. 152

272   *'If I speak to the emperor'* Quote from Bartlett, *Why Can the Dead Do Such Great Things?*, 395, from Thomas of Celano, *Vita Secunda sancta Francisci* 151, 244

274   *'The great sign by which'* E. Renan, *Nouvelles études d'histoire religieuse* (Paris, 1884), 332, quoted in André Vauchez, *Francis of Assisi*, trans. M.F. Cusato (Yale UP, 2012), 275

278   *'In somer when the shawes be sheyn'* From 'Robin Hood and the Monk' in T.H. Ohlgren and L. Matheson, *Early Rymes of Robyn Hood*, quoted in S. Harlan-Haughey, *Ecology of the English Outlaw* (Routledge, 2016), 182

278   *'Itt is merry, walking in the fayre forrest'* From 'Robin Hood and Guy of Gisborne' in S.K. Knight and T.H. Ohlgren, *Robin Hood and Other Outlaw Tales* (Kalamazoo, 1987), quoted in Harlan-Haughey, *Ecology of the English Outlaw*, 183

279   *'a royal prince'* Chadwick and Hill, *Olivier Messiaen's* Catalogue d'oiseaux, 84–5

279   *finally removed from the list of English breeding natives* Andrew Stanbury et al., *The Status of Our Bird Populations: The Fifth Birds of Conservation Concern in the United Kingdom, Channel Islands and Isle of Man and Second IUCN Red List Assessment of Extinction* (BTO, 2021)

279   *moving north at about two miles a year* J.W. Pearce-Higgins, *Climate Change and the UK's Birds*, British Trust for Ornithology Report (Thetford, Norfolk, 2021)

279   *'constant persecution by gunners of every description'* William Borrer, *The Birds of Sussex* (London, 1891), 8, 13

279   *'Forky-tailed kites'* Ibid., 15; they only returned to Sussex to breed in 2004, see M. Mallalieu (ed.), *Sussex Bird Report No. 75* (Steyning, 2022), 115

280   *Choughs and buzzards had both* Borrer, *The Birds of Sussex*, 16

280   *'victims of insensate persecution'* John Walpole-Bond, *A History of Sussex Birds*, 3 vols (1938), Vol. II, 223

280   'much sought for making fire screens' Borrer, *The Birds of Sussex*, 34
280   *shot out by 1895* Ibid., 144, 146
280   'inland in Sussex the Raven' Walpole-Bond, *A History of Sussex Birds*, Vol. I, 11
280   'from its persecution by the gamekeeper' Borrer, *The Birds of Sussex*, 150
280   'from constant persecution' Ibid., 154
280   *beginnings of a recovery* Walpole-Bond, Vol. I, 19
280   *Cuckoos became rare* Borrer, *The Birds of Sussex*, 167, 181
280   'not a hundred may now be seen' Ibid., 130–1; Walpole-Bond, Vol. I, 76
280   *At least until 1900, skylarks and greenfinches* Borrer, *The Birds of Sussex*, 109
280   '8 or 10 dozen linnets' Walpole-Bond, Vol. I, 201
281   'A steady traffic in Sky-Larks' Ibid., 201–2
281   'the whole length of the shore' Walpole-Bond, Vol. II, 111–12; Howard Saunders, *An Illustrated Manual of British Birds* (London, 1889), 40
282   'Farmland in the study area' Christopher F. Mason, 'Thrushes now largely restricted to the built environment in eastern England', *Diversity and Distributions*, 6, 4 (July 2000): 189–94, 193
283   *The requirement for builders now* https://www.gov.uk/government/collections/biodiversity-net-gain
283   'In the United Kingdom at least' Jamie Tratalos et al., 'Bird densities are associated with household densities', *Global Change Biology*, 13, 8 (2007): 1685–95
283   *disappeared from the British countryside* J.R. Krebs, J.D. Wilson, R.B. Bradbury and G.M. Siriwardena, 'The second silent spring?', *Nature*, 400, 6745 (1999): 611–12
284   *29 per cent of breeding birds have disappeared since 1970* K.V. Rosenberg et al., 'Decline of the North American avifauna', *Science*, 366, 6461 (2019): 120–4
284   *a drop of nearly a fifth* Fiona Burns, 'Abundance decline in the avifauna of the European Union reveals cross-continental similarities in biodiversity change', *Ecology and Evolution*, 11, 23 (December 2021): 1–14
284   'Modern arable agriculture captures energy' C.S. Dolton and M. de L. Brooke, 'Changes in the biomass of birds breeding in Great Britain, 1968– 88', *Bird Study*, 46, 3 (1999): 274–8
286   *more subtle dynamics are at work* D. Vanhinsbergh, R.J. Fuller and D. Noble, *A Review of Possible Causes of Recent Changes in Populations of Woodland Birds in Britain*, BTO Research Report No. 245

286 *40 per cent of all bird species use them* R.J. Fuller, S.J. Gough and J.H. Marchant, '11 bird populations in new lowland woods: Landscape', *Ecology of Woodland Creation* (1995): 163

286 *Those that go via Italy are doing better* Chris M. Hewson et al., 'Population decline is linked to migration route in the Common Cuckoo', *Nature Communications*, 19 July 2016

286 *over-managed fields and under-managed or abandoned woods* Fuller, Gough and Marchant, '11 bird populations in new lowland woods', 163

287 *the tits will begin to lay earlier* Will Cresswell and Robin Mccleery, 'How great tits maintain synchronization of their hatch date with food supply in response to long-term variability in temperature', *Journal of Animal Ecology*, 72, 2 (2003): 356–66

287 *migrants that fly to and from the African tropics* Chris B. Thaxter et al., 'Hypotheses to explain patterns of population change among breeding bird species in England', *Biological Conservation*, 143, 9 (September 2010): 2006–19

287 *Birds that eat insects* Diana E. Bowler et al., 'Long-term declines of European insectivorous bird populations and potential causes', *Conservation Biology*, 33, 5 (2019): 1120–30

287 *birds that nest in trees or bushes* M. Woods, R.A. McDonald, S. Harris, 'Predation of wildlife by domestic cats (*Felis catus*) in Great Britain', *Mammal Review*, 33 (2003): 174–88; Barry J. McMahon et al., 'European bird declines: Do we need to rethink approaches to the management of abundant generalist predators?', *Journal of Applied Ecology*, 57,10 (2020): 1885–90

288 *the weight of all the pheasants in England* C.S. Dolton and M. de L. Brooke, 'Changes in the biomass of birds breeding in Great Britain, 1968–88', *Bird Study*, 46, 3 (1999): 274–8

288 *about 40 per cent of the released birds* Deborah J. Pain, Ruth Cromie and Rhys E. Green, 'Poisoning of birds and other wildlife from ammunition-derived lead in the UK', *Oxford Lead Symposium*, 2014

288 *The other pheasants and partridges* J.R. Madden and R.B. Sage, 'Ecological consequences of gamebird releasing and management on lowland shoots in England: A review by rapid evidence assessment for Natural England and the British Association of Shooting and Conservation', Natural England Evidence Review NEER016, 20 August 2020; R.B. Sage, I.C. Ludolf and P.A. Robertson, 'The ground flora of ancient semi-natural woodlands in pheasant release pens in England', *Biological Conservation*, 122 (2005): 243–52; https://www.gwct.org.uk/research/long-term-

monitoring/national-gamebag-census/; N.J. Aebischer, 'Fifty-year trends in UK hunting bags of birds and mammals, and calibrated estimation of national bag size, using GWCT's National Gamebag Census', *European Journal of Wildlife Research*, 65 (2019): 64

288 *Half of the entire mass of wild English birds* This does not count the 29 million laying hens and 116 million broilers in the UK at any one time. In England alone there are 6.14 million breeding fowls, 4.9 million turkeys, 2 million ducks and 105,000 geese. Approximately 750 million broilers are slaughtered annually, producing 1.13 million metric tonnes carcass weight (www.defra.gov.uk *Poultry in the United Kingdom: The Genetic Resources of the National Flocks*)

288 *two-thirds of us* 64 per cent of British households put out bird food: Z.G. Davies, R.A. Fuller, M. Dallimer, A. Loram, K.J. Gaston, 'Household factors influencing participation in bird feeding activity: A national scale analysis', *PLoS ONE*, 7, 6 (2012)

288 *we put out 150,000 tons of bird food* Z.G. Davies et al., 'A national scale inventory of resource provision for biodiversity within domestic gardens', *Biological Conservation*, 142, 4 (April 2009): 761–71; M.E. Orros and M.D.E. Fellowes, 'Widespread supplementary feeding in domestic gardens explains the return of reintroduced Red Kites *Milvus milvus* to an urban area', *Ibis*, 157 (2015): 230–8

288 *We keep nine million cats which kill* Davies et al., 'A national scale inventory of resource provision for biodiversity within domestic gardens', 761–71

291 *The evidence is accumulating that wild birds* J.D. Shutt, U.H. Trivedi, J.A. Nicholls, 'Faecal metabarcoding reveals pervasive long-distance impacts of garden bird feeding', *Proceedings of the Royal Society B*, 288, 1951 (May 2021): 20210480

291 *a different man-engendered shape* Jack D. Shutt and Alexander C. Lees, 'Killing with kindness: Does widespread generalised provisioning of wildlife help or hinder biodiversity conservation efforts?', *Biological Conservation*, 261 (September 2021), with multiple references to other studies

292 *Nest boxes increase the size of populations* Ibid.

292 *makes the people who are providing the food and shelter* Daniel T.C. Cox and Kevin J. Gaston, 'Urban bird feeding: Connecting people with nature', *PLoS ONE*, 11, 7 (2016): e0158717

293 *They soon regurgitate what they try to eat* Hugh J. Hanmer et al., 'Habitat-use influences severe disease-mediated population declines in two of the

most common garden bird species in Great Britain', *Scientific Reports*, 12,1 (2022): 15055

13. Perch Hill: Reculturing

297 *'It might be interesting to watch'* Quoted by Richard Broughton in 'Monk's Wood wilderness: 60 years ago, scientists let a farm field rewild – here's what happened', *The Conversation*, 22 July 2021, https://theconversation.com/monks-wood-wilderness-60-years-ago-scientists-let-a-farm-field-rewild-heres-what-happened-163406

299 *'About half of the nests'* J. Wang, Y. Wei, L. Zhang et al., 'High level of extra-pair paternity in the socially monogamous Marsh Tits (*Poecile palustris*)', *Avian Research*, 12, 69 (2021)

311 *a vivid and vibrant present* Survey by RSPB birder Steve Blain reported on Twitter, 14 May 2023, after four hours at Strawberry Hill: 239 warbler territories: 59 willow warbler, 52 whitethroat, 43 blackcap, 30 garden warbler, 26 chiffchaff, 4 grasshopper warbler, 3 lesser whitethroat, 1 reed warbler, 1 sedge warbler. Also 30 nightingales and 2 cuckoos

312 *These acres may remain as song-filled shrubland* Another passive rewilding site that is even slower than Strawberry Hill, with fewer seed sources and dispersing birds, is at Noddle Hill, on the outskirts of Hull in East Yorkshire: R.K. Broughton et al., 'Slow development of woodland vegetation and bird communities during 33 years of passive rewilding in open farmland', *PLoS ONE*, 17, 11 (2022): e0277545

313 *'a formidable ally'* Nathalie Pettorelli, James M. Bullock, 'Restore or rewild? Implementing complementary approaches to bend the curve on biodiversity loss', *Ecological Solutions and Evidence*, 4, 2 (April–June 2023)

316 *'To exist is to change'* Henri Bergson, *Creative Evolution*, trans. Arthur Mitchell (New York, 1911), 7

317 *'ancient futures'* Helena Norberg-Hodge, *Ancient Futures*, 3rd edn (Local Futures, 2016)

328 *'Chew-chew chew-chew'* J. Clare, 'The Progress of Rhyme', lines 243–60

328 *'The alphabet [has] no letters'* J. Clare, Note C, Peterborough MS A58, in *Natural History Prose Writings*, 311–12

Roll-call of the Birds in Hollow Flemings, Perch Hill

B ird populations are full of variations in size and all the bird dimensions given here are averages and a rough guide only.

The QR codes in these mini-descriptions, when scanned into your phone, will connect with the relevant page in the Xeno-canto website (www.xeno-canto.org), which holds free-to-use recordings of wildlife sounds from across the world.

TITS

Blue Tit *(Cyanistes caeruleus)*

One of the birds everyone knows. Quite small, blue cap, blue-grey on its back, yellow below, with a black horizontal eyestripe running across its white face, which close-up can give it something of a Samurai air. The colours of the males can be stronger than those of the females.

Head to tail: 4.5 inches (11.5 cm)

Wingspan: 7 inches (18 cm)

Habits: Relentlessly perky and restless, never looking in one direction for more than part of a second, always curious to know what is going on above, below and beside it. One of the first to turn up at a bird feeder after a disturbance. In flight repeatedly whirrs and bounds with short rounded wings, evolved to flick in and out of thick broad-leaved woodlands.

Opportunistic feeders and diet is catholic throughout the year. Will eat any edible insect, spider or other invertebrate. Also resort to vegetable matter, if necessary, often with disastrous consequences (peanuts from feeders will kill nestlings).

Mostly associated with oak woodlands and specialise in feeding their young on oak leaf caterpillars such as winter moth (*Operophtera brumata*) and oak leaf roller (*Tortrix viridana*). Aphids can substitute if caterpillars are scarce. They will also take meat from dead animals and feed from ripe fruit at any time of the year. Uses aromatic herbs and nicotine (fag ends) to deter harmful pathogens in the nest.

Hangs upside down and pokes into crevices on the bark of trees and twigs.

Song & calls: High clear quivering song, extremely repetitive, with a hint of electric doorbell. When troubled by almost anything, it makes a harsh churring alarm or scolding call that sounds as if it comes from a larger bird. The Tit That Growls.

Seasonality: All year round in the same woods and gardens although in the winter outside the breeding season hangs out in large flocks hurrying between food sources. The following year's partners come from those winter flocks.

State of play: The 3.5 million breeding pairs are still many more than in the early 1960s and there is no concern for the blue tit's future but the UK population, after many years of expansion, has now entered a slow decline, for which there is no apparent cause.

Coal Tit *(Periparus ater)*

A small, slight tit with a slightly tweedy Bohemian air compared with the suave plumage of the marsh tit and the merry-go-round get-up of the blue tit. Dressed like a miniature Wessex farmer in a Hardy novel. Darkish-grey above, yellowish-grey below, distinguishable from the marsh tit by the white patch on the nape of its neck.

Head to tail: 4.5 inches (11.5 cm)

Wingspan: 7 inches (18 cm)

Habits: Behaves like the other tits, poking and looking into cracks and crevices, minutely examining and probing into any place a small invertebrate might be available. Its smallness means that it is always well down the pecking order and jumps away when a great tit or blue tit claims its place on the branch. Has a preference for conifers.

Song & calls: It does not make a churring alarm call like the other tits but sings pure silver-sweet songs, sounding something like a more honeyed version of the great tit's insistent two-note *dee-da dee-da* anthem.

Seasonality: Spending all year in the same English woods and gardens. In Europe it prefers pine forests to broad-leaved woods but in England makes little distinction. In some years giant 'eruptions' of coal tits arrive in Britain from continental Europe in early autumn.

State of play: With some variation from year to year, its numbers seem to be quite stable when measured over decades.

Great Tit *(Parus major)*

The muscled-up bruiser of the tit world, at least 20 per cent bigger and broader than the blue tit, easily displacing coal and marsh tits on arrival at a branch. Big black glossy cap on its head, yellow chest with a black stripe down the middle, like a wrestler's leotard, wider and blacker in the more successful males. Next to the other tits, the great tit can look like something of a tractor among runabouts.

Head to tail: 5.5 inches (14 cm)

Wingspan: 9 inches (23 cm)

Habits: Despite its bulk, can be shooed away by a dynamic and aggressive blue tit. Likes nest boxes and thrives in the Bird School accommodation. Eats insects in summer, seeds (including bird feeder food) in winter. Diet similar to blue tits, with a preference for beech woods and their nuts.

Song & calls: The unmistakable sound of the unoiled handle of a pump, or an electronic donkey *ee-awing* away in the tops of trees, conventionally portrayed as *teacher-teacher*, as well as lots of other *pees, tinks, churrs* and *buzzes.*

Seasonality: Lives in mixed flocks with other tits over the winter but pairs up in the early spring when the so-called singing begins.

State of play: Thriving all over Europe with 2.4 million territories in Britain.

Long-tailed Tit *(Aegithalos caudatus)*

The prettiest of woodland birds, a feathered canapé in soft, thick layers of pink, white and dark chocolate carnival colours: interior decorators would say salmon fillet with cocoa mousse and creme fraiche. An extraordinary body-form, like a truffle on a stick, whose flight is somehow a little frantic, unable to bound from wingburst to wingburst as other tits do.

Head to tail: 5.5 inches (14 cm)

Wingspan: 6.7 inches (17 cm)

Habits: Not a close relative of the other tits, but evolutionarily nearer to the flycatchers and some warblers. Behaves in the trees like a tit, busy about the branches, always on the move, bouncing from one twig to the next in an especially restless way. Eats insects and spiders in spring and summer, seeds and berries in autumn and winter.

Flocks of ten or twelve of them, strung out in a line across the sky like a school outing, make their way across the narrow fields from one wood to another and up and down the hedgerows. The pairs make carefully woven and cobwebby domed nests, camouflaged with lichen and difficult to find.

Song & calls: Such a high trilling song that it is difficult for listeners of a certain age to catch it. Merlin is the reliable standby.

Seasonality: Makes flocks in the winter of families from the previous breeding season (both parents and offspring), large numbers of them roosting together for warmth. They pair up in February and March, with young birds helping the breeding pairs to rear their chicks.

State of play: 380,000 breeding territories in the UK, a number that is quite stable.

Marsh Tit *(Poecile palustris)*

A delicate dandy some 4 to 5 inches long among the trees. Very difficult to tell from the willow tit, but as willow tits are now rare, if you see a slightly chubby-looking tit with a glossy black cap, white cheeks and a pale brown to morning-coat-grey back and wings, it is likely to be a marsh tit. Exudes an elegance and gentlemanliness. Not entirely common and so always a welcome sight. Both sexes look the same. The lack of a white patch on the nape of its neck distinguishes it from the scruffier coal tit.

Head to tail: 4.5 inches (11.5 cm)

Wingspan: 7.5 inches (19 cm)

Habits: Slightly tentative around bird feeders but takes its opportunity when it can, flying off with a seed in its mouth. Often goes to hide it somewhere for later. Has an intriguing habit of staring at you very hard if you are watching with binoculars. Will almost never use a nest box.

Song & calls: Makes all sorts of calls, sometimes a *pitchoo*, or a *pitch-pitchoo*, sometimes a very repetitive *dibidi-dibidi*. Can be summoned if its call is played loud on a phone when it will dance around you, ten yards away, telling you that the territory is already occupied.

Seasonality: Lives in the same territory all year round, super-loyal to spouse.

State of play: Under pressure from competition with other more aggressive blue and great tits, which benefit more from bird feeders. A catastrophic 80 per cent decline since the 1960s in the United Kingdom and not much better in other parts of NW Europe. Hanging on in the Balkans, Ukraine and southern Russia.

WOODLAND COMPANIONS

Goldcrest *(Regulus regulus)*

The smallest bird in Europe, whose Latin name means 'Little King Little King', with miniature wings, miniature tail and miniature body. Olive green above, with a gold crest on its head, and a caramel buff brown below with white wing bars. It used to be called the Goldcrested Wren and might be mistaken for a wren except it is paler overall. The gold crest on the heads of males is visible only when they are displaying.

Head to tail: 3.5 inches (9 cm)

Wingspan: 5.5 inches (14 cm)

Habits: It needs a conifer or two to feel happy. Flies like a slightly indecisive helicopter 'giving impression of more effort than resultant progress', as the Oxford ornithologists David Snow and Chris Perrins described it. Its lack of weight (a fifth of an ounce) means that it can hover-creep-perch on branches as if it were effectively weightless. Eats little aphids, spiders, mites and moth eggs. Few seeds.

Song & calls: A very high call and song. Was thought to be rare and endangered until conservation organisations sent out people in their twenties and thirties with undiminished hearing who found them everywhere.

Seasonality: Present in England all year but, extraordinarily, migrates to summers in Arctic Russia at one end and warmer winters in Tunisia at the other. Stragglers turn up in Iceland (630 miles from the nearest point of the continent). In the Azores (850 miles out in the Atlantic) it is common.

State of play: 790,000 territories in the UK and the population stable.

Nuthatch (*Sitta europaea*)

A rather impressive, gangsterish look, with a long black eyestripe extending the line of the bill back over the head towards the broad neck, like wraparound shades. Its bill is thick, strong, sharp and penetrative, its back and wings iron grey, its long round belly caramel-brownish. The whole effect is to make it seem dominant and bigger than it is. Looks charmingly loose and tufty round its back end.

Head to tail: 5.5 inches (14 cm)

Wingspan: 9.5 inches (24 cm)

Habits: Has the wonderful ability, with strong, grasping feet, to travel down tree trunks upside down, from which position it bends its head upwards towards an observer, as if to ask what they are looking at. Not at all sociable: can attack and harry other nuthatches at the bird feeders and when the young fledge they never flock together. Eats insects when available, seeds and nuts otherwise. Re-users of old woodpecker cavities, whose entrances the bird part-closes with a hard mixture of mud and saliva to make an entrance hole perfectly fitted to a nuthatch.

Song & calls: Loud, simple double note *tu-it* shouted in groups of four or five, audible over long distances in the wood, as endearing and bullish as the bird looks.

Seasonality: Almost entirely living in the same woods it was born in, although after very good breeding seasons in Europe large numbers of birds can make long expeditions across the continent.

State of play: Thriving in the modern world, now with 250,000 territories in the UK and almost triple the numbers of the 1960s.

Treecreeper *(Certhia familiaris)*

The most mouse-like of birds, often seeming to appear at dusk like a little quiet ghost, its back mottled and flecked as though made of lichened bark, its chest and belly a wonderful bright clean white (not usually dirtied like the woodpecker's). Its bill, used for poking into the crevices of the bark, looking for spiders and beetles, is long, pointy and downward-curved like a short bumkin on the bow of a yacht. In winter turns to seeds and small grains.

Head to tail: 5 inches (12.5 cm)

Wingspan: 8 inches (20 cm)

Habits: The bird climbs carefully up each trunk – or horizontally along the body of a fallen oak – spiralling around the circumference while hopping from stance to stance. Once it has reached a fork in the tree, it drops fluttering like a feathered stone to the foot of the neighbouring tree where it begins to climb again. Unlike the nuthatch, it always points upwards. The tail feathers are long and stiff and so in a woodpeckerish way act as a strut to brace the bird as it climbs with feet widely spread to give it a tripod platform. Often nests in a crack under the damaged bark of a tree and roosts by squeezing its body vertically into the soft or fissured bark of trees such as a sequoia. When comfortably lodged, the tail sticks out perpendicular to the tree trunk like a snapped twig.

Song & calls: The treecreepers have always been very quiet when I have seen them but they do have a simple, thin high-pitched song that drops in pitch as the bird runs through its phrases. Both male and female sing.

Seasonality: Lives all its life in the woods near where it was born.

State of play: For such a secret bird, there are far more in Britain than one might imagine, about 225,000 territories, a number that despite winter mortalities is quite stable.

Wren *(Troglodytes troglodytes)*

The shortest bird of all but with a tiny cock-a-hoop air, helped by the look-at-me gesture of its raised tail (always up in pictures, if not in life) as if it owned the world in which it lives. Close-up, a dark chestnut brown, with an elegant tailored selvedge to the wings. Its flight is a wonderful bee-like whirring zip from spot to spot.

Head to tail: 3.5 inches (9 cm)

Wingspan: 6 inches (15 cm)

Habits: Usually very shy. Lives mostly near the ground, feeding on beetles and spiders, but happily flies and hops up 25 feet or so to get into the top louvre of the birdhouse. Usually disappears into dark hollows and log piles. Likes to build its nest in any cavity it can find. At Perch Hill, in the hole left by a fallen brick, in the chassis of a van, the pocket of an old pair of chainsaw trousers, under the cover of a hose reel and inside the insulation around the top of an outside tap. Commonest native bird with 11 million pairs. The only British bird that has its origins in the Americas.

Song & calls: Extraordinarily loud song, especially in otherwise loud places, clear, shrill and vehement. Also a *click-click* warning note.

Seasonality: Migratory in much of Europe, moving south and west away from cold winters, but in England resident all year round. Eggs are laid in late March or early April.

State of play: Savagely vulnerable to harsh winters, which can knock back the population by three-quarters or more. Recovery over the following years so that the population follows a switchback course. 2020s numbers: about 11 million territories in Britain.

RESIDENT SINGERS

Blackbird *(Turdus merula)*

Cocks in the densest of blacks, hens in rich chocolatey brown. In spring the male's bill and a ring around the eye become a brilliant orange yellow, dulling in winter. Alert and sprightly, with strong confident surging flight at low level through the wood but also capable of torpedo-rapid shooting into cover if troubled. Can sit hunched a little mournfully in the rain as if in a semi-effective raincoat. Also stands on high points of trees or buildings with tail cocked up to assert its presence particularly in springtime when claiming territory.

Head to tail: 10 inches (25 cm)

Wingspan: 14 inches (36 cm)

Habits: Eats insects and earthworms as well as fruit, above all in the autumn. Eats in trees or on the ground where it shuffles its way through leaf litter. Can hear worms moving about underground. Woodland birds are very shy but in the garden much more confident. Husbands and wives stay together from one season to the next.

Song & calls: Incomparable. An oloroso of mellow roundedness, overspilling into the hedges and fields with a masterful languor no other bird can match. Chuckles are thrown in now and then. The blackbird does not shout like a song thrush but *chooks* if mildly alarmed and screams like a lunatic if seriously agitated.

Seasonality: Resident and sedentary in Britain but a migrant in north-eastern Europe.

State of play: About 5 million pairs in the UK but with strange and rather unexplained dips and rises in the population over the last few decades. Blackbirds in London in particular have been dying recently from the mosquito-borne Usutu virus, with no known cure.

Dunnock or Hedge Sparrow *(Prunella modularis)*

A very ordinary-looking bird, whose medieval name (1485) means 'little brown job'. Mostly brown and grey plumage. Their backs are streaked brown with black markings, making them look like a sparrow, to which they are not related. Underneath they continue the theme: mostly dull grey, with the sides tinged brown. Distinctive pinkish-red legs, as if in slightly dirty flesh-coloured stockings.

Head to tail: Smaller than a robin and less bulbous, 5–5.7 inches (14.5 cm) long

Wingspan: 7.5–8.5 inches (19–22 cm)

Habits: Quite shy, hopping about on the ground or up into the branches of a hedge or bush, feeding on insects, spiders and seeds. They have a chaotic love life, with set-ups of multiple husbands for one wife and multiple wives for one husband. Alpha, beta and even gamma males can serve either a single breeding female or even two. The relationship between the males is usually bad, as the alpha tries to exclude the beta and the beta the gamma but they will cooperate in keeping stranger males at bay. Polygynous set-ups – one male with two females – don't often last as one of the females usually recruits another male to her household. Often described but rarely witnessed except by the dedicated is its sexual behaviour: before copulation, the female crouches in front of the male, fluffs up her feathers, shakes a little and lifts her tail. The male responds by hopping from side to side and pecking at her cloaca. Stimulated by this, she ejects some of the sperm from a previous encounter, so that the new and present male has a greater chance of fertilising her eggs.

Song & calls: The sweetest thing about a dunnock is its song, a fast, high-pitched warble, relatively short but clear and sparkling in sharp little piccolo phrases. Sounds thinner than a robin.

Seasonality: Resident all year but tends to skulk in hiding when moulting at the end of summer.

State of play: Although there are 2.5 million territories in the UK, the welfare of the dunnock is a little uncertain. Its numbers fell in the 1970s and 1980s probably because farmers began to plant winter wheat, ploughing up the stubbles on which the birds had fed. They recovered a little in the early twenty-first century but have now begun a further unexplained decline.

The dunnocks are here but their near-lookalikes the unrelated House Sparrows (*Passer domesticus*) are not. There are still 5.3 million pairs of them in the UK, but numbers have dropped particularly in the south and east of England. The rural population had already halved nationally by 2000, and in the cities and suburbs had fallen by 60 per cent. The graph continues downwards and is now at about 20 per cent of its level in the 1970s. Intensification of farming systems, cleaner farmyards with less spillage, domestic cats, off-street parking, air pollution and in London avian malaria have all had their effect. In general, the more expensive the housing and the more modernised, the fewer house sparrows. Overall, both the number of chicks and their survival in the first year of life have declined.

Seedy planting and the provision of an open but sheltered porch might bring them in.

European Robin *(Erithacus rubecula)*

The Robin Redbreast or ruddock as it was known in medieval and early modern England (quite different from the American robin (*Turdus migratorius*), which is a dark-grey and brick-red thrush) with a surprisingly large head for its little body. Large, dark and highly expressive eyes. Both sexes look the same but young birds are an all-over speckly reddish brown with no red breast. Thin legs like a lawyer in a kilt. When cold it fluffs up its plumage and can look like a puffball on a stick. When warm much sleeker.

Head to tail: 5.5 inches (14 cm)

Wingspan: 8 inches (21 cm)

Habits: Nests low down in hollows. We found one robin nest in an old terracotta pot under a bucket. Not at all shy. Stands next to you and does curtsey-like bobs, coming up and down like an office chair on suspension springs. Ferocious singing duels with rival males, also involving a macho power dance and very occasionally a physical fight. A largely carnivorous diet of small invertebrates but in autumn and winter add fruits, berries and human-provided seeds and suet.

Song & calls: Wonderful bright songs in the winter (from both male and female) as clear as water illuminating the evenings and mornings when little else does. Can sing at night under street lights in cities or at rural railway stations.

Seasonality: Almost entirely resident in one place in England but many of our winter robins have come in from further north and east in Europe where they are much more migratory, wintering as far south as the oases in the Sahara, summering as far up as the North Cape of Norway.

State of play: About 7.5 million UK breeding territories, everywhere except the very tops of high hills. They did well in the late twentieth century and their numbers are now stable.

Mistle Thrush *(Turdus viscivorus)*

Not unlike the song thrush but bigger, longer, paler and rarer. The bird is aggressive to other birds but shy and wary of us, especially in the winter. More likely to be known by its song than by any clear sight of it.

Head to tail: 10.9 inches (28 cm)

Wingspan: 18 inches (46 cm)

Habits: Loves a holly tree and mistletoe after which it is named. It will defend these winter resources against other birds. In spring and summer eats insects, earthworms, snails and beetles, either on the ground or in trees and bushes.

Song & calls: Its desolate and beautiful 4-, 5- or 6-note song is sung from high in the tops of trees, here in the ashes on the edge of Great Flemings. Especially loud in the early morning, audible all over the rough grounds. Sings from late winter until early June.

Seasonality: Some are sedentary and spend all year in the same places. Others move with the seasons, especially southwards in autumn from northern Europe. Those in Britain might move a few tens of miles to more sheltered spots.

State of play: 165,000 British territories but the numbers have crashed by almost two-thirds with the degradation of farmland since the 1970s.

Song Thrush *(Turdus philomelos)*

The strident soloist that likes to adopt high branches from which to proclaim his position in the world. A medium-sized thrush, palish brown on its back but with a wonderful speckled pale chest. Stands upright to address its audience. Apricot orange lining of mouth visible when it opens its beak wide to sing.

Head to tail: 9 inches (23 cm)

Wingspan: 13 inches (33 cm)

Habits: When on the ground looking for worms seems like a canny operator, hopping from stance to stance, turning its head sideways to listen to the worms underground. Likes to pick up snails and smash them on to stones, eventually flicking the body out with its beak.

Song & calls: The dawn and dusk jazzmeister of the woods and hedges. Not as richly sonorous as the blackbird but more inventive with strings of different phrases, almost always repeated.

Seasonality: Spends all year in the same place in England but is highly migratory in Europe, and many of the northern European thrushes spend the winter in southern England. Those from further north in Scandinavia winter further south in Europe. They all head back north in late March, early April.

State of play: Modern agriculture devastated song thrush numbers which although still quite high and apparently stable at 1.3 million British territories is still some 48 per cent lower than in the 1960s. A lower survival rate among fledglings in a less protective and food-rich environment may have knocked them down.

FINCHES

Bullfinch *(Pyrrhula pyrrhula)*

Garbo-ish, glamorous, shy, the male with a bright rosy-red chest, the female greyer and more muted, but both with high-chic black skullcaps like Renaissance churchmen. Impressively powerful black beak for crushing seeds.

Head to tail: 6–6.5 inches (15.5 cm)

Wingspan: 8.5–11 inches (27 cm)

Habits: The pair usually turn up together so that if you see one look for the other. They can hang off high summer grasses, picking the seeds from the flowerheads. But be careful as they are easily disturbed. Orchard keepers do not love them because they pick the blossom off fruit trees. In Hollow Flemings they strip the blackthorn buds in early spring and in the summer meadows the little red seeds on the sorrel.

Song & calls: Their song is a soft and gently forlorn series of low, fluty whistles, sung from hiding among the trees.

Seasonality: Here all year round.

State of play: A huge drop in numbers in the 1970s, a slight recovery but now a renewed decline. Currently 265,000 territories in the UK but the population is down by half from its first count in the 1960s.

Chaffinch *(Fringilla coelebs)*

A subtle and complex colour system in the males, sliding from a blue-grey head into rusty brown on its upper back and an elegant citrine-green on the lower back, often concealed by the folded black and white wings. Its chest feathers have a pinkish-reddish-orange glow. The female is an equally subtle fusion of greys and browns on the edge of olive green. In flight you often catch only the striking white wing and tail bars as they scoot away.

Head to tail: 5.5–6 inches (14.5 cm)

Wingspan: 9.5–11 inches (27 cm)

Habits: Their main food is plant seeds, which they pick from the ground. Before the age of chemical agriculture they were regularly seen picking out the fallen seeds at the barn door and from the chaff of the barn-sweepings, from which they got their name.

Song & calls: They often call '*pink pink pink*' as they fly through the trees. The male song in breeding time is a descending trill, starting high and rapid and dropping over two or three seconds to a lower, longer final note, often with a flourished *churr* at the end.

Seasonality: Breeding from April to July in neat, cup-shaped nests made of moss, grass and spider webs, often camouflaged with lichen, in trees or dense shrubs. Difficult to find. Like many birds, resident here but migratory in northern Europe.

State of play: They boomed between 1970 and 2010 but then numbers started to fall sharply as the chaffinches were afflicted by trichomonosis, one of the diseases spread on dirty bird feeders. Nevertheless the UK still has 5 million breeding pairs.

Goldfinch *(Carduelis carduelis)*

Male and female look the same: a bright red face (with the red splotch slightly bigger in the male) and a white patch around the eye and chin. When in aggressive mode can look like pantomime devils. The wings are black with startling No Parking Yellow flashes, which come particularly clear when the bird is flying. The underparts are a soft pale caramel and white and in the young birds are as fluffy as a powder puff. From behind, the barred black and white markings look like the threatening face of a larger bird. Their bills, unlike other finches', are pointy to allow them to get at the narrow seeds of thistles, dandelions and teasels. The birds look white when flying above you. Most often seen in flocks despite mutual antagonism.

Head to tail: 5 inches (13 cm)

Wingspan: 8.5–10 inches (23 cm)

Habits: They roost up in the high branches of the ash trees where the early sun warms them. Travel in a dominant gang of 10 or 12, from which the tits shudder away. Can be aggressive to nearly all other birds, opening their bills in displays of red-faced ferocity. They build neat, carefully rounded if quite shallow nests made of moss, grass and other fine materials, usually in the forks of tree branches or in thick shrubs.

Song & calls: A rapid quickstep of a song, high and twitter-tinkling, repetitive and sung for hours at a time. Their calls when sitting together in the trees are straightforward *eets*, doing little more than announcing their presence to friends and relations. Slight sense of fingernails dragged down glass.

Seasonality: Here all year.

State of play: One of the boomers with 1.7 million pairs in UK and a tripling in numbers since the 1960s. Hugely stimulated by the bird-food revolution.

Greenfinch *(Chloris chloris)*

A wonderful, almost Amazonian shimmer to the green-yellow-lime-lemon colour-flicker in the male. Apart from strong yellow bars on wings and tails, that range of colours is mottled across their whole back, chest and head like a citrus mash. Big black eyes and a powerful pale seed-crushing beak. Females are similar but duller.

Head to tail: 5.5–6.3 inches (15 cm)

Wingspan: 9.6–10.8 inches (26.5 cm)

Habits: They eat big seeds, very fond of sunflowers and berries. Can rush from spot to spot in small flocks, all settling into the same one tree. Or then dropping to the ground to find the seeds.

Song & calls: A not very inventive song that chips and squeezes its notes, often from the very tops of small hawthorns or young oaks. Can sound as if it is singing through its nose. Or dragging a fingernail along the teeth of a comb. Once it has begun can continue for minutes at a time.

Seasonality: Resident all year round, with winter numbers boosted by migrants arriving from Scandinavia.

State of play: Down by 70 per cent since the 1960s, most of that damage being done by trichomonosis from dirty feeders in the last ten or fifteen years. Still, there are now more than three-quarters of a million pairs in Britain and numbers seem to be increasing slightly at Perch Hill.

Redpoll *(Acanthis flammea/cabaret/hornemanni)*

Used to be divided into Common, Lesser and Arctic Redpoll but since 2024 have been lumped together as simple Redpolls, named after the raspberry splash on their foreheads (poll: Old English for 'head'). The males in their breeding finery also have a pink or red flush spread rather haphazardly across their chests as if a three-year-old had spilled summer pudding down his bib. The wings and backs are brown with dark bars like a dunnock or sparrow. They are the prettiest of birds, in the past much caught by London birdcatchers for drawing-room cages.

Head to tail: 4.7–5.5 inches (12.5 cm)

Wingspan: 8–9 inches (23 cm)

Habits: Loves the birches and alders of Hollow Flemings but will also come to the feeders for sunflower and nyger seeds. Not at all fierce with each other, as other finches can be, and have even been known to nest in loose colonies.

Song & calls: A sharp, fast, jumbled song, more a chatter than a song and with finchy *churrs* scattered through it.

Seasonality: Our redpolls at Perch Hill are resident but their numbers are increased by European visitors, particularly in cold winters.

State of play: In a sorry state, after a boom in the 1970s, then a catastrophic crash from which they have yet to recover. The UK population is stable at 260,000 pairs but about 90 per cent down on its 1960s numbers.

Siskin *(Spinus spinus)*

Small and delicate finch, a bright clear yellow in the male with a black crown and black bib. The females are out of the same design studio but slimmer and with their colours silvered and frosty. Closely related to canaries with which they can hybridise.

Head to tail: 4.5 inches (12 cm)

Wingspan: 8–9 inches (23 cm)

Habits: Traditionally a bird of mixed conifer woods, picking the seeds from the pine cones and from alders and birches. Once confined largely to the north but with commercial plantations of these soft-woods have spread south. At Perch Hill they live in stands of Western Hemlocks in the neighbouring woodland. Happy at bird feeders where they compete with the goldfinches.

Song & calls: Quick, high, warbling twitters and trills, with some buzzes mixed in. Often a burbling stream of *tseet* calls when a flock of them is sitting above you unseen in the trees. They go quiet if they know you are there.

Seasonality: At Perch Hill all year but migrant elsewhere in Europe.

State of play: Expanded its numbers as more of the pine forests it loves were planted in England but the graph has not been an uninterrupted climb. Big fluctuations on a decade-long rhythm have slowed the Siskin's increase to what is now about 445,000 pairs, most of them in the north and west of the country.

PIGEONS

Stock Dove *(Columba oenas)*

Smaller than the wood pigeon and although both birds are overall a soft, slatey bluish-grey, stock doves do not have the white neck patch and white wing bars of the adult wood pigeons. On the back of their necks a glimmery iridescent smear of metallic submarine green, like a sea-opal wiped across the feathers. The slightest clouded pink tinge to their breasts.

Head to tail: 12–13 inches (33 cm)

Wingspan: 26 inches (66 cm)

Habits: Seed and plant eaters and so usually on the ground, picking for grains. In autumn they will also eat acorns and beech mast and in spring sometimes forage on young shoots and buds. They nest in natural holes in trees – at Perch Hill they seem to choose the high ashes – rather than in the open stick nests made by wood pigeons. The female also lays two white eggs. Both parents incubate the eggs and like other pigeons feed the chicks with 'pigeon milk', a liquid secreted from the lining of their crops, the bulbous chamber at the top of their gut in which food is also stored.

Song & calls: The stock dove's song can be an almost monkey-like hooting, or at least a monkey exhausted after a night on the tiles: *oo-oo-oo*, repeated six or seven times, much less rhythmic than the wood pigeon's. Somewhere between gently pained and gently ecstatic.

Seasonality: Present all year.

State of play: 320,000 territories, with a rapid expansion in the last twenty years, recovering after damage done by toxic seed dressings in the twentieth century.

Wood Pigeon *(Columba palumbus)*

Stalks about on the ground as a waistcoated beadle. A little bobble head on a bulbous body. White stripes on the wing and the white collar patch (present only in adults) distinguishes them from the stock dove. Male and female look the same.

Head to tail: 15–17 inches (41 cm)

Wingspan: 27–31.5 inches (80 cm)

Habits: Feed on the ground on plants and seeds. They have a large crop in which hard grains can be stored for digestion later. Nests are slightly messy and surprisingly happy jumbles of sticks and twigs in which the two white eggs are laid. Can breed in any month of the year and is most productive in August. Escape from the trees in a fluster of noisy clapping wingbeats but are capable in flight of a beautiful breasting-the-air gesture, interrupting their flapped flight with a long dipping mid-air glide.

Song & calls: Deep repetitive strum of English woods, less a cooing than a bass-line sustained for hours at the back of the stage, rhythmically and lullingly wallpapering the summer days:

Hallo my dear: I love you too.

Why don't you: now love me too?

I long for you: to be here too.

Come here now: I want you so-o

Seasonality: Present all year round.

State of play: Very common with more than 5 million pairs in the

UK. A huge increase in numbers since the 1960s, which only recently has been seen to level off.

PREDATORS

Buzzard *(Buteo buteo)*

A big dominant bird if smaller than any eagle. Soaring, circling, a round heavily beaked head on a thick neck and strong-looking body slung between broad, finger-tipped wings. A short fanned tail. Some buzzards are paler, some darker brown, almost black, the lower side always paler than the upper. In the binoculars a large dark observant eye. At a distance, a coasting invigilator.

Head to tail: 20–22 inches (55 cm)

Wingspan: 44–50 inches (128 cm)

Habits: Soars with wings raised in a shallow V and glides with wings flat, often circling. Likes a mixed landscape of wood and open ground. Eats all kind of prey from rabbits, other small mammals and birds to insects and earthworms. Can casually survey the ground from the air or a viewing post or sometimes more surreptitiously ambush its victims. To be seen stalking about the fields like a security guard looking for malefactors – or worms. Thrives in the margins of wood and field. Often solitary but also in pairs. Can make dramatic territory display flights in the spring, two birds or more soaring and diving together, wings aloft.

Song & calls: All year but above all in the breeding season a plaintive mewing or a high ringing *ca-ow*, often repeated, with gaps between calls.

Seasonality: Resident all year.

State of play: An extraordinary recovery since a low point after massive destruction by gamekeepers and agricultural poisons in the mid-twentieth century. Its numbers have increased tenfold since the mid-1980s to about 63,000 breeding pairs in Britain. Despite a small recent decline, buzzards are now to be found almost everywhere except the cities.

Great Spotted Woodpecker *(Dendrocopos major)*

Nothing cryptic about it, bigger than the songbirds, with a blazing zigzag pattern of black and white bars and patches, and a traffic-light red patch under its tail. The juveniles add to that a bright cardinal-red cap that fades as they age. All males have a red nape. A big black bill. It 'swees' in flight, to use John Clare's word – a form of 'swaying' – making long, looping, undulating, closed-wing bounds between wingbursts. Exudes a kind of frantic energy when confronted with a tree trunk.

Head to tail: 8–9 inches (23 cm)

Wingspan: 13–15 inches (38 cm)

Habits: Feeds on insects and tree seeds in winter but in the breeding time takes small birds, their eggs and nestlings. Can chisel its way through an inch of timber with no problem. Makes a new nest cavity each year. Equipped with a miracle tongue stored in a cavity wrapped around its brain which it extends into tree holes and nest boxes where its harpoon tip can impale soft-bodied victims. Insects become glued to sticky bristles with which the tongue is coated. Each pair has a territory of about 25 acres or 10 hectares.

Song & calls: Loud drumming in the first half of the year declares presence and territory over wide areas. The bird clings to the tree and delivers its head at the wood like a bowler flinging his arm at his adversary. Up to 25 hammer blows a second. The force has been measured at 400–600 G. (100 G causes concussions in human beings.) Despite earlier suggestions, it now appears that woodpeckers do not have inbuilt shock absorbers. No one is sure how they avoid brain damage. At other times of year a harsh *tchik*, quite often loud and repeated.

Seasonality: Resident year round wherever it lives in Europe.

State of play: Increasing in the UK, thanks in part to milder winters, the abundance of garden feeders and plenty of standing dead wood. There are now about 130,000 pairs in Britain, almost four times the number that were here in the 1960s.

Kestrel *(Falco tinnunculus)*

A small and delicate-looking falcon, with a reddish impression overall, long wings, pale below and with a brown and dark-spotted back that in some birds can look like a ploughed field or the floor of a wood in autumn. The hovering bird, often seen over motorway verges, its wings trembling beside its head, balancing on the wind, holding still its observing eye while everything in the rest of its body is in motion. The windhover, master of poise afloat and of long silk-lined glides from stance to stance.

Head to tail: 12–15 inches (34 cm) (female larger than male, as in most raptors)

Wingspan: 25–32 inches (81 cm)

Habits: Feeds on small mammals and occasionally small birds. When it spots a victim, steps down through the air towards it, one swoop after another, punctuated with still hoverings, before finally plunging fast and hard for the kill.

Song & calls: Almost silent except when giving sharp warning calls to other kestrels or with their own young.

Seasonality: Year round.

State of play: The kestrel population has been declining, largely due to loss of habitat, loss of grasslands and the absence of small mammals on which to prey. There are now about 30,000 pairs in Britain, fewer than in the 1960s. They have also been declining in Europe since 1980.

Red Kite *(Milvus milvus)*

Large and masterly raptor. Floats high and lofty above wood and field. More mobile, less stately than a buzzard. Turns like a dancer, its forked tail and long fingery wings flickering in the way of a flamenco hand. Often no more than a dark silhouette but close-to a rich reddish brown on the chest, white and dark in the wings.

Head to tail: 24–28 inches (61–71 cm)

Wingspan: 69–77 inches (175–195 cm)

Habits: Primarily a scavenger, feeding on dead animals, roadkill and small mammals but also birds, insects and even earthworms.

Song & calls: A long rocking reverberant wolf-whistle whistling '*wee-ooo*'.

Seasonality: Resident all year round.

State of play: Was heavily persecuted by farmers and game enthusiasts all across Europe and only just hung on in Wales with a low point of ten breeding pairs in the 1940s, all birds descended from a single fertile female. In the late twentieth century reintroduced in the Chilterns and the Black Isle and have been spreading since. Now approaching 5,000 pairs in the UK and have recently arrived, at least as visitors, at Perch Hill.

Sparrowhawk *(Accipiter nisus)*

Slender, bluish grey above in the males, barred reddish orange on the chest. Unforgiving orange-yellow eyes. Females are larger, browner below and brown-grey above. Sharply armed with long narrow talons.

Head to tail: Males 11–13 inches (33 cm), females 14–16 inches (41 cm)

Wingspan: Males 23–26 inches (66 cm), females 26–31 inches (78 cm)

Habits: An ambush predator, almost entirely preying on small birds, quick and sneaky by habit, leaping on to sparrows and finches from hidden spots, with sudden flight turns, around the corner of a bush or over the top of a hedge and down on to the unsuspecting victims. The ultimate dash-raider. Lives a solitary life. Breeding pairs do not remain together once the chicks have been raised.

Song & calls: As suits them, no song at all and only occasional quick high-pitched '*kek-kek-kek's*. The silent killers.

Seasonality: Resident in Britain all year. Migratory in Europe.

State of play: Pesticides very nearly destroyed them all in the 1950s and 1960s and although they have recovered since the banning of the toxins, there are still only some 30,000 pairs in the UK, evenly spread across the country.

Tawny Owl *(Strix aluco)*

Dark-eyed and broad-winged with mottled brown plumage, which can vary from almost ashy grey (especially further east in Europe) to reddish dried-oak-leaf brown. You don't see them often, but if you are lucky enough to catch one off guard, endearingly tubby. Big dark receptive eyes in a dark face. Silent, long, flat glides like the dream of flight through wood clearings. Very little flapping. An occasional strong wingbeat.

Head to tail: 15 inches (38 cm)

Wingspan: 37–40 inches (102 cm)

Habits: Mostly eats small rodents and the occasional rabbit, as well as small birds, worms and beetles. Mainly hunts at night but not at all rare to hunt in the daylight. Sits on familiar perches and drops on to prey from above. Solitary or in its long-bonded pair. Sleeps in the daytime on a branch near the trunk of the tree. Eyes shut. They nest deep in the woods, not near any clearing.

Song & calls: The unmissable music of the woods. A *hoo*, followed by a low short *hu* and finally by a long wavering *hoo-oo-oo*. The contact call made by both sexes is a high tense *ke-wick*.

Seasonality: Highly sedentary, commanding their patch of wood for years and even decades at a time.

State of play: 50,000 pairs in Britain, down 36 per cent from its numbers in the 1960s. The causes are unclear: the breeding success of tawny owls increased with the reduced impact of pesticides, but still the population has gone steadily down nevertheless. Maybe a decline in the numbers of voles and other prey; maybe increased road deaths or fear of roads; maybe a fragmentation of woodland cover.

CORVIDS

Carrion Crow (*Corvus corone*)

25 per cent smaller than raven, sleek and nowhere shaggy, shorter wings and tail. But just as black. A stranger to grace. On the ground does a stalking walk and an occasional sidling hop. A robust body, a strong bill and a relatively short tail compared to other crows. Its overall appearance is sleek and solid. The glossy sheen can appear purple or green in sunlight.

Head to tail: 18–20 inches (51 cm)

Wingspan: 33–39 inches (84–100 cm)

Habits: Highly adaptable and opportunistic feeders, scavenging carrion, feeding on invertebrates, small mammals and rubbish in cities. Picks at grains on the ground. Typically solitary, but also hangs out in social groups, especially in large communal roosts during the winter.

Song & calls: The familiar loud hoarse 'caw', often repeated. Finds it difficult to stop talking.

Seasonality: Resident year round.

State of play: Population is stable and widespread throughout the UK, with over a million territories.

Jay *(Garrulus glandarius)*

A bold, clever, gawky, jumpy relative of the crows, not as big as some of the others. Pinkish-brown body with a striking black moustache across its face and vibrant blue-and-black streaked wing patches. A white rump and black tail feathers, seen as it disappears in front of you.

Head to tail: 13 inches (33 cm)

Wingspan: 21 inches (53 cm)

Habits: A rather clumsy bird. Eats insects and seeds, especially acorns, which it likes to hide in caches. Quite a few of the young oaks in Hollow Flemings have grown there in the sort of clusters that mark an abandoned or forgotten jay hoard. Most oak woodlands in Europe from the south of France to Scotland began through jays planting acorns as the ice retreated north. Birds remain bonded to their partner for life. They also feed on insects, small animals, and occasionally bird eggs and chicks.

Song & calls: The least tuneful bird in the wood. A loud, harsh screeching rasp, often heard before the bird is seen. Is said to whisper love songs to its mates. Can also mimic the calls of other birds – often the predators: buzzards, goshawks, sparrowhawks and tawny owls. Some jays can mew like cats. They are good pets and can end up talking like their human companions – or their hoovers.

Seasonality: Resident year round.

State of play: Population of about 170,000 pairs seems to be stable although numbers have fluctuated widely in recent decades.

Magpie *(Pica pica)*

Catwalk-level chic in black and white. A long tail in flight and relatively short wings. Does not look well designed for flying. David Snow and Chris Perrins, the Oxford experts, say: 'Flight action alternates slightly "desperate" bursts of rapid wing-beats with stalling glides, bird appearing to drag long straight tail.' When at ground level, brassy style of pacing with long legs on a short body. Only close-up can you detect the shimmering deep-river-pool green and blue of the sheen on wings and tail.

Head to tail: 18 inches (46 cm)

Wingspan: 22 inches (56 cm)

Habits: Eats anything: roadkill, insects, mice and voles, dead deer, berries, seeds, your leftovers. An exaggerated reputation for killing small birds which has been the basis for their persecution. Gamekeepers hate them. Often seen in pairs or small groups, and are as clever as most corvids, performing well in problem-solving and tool-using tests.

Song & calls: Noisy, especially when in groups or when alarmed. A harsh rattling and far-carrying *cha-cha-cha*. Plus all sorts of *yelps, clicks* and *shrak-aks.*

Seasonality: Resident year round.

State of play: Doubled in numbers 1960s–1990s, at home in modern farmed and urban landscapes, and since then the population has been stable. Now with about 600,000 breeding pairs in Britain. Many shooting estates still kill them but there is no evidence that their predation on eggs and young has any effect on bird populations. Adaptability to human environments has helped them thrive.

Raven *(Corvus corax)*

King of Sussex skies. Entrancing at any appearance. As big as a buzzard with an enormous all-power bill, shaggy throat and an unmistakable sense of potency and significance. Playful acrobat and attention-seeker, aerial prodigy and tumble-artist. Often flies so high (1,000 feet) that it is heard but scarcely seen. A grandeur in its presence. The raven is entirely black, with a wedge-shaped tail, especially noticeable in flight. Like the crow's, in sunlight or close-up, its plumage can gloss blue and purple.

Head to tail: 21–26 inches (66 cm)

Wingspan: 45–59 inches (114–150 cm)

Habits: Nests on tall trees or, where they exist, cliff faces. Doesn't like intensively farmed land. Eats anything, often scavenging the dead. Has an effective but loathable habit of taking out the eyes of weak and injured animals, thus guaranteeing their deaths. Never attacks the eye of other ravens, despite bouts of intense fighting.

The young live in vagrant gangs but at three years old or so birds pair up for life and hold to a fixed territory from which their young are expelled at the end of the first summer.

Song & calls: A low-pitched and majestic *hark hark*. Much more impressive than the squawks of crows. It is unknown if only the male sings. Also a range of other remarks, including knocks, clicks and gurglings, often used for communication between friends and mates.

Seasonality: Resident year round. Breeds early in the year, some laying eggs in late January.

State of play: Ravens were driven into the remote places of the north and west after sustained persecution in the nineteenth and twentieth centuries. In the last forty years the population has begun to increase, gradually spreading out across the country, where there are now about 10,000 pairs.

SUMMER VISITORS

Barn Swallow *(Hirundo rustica)*

Narrow and long in body and wing, as if streamlined by the wind, a tapering sleekness, dark above, pale below, a wind-sculpted form. Long streamers in the tail distinguish it from its cousin the house martin. Avoids the woods but out in the open performs balletic darting acrobatics inches above the grass.

Head to tail: 7 inches (18 cm)

Wingspan: 13 inches (33 cm)

Habits: Feeds on small flying insects when in flight. Makes shallow half-cup nests of muddy blobs usually mixed with grass or straw and lined with feathers, stuck as an agglomeration against a beam or window ledge.

Song & calls: The sound of the light high song hardly carries and is inaudible in any wind but near-to or as they pass overhead is a bright chirruping.

Seasonality: Spends the winter in Africa south of the Equator, many as far as South Africa, leaving England in late September and early October. Return in mid-March to late April. For many decades, some swallows have overwintered in south-west England, a number that may increase with climate change.

State of play: Now about 700,000 territories, but that is a decline of 24 per cent since 1995. No one knows why. Widescale improvement and sealing up of barns may have reduced nesting sites. Shrinking English pastures will not have helped. Pressures may be coming to bear in the swallows' wintering grounds in Africa or on their migration routes between here and there. The disastrous crash in the insect population of Europe will have starved many.

Blackcap *(Sylvia atricapilla)*

Dusky brown above, pale grey below, with a smart cap, in proportion like a schoolboy's cap but without the peak, black in the cock, rufous brown in the hen. The male stands upright in his tree to sing. No skulking.

Head to tail: 5 inches (13 cm)

Wingspan: 8–9 inches (22 cm)

Habits: Spends its life in trees feeding and singing but nests lower down in undergrowth.

Song & calls: One of the most life-enchanting of all songs, beginning with a high chatter, finessing into gleaming flute music, like a blackbird that has dropped its woody undertones and brightened and lightened into silver.

Seasonality: All kind of varied strategies across Europe, both resident and migratory. Those in the west and south largely resident, those in north and east migratory. Leap-frog migration, so that those that summer furthest north spend the winter furthest south, beyond the Sahara. Those that winter in Britain from continental Europe are probably sustained by garden feeders.

State of play: The warbler that is thriving in the modern world. Numbers in the UK have risen by 360 per cent since the 1960s, now with 1.7 million breeding pairs.

Chiffchaff *(Phylloscopus collybita)*

Very like the willow warbler if a little smaller and more compact. Difficult to tell the difference by sight alone: sort of greeny-brown above and sort of browny-green below; *usually* darker legs than the willow warbler. Generally browner than a willow warbler, which shows more yellow. Both sexes look the same.

Head to tail: 4.5 inches (12 cm)

Wingspan: 6–8 inches (17 cm)

Habits: Eats insects and spiders and sometimes berries.

Song & calls: Just as a kittiwake says *kittiwake*, a chiffchaff says *chiff-chaff*. At Perch Hill, it can spend most of its time saying *chiff, chiff, chiff*. Germans think it says *zilp zalp*. The song is one of the first signs of spring, filling the bare woods as early as February. The equivalent of an avian snowdrop. Simple, rhythmic and unmistakable during the breeding season. Its call is a soft but strangely imperious *hweet*, like an impatient high-pitched diner to a waiter.

Seasonality: Mostly a summer migrant in the UK, arriving in March and leaving by October. But increasing numbers of chiffchaffs are now overwintering in the UK, especially in the south where it is milder. Welcome sight outside the bathroom window at Perch Hill. In Europe all of them are migratory, travelling to winter in southern Spain and north Africa. In high summer migrates all the way up into northern Russia.

State of play: Numbers climbing, now 1.8 million territories in the UK, perhaps reaching a peak. They may have benefited from global warming, which has allowed them to dispense with the stress of migratory voyages. Nowadays lay their eggs as early as mid-April, two weeks earlier than before.

Common Nightingale *(Luscinia megarhynchos)*

Dark russet brown above, pale brown-grey below but rarely seen and is largely only heard, especially at dawn and dusk but also deep in the night, in the thickety scrub in which it hides.

Head to tail: 6 inches (15.5 cm)

Wingspan: 9–10 inches (25 cm)

Habits: Eats beetles and ants and berries. Feeds on the ground and in the leaf litter. Also catches insects in flight. Sings low in the undergrowth. Nocturnal song is the male's long-distance signal to females flying overhead. The most voluble come-hither in nature. The song stops before mid-May or at least begins to taper off. No song from the beginning of June onwards. Very difficult to see in its chosen hiding places in dense vegetation.

Song & calls: The great variationist, a pumped-up protean, loud, kaleidoscopic song. More passionate than smooth. The one bird you have to hear before you die. Bubbling piping chuckling sequences of *tuctcucuctcuc* followed by mournful groaned sighings. A tiny sub-breath, *chuck chuck chuck* in the scrubby hedge. Then a hammering before ending with an upcurving trill. A note of surprise. Then sigh-weeping. And then *dough dough dough*. For Olivier Messiaen, the nightingale was 'brilliant and biting ... like a harpsichord blended with a gong' or, like the woodlark, 'distant, lunar', like 'something that had fallen from the stars'.

Seasonality: Winters south of the Sahara but north of the rainforest, spending from November to April there. Summers and breeds in much of Europe and in south-east England from April to July. Males arrive alone and start to sing from their territories. The best places are always those occupied first, successful males coming back to same territories for years in succession.

State of play: Catastrophic. A 90 per cent decline since the 1960s and a 35 per cent decline between 2017 to 2022, with a huge loss of territory, gradually shrinking back southwards and eastwards. The loss of thick shrubby cover, the increase in deer clearing out the understorey of woods and worsening winter conditions in Africa may all contribute to decline.

Cuckoo *(Cuculus canorus)*

Sometimes mistaken for (and so shot as) a bird of prey in flight. A falcon-like bird, with a small head, pointed wings and strikingly long tail. Greyish-blue and dark grey above, barred black and white below.

Head to tail: 12.5–14 inches (33 cm)

Wingspan: 21–23 inches (58 cm)

Habits: To be found in every kind of habitat, very mobile and very loud. If there is a cuckoo in the area you will know about it. A brood parasite, meaning it lays its eggs in the nests of other bird species, particularly those of dunnocks in the shrubby woodlands, meadow pipits and reed warblers in seedbeds. When the female cuckoo lays its egg in the host's nest, it picks up one of the host's eggs and holds it in its bill while laying its own. Then flies off with the stolen egg, which it either swallows whole or crushes and eats. The host birds unwittingly raise the cuckoo chick, which often ejects the host's own eggs or young from the nest. Cuckoos are subdivided into inherited host specialists: reed warbler cuckoos, dunnock cuckoos, meadow pipit cuckoos. There has even been a blue tit cuckoo recorded. All eat caterpillars and beetles.

Song & calls: Unmistakable call given by males to attract mates. With a strangely ventriloqual quality as if singing from somewhere else in the wood. Audible over at least 2,000 acres.

Seasonality: Arrives in the UK from April and mostly leaves by June, much earlier than previously thought. Research by the British Trust for Ornithology has shown that a cuckoo spends roughly 47 per cent of its time in Africa, 38 per cent on migration and 15 per cent in Britain. 'Cuckoos are truly African birds which make a short and dangerous excursion to northern climes, purely for the purposes of breeding.' Fledglings never encounter their parents but have the innate knowledge that their winter must be in Africa.

State of play: 70 per cent decline since the 1960s, half of that since 1995 and most of the decline in England. Scottish cuckoos are relatively stable, even increasing, but there are now only 18,000 breeding pairs in the UK as a whole. The British decline has been matched across the whole of Europe since 1980. Much of the trouble may occur in the migration routes through southern Europe, particularly in Spain. Climate change may also be playing havoc with the cuckoo's subtle timing mechanisms, where its own egg-laying has to be synchronised

with those of its host birds, all subject to subtly shifting climatic and
environmental cues.

Garden Warbler *(Sylvia borin)*

To look at, the least demonstrative and most characterless of
all the woodland birds. Both hen and cock are dun and buff dumplings
with no distinguishing characteristics, no black cap, dressed in
modulations of dried-mud brown and business-suit grey. You
would not be drawn to them at a drinks party. Strangely confident
with none of the wing-flicking displayed by the more anxious
warblers.

Head to tail: 5.5 inches (14 cm)

Wingspan: 8–9 inches (22 cm)

Habits: Eats insects and fruits like the blackcap, living in thick
understorey, sometimes venturing up into higher branches from which
to sing but often deciding to sing from within the denser undergrowth.
Not much of a garden bird despite its name. More often found in
broad-leaved woodland.

Song & calls: The song is the thing, like a surprisingly good contest-
ant in a game show. A gentle even-flowing warble, not at all unlike a
blackcap's. An occasional harshness or churr in it. Called in French the
fauvette des jardins, the little wild thing of the gardens, fearless in its
stance high on its chosen tree declaring its arrival from the south. The
song is filled with rapid variations, a tireless virtuosity and a ceaseless
tide of invention seeming to make time stand still.

Seasonality: Arrives from deep in Africa south of the Sahara, coming to Britain between May and July.

State of play: The population is probably stable at about 145,000 territories, spread all over England, Wales and southern Scotland.

Willow Warbler *(Phylloscopus trochilus)*

Small, slight and graceful, shy, dancing from spot to spot, quite pale and bright, a yellowish green above, a greenish yellow below, with yellow-brown legs (different from the usually dark legs of the otherwise very similar chiffchaff).

Head to tail: 4 inches (10 cm)

Wingspan: 6.5–8.5 inches (22 cm)

Habits: Picks insects from the trees. Seems to like the birches and chestnuts where it picks spiders off the leaves and twigs. Males arrive ahead of females and sing while standing still to proclaim or defend territory. Stops singing by late June. Solitary.

Song & calls: David Snow and Chris Perrins call its song 'a lyrical dropping melody of gentle pure notes in silver, rippling phrases'. Otherwise a twinkly *tat-a-tat-tat*, its notes falling away as it reaches the end of each phrase. New energy as the song begins again, peaks and then runs away, slipping down and out like water from a basin. A sequence of many bubbled earrings for the trees.

Seasonality: Winters in Africa south of the Sahara and makes dazzlingly long migratory flights to the extremes of the north in Europe and Asia. Arrives in Britain mostly in April, starts to go south in late July.

State of play: Huge numbers arrive each year and set up 2.3 million territories in Britain. In decline across England and Wales but increasing in Scotland and Northern Ireland. The northern populations winter in a different area of the damp forests of west Africa and that difference might contribute to their different fates. The decline especially sharp in the south and east of England, where the sex ratio of birds is often skewed: males singing all season long in the hope of finding a female that is not there.

WINTER VISITORS

Brambling *(Fringilla montifringilla)*

A finch quite closely related to the chaffinch and often hangs out with them. Male brambling in winter, which is when we see them, a spotty grey and black head and face, with splashes of black over its upper back. A beautiful cooked-apricot flush over the open parts of its chest. Creamy white further down. Females are browner and duller overall but still display some orange on breast and shoulders.

Head to tail: 5.5 inches (14 cm)

Wingspan: 9–11 inches (25 cm)

Habits: Eats insects in the breeding season, seeds at other times of year. Spends the summer in the high latitudes, further north than

Denmark or southern Sweden, comes far south to Greece, Cyprus and even Palestine in winter. Especially fond of beech mast during the winter. They are often seen in large flocks in woodlands and farmland. In winter, they may also visit garden feeders.

Song & calls: A repeating *tzeek tzeek tzeek* which in some of the enormous European roosting flocks is said to be audible for miles.

Seasonality: Winter visitor to the UK from October to March.

State of play: Apparently thriving but very uncertain in winter numbers, depending on the severity of the weather in Europe. Estimates vary from 45,000 to 1.4 million visiting each winter, a sign that the truth is not really known.

Redwing *(Turdus iliacus)*

A small rakish thrush with longer and more pointed wings than the song thrush, with brown upperparts and a distinctive red chestnut patch on its flanks. Underneath white with brown streaks. Flies fast and into cover, looking almost starling-like, dashing down into the shelter of a blackthorn thicket.

Head to tail: 8–9 inches (21 cm)

Wingspan: 13 inches (34 cm)

Habits: Redwings feed on berries and invertebrates, often seen in large flocks during the winter, foraging in open fields, hedgerows and gardens. Eats invertebrates, flies and berries, migrates in loose flocks and hang out together in thick hedgerows.

Song & calls: Their call is a high-pitched *tseep*, often heard during their night-time migrations as they arrive from the north in their thousands. Can be slightly rough and raspy, as with a catarrhy winter cold.

Seasonality: Arrives from late September onwards and starts to return in late February. Breeds in northern and eastern Europe and much further east into Siberia. Also very minimally in the Scottish highlands. Arrives in the rest of Britain from late September onwards and starts to return in late February.

State of play: About 700,000 redwings come to Britain each winter, after their summers in Scandinavia and Iceland. A global population of about 150 million birds, but in decline in Europe and Asia, down about 30 per cent in fifty years.

Woodcock (*Scolopax rusticola*)

Big and bulky but magically secretive, a gamebird relative of the snipe, a wader that has wandered up into the woods. The woodcock is a chunky, well-camouflaged bird with mottled brown and black plumage, a long straight bill, and large dark alert eyes high on its head. The camouflage blends into the wood floor. Often almost invisible on the ground until you nearly step on them when they bang away from you in a loud and sudden departure, twist-zagging, cutting a sharp italic nib's path through the trees.

Head to tail: 13–15 inches (34 cm)
Wingspan: 21–25 inches (58 cm)

Habits: Loves brackeny dank places for cool and softness. Feeds on the wood floors and at night out in the pastures, probing underground for earthworms and insect larvae. The tip of its bill, like most waders', can detect movement. The positioning of its eyes mean it has a range of binocular vision behind its head. During the breeding season, males perform a display flight to females on the ground known as 'roding', accompanied by a deep croaking call as they fly. Very solitary for most of its life.

Song & calls: In addition to the croaking call during roding flight displays, woodcocks produce a distinctive squeak – *pist.*

Seasonality: Arrives in October–November and leaves during March. The woodcock is both a resident breeder and a winter visitor to the UK. A few are present year round, but the flood of winter arrivals from northern Europe is on a different scale.

State of play: A secure global population of about 26 million birds. The small British population of resident and breeding birds (about 57,000) is in trouble and in long-term decline, the numbers dropping by almost 30 per cent in ten years. The number of winter visitors remains huge: about 1.4 million.

ASSORTED OTHERS

Common Pheasant *(Phasianus colchicus)*

A dramatically long tail on a dramatically fat body, its roundness emphasised by the long neck and smallness of the head. The most beautiful colours of any bird in England but too familiar to be appreciated. A red splash on the face of the male, with a dark blue head and neck, a white ring above body plumage mottled amber and bronze, with silver-gilt dabs on burnt umber grounds. The female a dark and pale crypto mottled brown.

Head to tail: 24–25 inches (64 cm)

Wingspan: 27–35 inches (80 cm)

Habits: Explodes into flight with a loud frightened squawk, making height until it reaches a safer altitude and then flaps and glides with stiff wings and long held out tail. Straight flight makes it easy to shoot and so is raised in its sacrificial battalions for target practice. The genetic origins of the native pheasant from southern Russia and Ukraine now hopelessly confused with the millions of introduced birds from a variety of Asian origins. Omnivorous eaters.

Song & calls: Eruptive bellow like a drunk who has sat on a drawing pin. Not unlike farmyard cockerel and of disturbing loudness if nearby and unexpected. Said to be audible a mile away. Also performs a low groaning croon when going for a walk with its mate, *roo-roo-roo.*

Hearing one below the birdhouse, I thought for a moment it was a wild boar muttering in its sleep.

Seasonality: Present all year round. In summer moves out into fields. In winter retreats to the protection of the woods.

State of play: The grand distorters of the picture. Easily the most common bird in the UK (if you forget the farmed chickens). 2.4 million breeding females, but 47 million non-breeders or more are released to be shot each year. Around 15–20 million of the released birds are killed for fun. The rest die from other causes.

Common Snipe *(Gallinago gallinago)*

Very long billed, dark brown striped back, probably met with as you almost step on it in wet marshy places. Crouches silently until it suddenly tacks hard away from your toe caps. Seems to be digging into the air as it drives for acceleration while staying as close to the ground as an intruder jet.

Head to tail: 9–11 inches (28 cm)

Wingspan: 16–19 inches (46 cm)

Habits: Likes its mud soft, into which it can probe for invertebrates with its long bill. Most food eaten underground with the bill buried up to the socket. Lives alone but occasionally found in small groups for which the collective noun is the best in English: a wisp of snipe.

Song & calls: Its most distinctive sound is made not by the voice but by the vibrations of a pair of stiff tail feathers it can hold out at 90 degrees to its body. These display flights rise and fall in a switchback over its territory, the feathers vibrating on the 45-degree descents, a high haunted fluting filling the air below them. Their call is a sharp squeak.

Seasonality: All year round here but also migratory, coming in for the winter further north and east.

State of play: A relatively stable population with 67,000 breeding pairs in the UK. But that is at a low level compared with the past. With the twentieth-century mania for drainage, snipe now lack the wet places they need and numbers have fallen dramatically since the 1970s. Numbers of breeding birds in wet meadows between 1982 and 2002 crashed by two-thirds. Declines continued into the twenty-first century. There has been a decline across Europe since 1980.

Skylark *(Alauda arvensis)*

Greyish brown, streaky, with a low, blunt crest on its head. Crouches low to the ground until you disturb it when it lifts into the most unmistakable aria flight of any bird.

Head to tail: 7 inches (18 cm)

Wingspan: 12–13 inches (33 cm)

Habits: Lives in the grassland of the pastures on the farm. Perhaps originally came from the great open spaces of the steppes. Once airborne, it climbs up and up in stages, 300 feet at the height, a tower of song, throwing its music into ever-widening circles until it is so high it is as good as invisible. Catch it in the binoculars and you will see the lark fluttering like a mosquito a thousand feet above you. Finally, after up to a quarter of an hour, it descends while singing, spiralling, wings fully spread and unmoving, as if using them as a parachute, and suddenly at about 30 feet falls silent and drops with wings folded.

Feeds on seeds and invertebrates, insects in summer, seeds and weeds in winter and spring.

Song & calls: The most uninterrupted and unbroken of songs, rolling like waves on to a beach, coming back to its ecstatic pitch again and again. A voice that seems to belong to the upper air.

Seasonality: All year round in Britain, France and Spain but migratory in the north and west of Europe, making its way south to Mediterranean winters. In the winter, flocks come in to Perch Hill from the north.

State of play: A 60 per cent drop since the 1960s, now down to 1.6 million breeding territories. Most of the crash happened in the 1970s and 1980s. The switch to autumn sowing, the ploughing up of the previous years' cereal fields and the loss of winter stubbles not only reduced the chances of breeding in the autumn but deprived the skylarks of a crucial means of winter support. The increase in raptors has also helped to make their life more difficult.

Acknowledgements

A list of the reams of people who over my time at Bird School have helped me in a wide variety of ways, both conscious and unconscious, practical and theoretical, with information and expertise, encouragement and labour. My heartfelt thanks to them all.

Liam Ashmore
Irene Baldoni
Nicola Bannister
Ian Barth
Laura Beatty
Susannah Black
Sylvia Bowden
Charlie Boxer
Kate Boxer
Richard Broughton
Michael Brooke
Martin Brown
Jonathan Buckley
Georgina Capel

Aurea Carpenter
Alexandra Chaldecott
Mark Cocker
Rebecca Cocker
Rachel Conway
Helen Crabtree
Nicola Crockford
Alasdair Cross
Peter Dear
Tim Dee
David Dimbleby
Prim Duplessis
Melody Foreman
Jonathan Galassi

Belinda Giles
Sarah Gillett
Victoria Gray
Polly Halladay
Frank Hamel-Cooke
Charlie Hamilton James
Tom Hammick
Sam Harding
Steve Head
Clive Hicks-Jenkins
Peter Hill
Julian Humphries
Iain Hunt
Tobias Jackson
Richard Lambden
Jason Lavender
John Leigh-Pemberton
Josie Lewis
Katharine Liptak
Rob Macfarlane
Clementine Macmillan-Scott
Alex McCaffrey
Jim McDowell
Kat McLaughlin
Kenny McLaughlin
Phil Marsh
Nick Measham
Laura Meyer
Deborah Needleman
Ben Nicolson
Juliet Nicolson
Molly Nicolson
Rebecca Nicolson
Rosie Nicolson

Tom Nicolson
William Nicolson
Anita Oakes
Nick Oakes
David O'Rorke
Alice Oswald
Zoë Pagnamenta
Andrew Palmer
Gary Parker
Nicolet Pascale
Arabella Pike
Colin Pilbeam
Charles Rangeley Wilson
Vicky Rangeley Wilson
Lisbet Rausing
Sigrid Rausing
Hugh Raven
Sarah Raven
Robert Sackville-West
Charlotte Scott
Ivan Samarine
The staff at the East Sussex and
    Brighton and Hove Record
    Office
Martyn Stenning
Kirsty Todd
Isabella Tree
Nick Walsh
Mark Wells
Jacob Weisberg
Stevie Wishart
Mark Wormald
Klara Zak
Sofka Zinovieff

List of Illustrations

Photographs by Adam Nicolson unless otherwise stated

page 73: Robin singing spots (Google Earth/Martin Brown)

page 74: Robin territories (Google Earth/Martin Brown)

page 88: Tawny owl (Graham Eaton/naturepl.com)

page 90: Owl territories (Martin Brown)

page 91: Hoot of the tawny adapted from Paolo Galeotti, 'Individual recognition of male Tawny Owls (*Strix aluco*) using spectrograms of their territorial calls', *Ethology Ecology & Evolution*, May 1991 (Martin Brown)

page 98: Owlets' map: adapted from H.N. Southern, Richard Vaughan and R.C. Muir, 'The behaviour of young tawny owls after fledging', *Bird Study*, 1, 3 (1954): 101–10 (Martin Brown)

page 100: Eric Hosking's 1938 Tawny photograph (FLPA/Alamy Stock Photo)

page 104: Raven (imageBROKER.com GmbH & Co. KG/Alamy Stock Photo)

page 120: Stone relief: M. Aldhouse-Green, *Dying for the Gods: Human Sacrifice in Iron Age and Roman Europe* (History Press, 2002), fig 74

page 123: Great Northern Diver (Public domain)

page 125:Raven sculpture (Felix Choo/Alamy Stock Photo)

page 128: Raven territory: adapted from William C. Webb, John M. Marzluff and Jeff Hepinstall-Cymerman, 'Differences in space use by Common Ravens in relation to sex, breeding status, and kinship – Diferencias en el uso del espacio por *Corvus corax* con relación al sexo, estatus de cría y parentesco', *The Condor*, 114, 3 (August 2012): 584–94 (Martin Brown)

page 130: Raven journeys: adapted from Matthias-Claudio Loretto, Richard Schuster and Thomas Bugnyar, 'GPS tracking of non-breeding ravens reveals the importance of anthropogenic food sources during their dispersal in the Eastern Alps', *Current Zoology*, 62, 4 (2016): 337–44 (Martin Brown)

page 149: A flying dinosaur, *Zhenyuanlong suni*, reproduced in Stephen L. Brusatte, Jingmai K. O'Connor, and Erich D. Jarvis, 'The Origin and Diversification of Birds', *Current Biology 25*, R888–R898, October 5, 2015 p R890 Photo by Junchang Lu (Creative Commons CC by 4.0); *Anchiornis huxleyi* (Michael DiGiorgio)

page 160: Wing diagram (Public domain)

page 186: Birds' eggs: M.-J. Holveck et al., (2012) 'Eggshell spottiness reflects maternally transferred antibodies in blue tits', PLoS ONE, 7, 11 (2012): e50389

page 203, 207: Blackbird singing: adapted from J. Hall-Craggs, 'The development of song in the blackbird *Turdus merula*', *Ibis*, 104, 3 (1962): 277–300

page 204: Blackbird phrase: adapted from J. Hall-Craggs, 'The development of song in the blackbird *Turdus merula*', *Ibis*, 104, 3 (1962): 277–300 (Martin Brown)

page 207: Blackbird singing: adapted from J. Hall-Craggs, 'The development of song in the blackbird *Turdus merula*', *Ibis*, 104, 3 (1962): 277–300

page 227: 'Lever du jour': from Maurice Ravel's score of 'Daphnis & Chloé', *Ballet en un acte, Fragments Symphoniques*, Durand et Cie, Paris 1912

page 228: *Vogel als Prophet*: from Robert Schumann's opening to '*Vogel als Prophet*', in G Minor, Op. 82 No. 7 from *Waldszenen*

page 237: Migration routes: adapted from Andrew N. Hoodless and Christopher J. Heward, 'Migration timing, routes, and connectivity of Eurasian woodcock wintering in Britain and Ireland', *Proceedings of the American Woodcock Symposium*, 11: 136–45 (Martin Brown)

page 238: Woodcock on oil platform: 'Migration and movements of Woodcocks wintering in Britain and Ireland', *British Birds* 113, May 2020

page 241: Autumn woodcock migrations: adapted from A. Tedeschi et al., 'Interindividual variation and consistency of migratory behavior in the Eurasian woodcock', *Current Zoology*, 2020 (Martin Brown)

page 244: Mecklenburg stork (Public domain)

page 247: Shrike migration: adapted from A.P. Tottrup, L. Pedersen, A. Onrubia et al., 'Migration of red-backed shrikes from the Iberian Peninsula: Optimal or sub-optimal detour?', *Journal of Avian Biology*, 48, 1 (2017): 149–54 (Martin Brown)

page 254: Mist nets: Plan of action to address bird trapping along the Mediterranean coasts of Egypt and Libya, March 2014, Nature Conservation Egypt, Dr Holger Schulz

page 258: Common pheasant (John MacTavish/Alamy Stock Photo)

page 262: Julian Huxley (IanDagnall Computing/Alamy Stock Photo)

pages 273, 276, 277: Bird trends: adapted from the Bird Trends Explorer on the British Trust for Ornithology's website (https://data.bto.org/trends_explorer) (Martin Brown)

page 320: Perch Hill (Google Earth/Martin Brown)

page 322: Perch Hill garden (Jonathan Buckley)

page 364: Man leaning on a stick watching a flight of birds: Guercino (1591–1666) (Royal Collection Trust/© His Majesty King Charles III, 2025/Bridgeman Images)

Appendix illustrations: From Thomas Bewick, *A History of British Birds*, 2 vols (1797 and 1804)

Plate sections

All images by Adam Nicolson except for ring ouzel, goldfinch on teasel and great tit on sunflower (Jonathan Buckley); Goldcrest (Rebecca Cocker); Woodcock (Jean-Lou Zimmermann and Serge Santiago); and Giotto's depiction of St Francis's sermon to the birds (Alburn/Alamy Stock Photo)

Reading List

M ost of the references in the notes are to individual papers on different aspects of bird life. Below is a list of books and websites that have been especially useful and inspiring when in Bird School.

Guides
M. Cocker and R. Mabey, *Birds Britannica* (Chatto, 2005)
D.W. Snow, C.M. Perrins et al., *The Birds of the Western Palearctic*, Concise edition, 2 vols (OUP, 1998)
L. Svensson et al., *Collins Bird Guide* (William Collins, 3rd edn 2023)

Ecological history and theory
Mark Cocker, *Our Place* (Jonathan Cape, 2018)
J. Huxley, A.C. Hardy and E.B. Ford (eds), *Evolution as a Process* (Allen & Unwin, 1954)
B. Macdonald, *Rebirding* (Pelagic, 2019)
A. Zahavi, A. Zahavi, *The Handicap Principle: A Missing Piece of Darwin's Puzzle* (OUP, 1997)

Relationship to nature and the spongy boundary

V. Despret, *Living as a Bird* (Polity, 2022)

A. Eastham, *Man and Bird in the Palaeolithic of Western Europe* (Archaeopress Archaeology, 2021)

E. Hosking, *An Eye for a Bird* (Hutchinson, 1970)

K. Lorenz, *King Solomon's Ring*, trans. M.K. Wilson (Methuen, 1952)

T. Morton, *Humankind: Solidarity with Nonhuman People* (Verso, 2017)

The inspirers

J.A. Baker, *The Peregrine, The Hill of Summer & Diaries*, edited by John Fanshawe (Collins, 2011)

R. Bartlett, *Why Can the Dead Do Such Great Things? Saints and Worshippers from the Martyrs to the Reformation* (Princeton UP, 2015)

J. Bate, editor, *John Clare: Selected Poems* (Faber, 2003)

L. Beatty, Introduction to H.E. Bates, *Through the Woods* (Little Toller, 2011)

U. Brunforte (1260–1345), *Fioretti di San Francesco* (*The Little Flowers of Saint Francis*), 1864 translation revised by Dom Roger Hudleston 1930

J. Clare, *Major Works*, edited by Eric Robinson and David Powell (OUP, 1984)

J. Clare, *By Himself*, edited by Eric Robinson and David Powell (Carcanet, 1996)

T. Dee, *The Running Sky: A Birdwatching Life* (Cape, 2009)

T. Dee, *Greenery: Journeying with the Spring from Southern Africa to the Arctic* (Cape, 2020)

E. Dickinson, *The Letters of Emily Dickinson*, ed. Thomas H. Johnson (Belknap Press of Harvard University Press, 1958)

S. Harlan-Haughey, *Ecology of the English Outlaw* (Routledge, 2016)

T. Hughes, *Winter Pollen: Occasional Prose*, ed. W. Scammell (Faber, 1994)

J. Huxley, *Bird-Watching and Bird Behaviour* (Chatto, 1930)

J. Mynott, *Birdscapes: Birds in our Imagination and Experience* (Princeton, 2009)

R.D. Sorrell, *St Francis of Assisi and Nature* (OUP, 1988)

L. Sterne, *The Life and Opinions of Tristram Shandy, Gentleman: … [pt.2]* (London, 1760)

T.W. Thompson, *Wordsworth's Hawkshead*, ed. Robert Woof (OUP, 1970)

I. Tree, *Wilding: The Return of Nature to a British Farm* (Picador, 2018)

The Journals of Gilbert White, ed. Francesca Greenoak, General Ed. Richard Mabey, 3 vols (Century Hutchison, 1986–9)

W. Wordsworth, *The Prelude 1798–1799*, ed. Stephen Parrish (Cornell UP, 1977)

Particular birds

J. Ackerman, *What an Owl Knows* (Oneworld, 2023)

E. Armstrong, *The Wren* (Collins, 1955)

R. Broughton, *The Marsh Tit and the Willow Tit* (Poyser, 2025)

B. Heinrich, *Ravens in Winter* (Summit, 1989)

D. Lack, *The Life of the Robin* (4th edn Witherby, 1965)

J.R. Martin, *The Tawny Owl* (Poyser, 2022)

I. Newton, *Bird Migration* (Collins, 2010)

I. Newton, *Finches* (Collins, 1972)

C. Perrins, *British Tits* (Collins, 1979)

D. Ratcliffe, *The Raven* (Poyser, 1997)

E. Simms, *British Thrushes* (Collins, 1978)

E. Simms, *British Warblers* (Collins, 1985)

D.W. Snow, *A Study of Blackbirds* (Allen & Unwin, 1958)

M. Stenning, *The Blue Tit* (Poyser, 2018)

S. Walls & R. Kenward, *The Common Buzzard* (Poyser, 2020)

Birdsong and music

R. Chadwick and P. Hill, *Olivier Messiaen's Catalogue d'oiseaux* (CUP, 2017)

A. Chaudhuri in *Finding the Raga: An Improvisation on Indian Music* (Faber, 2022)

C. Dingle, *The Life of Messiaen* (CUP, 2007)

P. Hill & N. Simeone, *Messiaen* (Yale, 2005)

P.R. Marler, *Nature's Music: The Science of Birdsong* (Academic Press, 2004)

J. Swafford, *Beethoven: Anguish and Triumph* (Faber, 2014)

Sussex

W. Borrer, *The Birds of Sussex* (Porter, 1891)

M. Mallalieu, *Sussex Bird Reports* (Sussex Ornithological Society, many dates)

J. Walpole-Bond, *A History of Sussex Birds*, 3 vols (Witherby, 1938)

Websites

Merlin
The best bird identification app, https://merlin.allaboutbirds.org/

Xeno-canto
A huge collection of birdsong recordings, https://xeno-canto.org/

British Trust for Ornithology
An unrivalled resource for understanding birds, their distribution and destiny, www.bto.org

European Breeding Bird Atlas
Maps for nearly 600 breeding bird species across Europe, where they breed, how many there are, how their distribution has changed since the 1980s, https://ebba2.info/

Index

BIRDSEYEVIEW

FERAL
PARTNERSHIPS

8 April – 21 May

San Mei Gallery